Black Finance

Black Finance

The Economics of Money Laundering

Donato Masciandaro

Paolo Baffi Centre, Bocconi University, Italy

Előd Takáts

Princeton University, NJ, USA

Brigitte Unger

Utrecht School of Economics, Utrecht University, The Netherlands

Edward Elgar

Cheltenham, UK • Northampton, MA, USA

Published by
Edward Elgar Publishing Limited
Glensanda House
Montpellier Parade
Cheltenham
Glos GL50 1UA
UK

Edward Elgar Publishing, Inc.
William Pratt House
9 Dewey Court
Northampton
Massachusetts 01060
USA

A catalogue record for this book
is available from the British Library

Library of Congress Cataloguing in Publication Data

Masciandaro, Donato, 1961–
    Black finance : the economics of money laundering / by Donato
Masciandaro, Előd Takáts, and Brigitte Unger.
        p. cm.
    Includes bibliographical references and index.
    1. Money laundering. I. Takáts, Előd, 1975– II. Unger, B. (Brigitte) III.
Title.
    HV6768.M265 2007
    364.16'8—dc22

                                                                    2007000734

ISBN 978 1 84720 215 4

Printed and bound in Great Britain by MPG Books Ltd, Bodmin, Cornwall

Contents

List of figures   vii
List of tables   viii
Introduction   ix

PART ONE   MONEY LAUNDERING: PRINCIPLES

1. Economics: The Demand Side   1
    Donato Masciandaro

2. Economics: The Supply Side   27
    Donato Masciandaro

3. International Economics   74
    Brigitte Unger

References   97

PART TWO   APPLIED MONEY LAUNDERING

4. Implementing Money Laundering   103
    Brigitte Unger

5. The Impact of Money Laundering   149
    Brigitte Unger

References   181

PART THREE   ANTI-MONEY LAUNDERING

6. Domestic Money Laundering Enforcement   193
    Előd Takáts

7. International Enforcement Issues 225
    Előd Takáts

References 242

Index 247

Figures

1.1   The alternatives for the criminal organization   9
1.2   The expected utility of the criminal organization   10
1.3   The optimal level of money laundering respect to
the probability of detection   12
1.4   The optimal level of money laundering respect to
the severity of the punishment   13
1.5   The optimal level of money laundering respect to
the value of the profitability   14
1.6   The optimal level of money laundering respect to
the cost of laundering operations   15
2.1   The Authority and the Bank: the optimal choice   46
2.2   The optimal choice with asymmetric information   49
3.1   Criminal money instead of raising taxes   92
3.2   Countries competing for criminal money   95
4.1   The three phases of money laundering   104
4.2   Money laundering and the shadow economy   122
4.3   Correspondent banking   135
5.1   Spending behaviour in 52 big Dutch criminal cases   152
5.2   The crime multiplier with an illegal interest rate of 50%   176
5.3   The crime multiplier with an illegal interest rate of 100%   177
6.1   Two kinds of money laundering   198
6.2   Reporting fee and optimal reporting   213
6.3   Modeling discretionary reporting   214
6.4   Information Laffer curve   214
6.5   Suspicious activity reporting by depository institutions   216
6.6   Money laundering prosecution   217
7.1   Prisoner's dilemma and the laundering externality   227

Tables

1.1	Money laundering: the determinants	16
2.1	Financial intelligence units: institutional models, agents and principals	67
3.1	Top 20 destinations of laundered money	80
3.2	Inflows of money and domestic laundering in the Netherlands in million US$	85
4.1	Money laundering definitions: their subject and laundering purpose	112
4.2	Types of crime in money laundering definitions	119
5.1	Spending behaviour of Dutch criminals from large datasets	153
5.2	Spending behaviour in 52 big Dutch criminal cases	154
5.3	Input-output multipliers, by sector of industry for Australia	163
5.4	Fiscal fraud and tax evasion	168
6.1	Money-laundering methods	195
6.2	Predicate crimes linked to money laundering	197
6.3	United States anti-money-laundering legislation	202
6.4	Reports	206
6.5	Information and fines	219

Introduction

Traditionally, monetary and financial economics has focused on legal financial transactions, while the economics of crime – following Becker – has neglected the financial aspects. Hence, black finance – finance that relates to illegal or criminal activities – has fallen between the two stools. Due to this separate development in the two sub-disciplines of economics, economic theory has not addressed financial crime sufficiently, so far. This creates a particularly disturbing gap in the literature, since lately, especially in connection with terrorist financing, the financial side of crime has become accentuated in the public and political debate.

A substantial part of financial transactions has a very special purpose: namely hiding the originally criminal or illegal source of the economic activity. The economics of money laundering aims at modelling the behaviour and process of making dirty money appear clean. It necessitates a multidisciplinary approach, since the behaviour and process of money launderers involves, beside economics, aspects of law, criminology, sociology and political sciences. To give an example, in order to model laundering one has to know how criminals behave, which legal restrictions they face, and which social and political consequences their activities can have.

This book wants to establish a framework to understand the mechanisms of black finance markets, or in other words to formally model the economics of money laundering. Part one deals with the microeconomics, macroeconomics and international economics of money laundering. Part two investigates the empirical aspects of the scale, techniques and impacts of laundering. Part three analyzes the economics of combating money laundering and enforcing anti-money-laundering measures.

We assume a rational criminal actor or organization, which derives revenues from an illicit or criminal activity. The criminal actor or organization wants to maximize the expected utility of his or its illicit proceeds. The expected utility increases with the average return and it decreases with the costs for laundering, with the probability of being caught and with the severity of the sanction when being caught. In addition to the expected market return and laundering transaction costs criminal financial investors have to take into account that they can be caught and sanctioned. This can be interpreted as additional transaction costs. In the case of being caught, the damage can be more than the amounts invested, like having the whole property seized or being sent to jail.

The macroeconomic effects of money laundering can be captured in a multiplier model. If criminals control an initial volume of illicit proceeds, they will decide to launder a specific proportion y of it. Subtracting the costs of laundering (share c), a specific amount is left for investment. Parts will be re-invested in illegal activities (share q), parts in legal ones (share f). The share of re-investment depends on the difference in returns between the illegal and the legal sector (r). Since the original criminal proceeds are re-invested partly in the illegal sector, this necessitates additional laundering. Money laundering triggers a multiplier process, which ends up with higher laundering and higher criminal activities (see Chapter 1). In Chapter 5 this multiplier is measured empirically. The most likely results are that money laundering will trigger additional money laundering activities of 6%-10% within the coming four years.

The banking and financial industry can play a pivotal role for the development of the criminal sector as a preferential vehicle for money laundering. The supply side of money laundering consists of regulatory agents who want to combat money laundering, and of financial intermediaries who can be either honest and compliant or dishonest and non-compliant. Asymmetric information and principal-agent problems are typical for this market. The design of anti-money-laundering regulations must take four aspects into consideration: the difference in information assets between the individual intermediaries and the agency, the non-verifiability of bankers' efforts to comply, the costliness of that effort for the intermediaries, and the non-verifiability of the influence of the effort on the performance of the regulation. The supply side (see Chapter 2) is modelled for two actors, the Authority and the Bank, which in one case is honest and in the other case criminal. The latter has to take into account the probability of being caught and sanctioned. The Authority can set the optimal regulatory effort, depending on the reputation costs and the required effort. From an economic point of view, the more specialized and financially trained the anti-money-laundering agency is, the more useful it will be. In this sense, the creation of the Financial Intelligence Units in 94 countries, who are specialized in combating money laundering, is a step in the right direction.

Chapter 3 shows how models of international economics and of tax competition can be applied to money laundering issues. The Gravity Model, developed by Newton (Newton's Law of Universal Gravitation also called Newton's Apple) and imported into economics by Tinbergen in the 1960s, has been very successful in predicting trade flows among countries. In its original version it stated that every object in the universe attracts every other object with a force directed along the line of centres for the two objects that is proportional to the product of their masses and inversely proportional to the square of distance between the two objects. This formula was imported into economics by Tinbergen, who redefined masses as GDP and interpreted the attracted forces as trade flows among countries. In recent years Tinbergen's formula has been very successfully micro-founded by international trade economists (see Head 2003; Helliwell 2000). Furthermore, John Walker (1995) in a pioneer approach applied such a type of model to measuring money laundering. Chapter 3 applies this model to predict the allocation of global money laundering among different countries. The 'masses' of Newton's objects are replaced by GDP per capita and by the amount of crime and criminal proceeds, the gravity is replaced by attractiveness indicators and the physical distance is augmented by cultural and economic distance.

The indicator of attractiveness has been derived from assumptions about the behaviour of launderers. At an international scale, money launderers are supposed to behave pretty much like normal people. They like to invest their money in well-developed countries, because it is easier to hide their transactions there. They like countries with low conflict and corruption, because otherwise they run the risk of losing their funds. They like easy and fast access as provided by countries that are SWIFT members, and they like high returns. Different from normal people, they prefer countries with high bank secrecy and lax anti-money laundering policy. A country will attract more global criminal money: the higher its GDP per capita; the higher its bank secrecy; the more developed its financial markets; if it is a SWIFT member; the lower its conflicts and corruption and the laxer its anti-money-laundering policy is. Apart from attractiveness, distance also matters. Geographic distance, linguistic and cultural differences matter, and whether countries have intense trade relations. This makes it easier for launderers to come to know the country, speak its language and do the laundering business there.

Chapter 3 applies this model to predict the inflows of money for laundering into the Netherlands. Major countries that send their money for laundering to the Netherlands are the US, followed by the Cayman Islands, Russia, China and Italy.

Seen globally, most of the top 20 countries receiving money for laundering are well-established, well-developed, and quite sizeable countries, the major laundering country being the United States. There are only a few microstate Offshore Centres such as the Cayman Islands, Vatican City, Bermuda and Liechtenstein amongst them. Countries of the EU are represented prominently in this list. Italy, Luxembourg, France, Germany, Austria, the Netherlands, the UK and Spain belong to the top 20 laundering countries in the world. Money laundering can, therefore, not be restricted to small countries and tax havens. It is a problem for well-established industrialized countries with successful financial markets. However, given the problems to work empirically on this field – as we will stress below – more than the usual caveats have to be applied.

The second part of Chapter 3 therefore asks the question whether it pays for countries to compete for criminal money. If crime stays in Colombia and only the drug money comes to Europe or the US, would that harm the European or US economy? The ancient Romans had already discovered that pecunia non olet – money does not stink . Using a model of tax competition, Chapter 3 (second part), shows that the original welfare gains from attracting additional (criminal) money, can easily be lost again once other countries decide to follow the same policy. A race to the bottom with regard to competing for criminal money is very likely. The model presented assumed that countries can make a deliberate choice whether to let laundering happen or not. This means it assumes that an anti-money-laundering policy can be implemented at will and that it is effective (and, therefore, can also be effectively removed in order to attract additional criminal money). Some countries, indeed, deliberately offered their services to criminals, such as the Seychelles in the 1990s (see Unger and Rawlings 2005). However, it can also happen, as Masciandaro (2000) pointed out, that countries establish big functioning financial markets that attract all kinds of investors, including criminal ones. Countries then start to combat money laundering in order to keep up their reputation as solid financial centres. Chapter 7 interprets the international money-laundering problem as an externality and a prisoner's dilemma and details how the international community can deal with it.

Chapter 4 shows some empirical problems when implementing money laundering. One major concern is with the definition of money laundering. What precisely does money laundering include and is it a stock or a flow? In our theoretical model (Chapters 1 and 2) we defined money laundering in a very general way: money-laundering activities can concern any proceeds generated by criminal or illegal activities. Laundering refers to all types of crime and illegal activities. The principle of peculiarity stated that the purpose of the laundering activity is to reduce peculiar transaction costs, concealing the illicit origin of the proceeds. So, we defined laundering as all transactions meant to conceal the illicit origin of proceeds from all types of crime. In Chapters 6 and 7 we follow the definitions of international organizations and define money laundering specifically as 'money transfer'. According to Chapter 6: 'The main idea behind all these transactions is to transfer funds from their present form or place to somewhere else, either to use it there or to conceal the origins of them'.

While Chapters 1 and 2 still leave some room for establishing whether money laundering is a stock or a flow, since 'transactions' can refer to both of them, Chapters 6 and 7 clearly opt for a flow approach to money laundering. Transfers are clearly a flow, not a stock. However, that approach might not be the best for empirical investigations. To measure money laundering with a transfer approach would mean that one has to estimate the velocity of money, or that one has to follow the illegal money around the globe. Due to reasons of privacy and of limited international cooperation, this is not possible. Criminal money can be measured at the first step, when criminals try to put it into the financial circuit. But once it is diluted in international financial transactions it is very difficult, if not impossible, to trace it any more.

This is why measurement of money laundering prefers to measure the stock of criminal money and use a bottom up approach. One calculates the amounts of crime (from criminal statistics) times the average prices obtained (for example for drugs) in order to calculate the proceeds of each crime. Summing up all types of proceeds from crime, and assuming a certain percentage of them, which will get laundered, gives the estimate of the stock of money laundered. With allocation models such as the gravity model one can find out to which countries this money will be sent at the first step. This is where the estimate stops. But to follow the money further would necessitate prosecuting each individual transaction. Although theoretically it is desirable to follow flows of money, empirically this would mean having to look for a drop of ink in a stream of water after it has been diluted. Legally, laundered money always stays illegal money, no matter how often it has been circulating the globe. It is, however, impossible to trace any more.

Beside the stock-flow problem, another problem occurs when working empirically. Which types of crime belong to money laundering? Theoretically it is wise to do what we did, namely to assume that the proceeds of all types of crime belong to money laundering. However, empirically one is bound to the countries' legislation and differences in legal definition. A person can only be prosecuted for money laundering if the underlying crime is on the list of crimes that are predicate crimes for laundering. To give an example: proceeds from tax evasion are a predicate crime in the US, in Germany only from business and criminal organizations, in Austria and Switzerland tax evasion is no crime at all, in the Netherlands tax evasion is no serious crime, only if it is clearly fraudulent. When measuring money laundering empirically, one would have to include tax evasion for the US, parts of it for Germany, none of it for Austria and Switzerland, and only the fraud part of it for the Netherlands. The same problems occur with proceeds from illegal gambling, copying and parts of fraud (see Table 4.2 for a tentative country comparison). Latest European efforts to harmonize money laundering definitions like the Third Anti-Money-Laundering Directive are a further step towards a more comprehensive approach. But the Directive does not do away with the differences of predicate crime in the diverse member states.

The disharmony in definitions in national laws also means that a clear differentiation between money laundering and the shadow economy is not possible. Money laundering includes on the one hand formal sector cross-border white collar crime (for example when it happens through fake invoicing and fake transfer pricing in regular companies), on the other hand it also includes part of the informal irregular sector shadow economy (like tax evasion and social fraud, which are illegal ways of producing goods and services in a legal product market), and parts of the criminal informal sector (like the underground economy). Table 4.3 gives a tentative framework to study the relation between money laundering, the shadow and the underground economy.

Another way of perceiving money-laundering activities is to distinguish phases of laundering and techniques used. In the first phase of laundering, the pre-wash or placement phase, money is being collected. By means of smurfing and structuring (breaking large deposits into smaller ones to avoid transaction reporting requirements), camouflage (using a false ID), or currency smuggling, buying traveller cheques or gambling in the casino one tries to bring it to a financial intermediary. The second phase of laundering, the main-wash or layering phase, necessitates circulating money around the globe in order to hide its origin. Techniques such as correspondent banking, bank cheques, collective accounts, payable-through accounts, loan at low or no interest, back-to-back loans, using money exchange offices and money transfer offices, fake insurances, fictitious sales and purchases, fake invoicing, using shell companies, abusing trust offices and special purpose entities, or underground bankers provide a great variety of complex ways of sending money around the globe. The third phase, the after-wash or integration phase, aims at parking the money permanently. Now it must be safe without the chance of being detected and with profit. Capital market investments, derivatives, real estate acquisitions, the catering industry, the gold and diamond market, buying consumer goods and luxury goods, doing cash-intensive business for further laundering, doing export-import business or transport business (for further drugs or human trafficking) are ways of parking the money permanently. New forms of money laundering can emerge in the electronic world, such as online banking, E-cash, E-gold, and through proprietary systems (see Chapter 4 sixth section). The first part of Chapter 6 summarizes the most important techniques that the Financial Action Task Force FATF has identified.

Given the great variety of money laundering techniques it is very difficult for the police to prosecute laundering. In many countries the police are trained to prosecute the 'real' criminals such as drug dealers, murderers and thieves. To prosecute an intelligent financially literate money launderer necessitates much more differentiated skills than the traditional police corps has. Special departments for money laundering prosecution are being established at the moment in some countries. Without such efforts, due to the complexity of the business, sophisticated laundering constructions are impossible to detect.

If laundering takes place, does it harm the economy? In Chapter 3 we saw that the competition for criminal money can lead to a race to the bottom, countries offering laxer and laxer anti-money laundering regulations in order to attract criminal money. But will this really happen? Which positive and negative impacts does money laundering have? Chapter 5 summarizes the empirical impacts of money laundering. As we have already stated, money laundering triggers additional money laundering activities of about 6%-10%. This also means an increase in crime, since laundering activities necessitate helpers. Bank employees, notary publics, real estate or insurance company agents who are willing to overlook discretely the suspicious behaviour of criminals are necessary for laundering activities. The buyer who shows up with a suitcase full of cash in order to buy a house, the smurfer who shows up ten times a day to deposit a sum which is just slightly below the reporting requirement, the insurance client who makes a deal with the broker to fake an incident, they all need collaborators.

Money laundering can contaminate legal professions. Money laundering can affect particular sectors. In the Netherlands, the real estate sector is very prone to laundering activities. Several killings in broad daylight in the last years have made it transparent that this sector is very popular among Mafiosi and launderers. Money laundering can affect growth, both positively and negatively. Positively, because additional funds flow through the economy, which means additional demand for goods and services. Negatively, because of its impact on crime, and crime dampens growth. Legal business tends to move out once criminal business steps in. The net effect of money laundering on growth is very small and negative. Our calculations for 17 countries show that an additional one billion US$ will reduce growth by between –0.03 and –0.06 percentage points. In the long run money laundering can also undermine politics, if criminals gain access to political institutions. Therefore, it seems important to combat laundering quickly.

Chapter 6 deals with anti-money-laundering (AML) enforcement problems. While Chapters 3 to 5 focused on money laundering in Europe, Chapter 6 focuses on the United States, the country where most monies are laundered in the world and the country which simultaneously took the international lead in fighting money laundering. It is, therefore, also no coincidence that most of the money laundering literature so far, has focused on the United States. Originally, money laundering referred to drugs money only. Eventually this was extended to fraud and other crimes, including terrorist financing. Lately, especially because of the fear of terrorist financing, the United States wants to tackle money laundering with greater severity.

In Chapter 6, money laundering is defined as an externality. For example, a bank might want to accept funds from drug dealing, as the social costs of drug trade are external to the bank. Given this externality, the government should intervene and set anti-money-laundering regimes to properly price this externality through the AML regime. However, it faces a trade-off: stronger enforcement yields increased costs and reduces the privacy of citizens. The ultimate goal of the AML regime is to deter criminals from laundering monies, and thereby deter them from committing predicate crimes in the first place. This goal is achieved through two intermediate objectives. First, the AML regime is supposed to directly deter and prosecute criminals (through use of customer due diligence procedures which aim at validating the client's background and identity, through currency and suspicious transaction reporting, and through providing client contact information to law enforcement agencies). Second, the AML regime is supposed to protect the integrity of the financial system. This means the regime must also emphasize, that banks are not the criminals themselves.

The most interesting finding is how excessive reporting of money laundering cases can dilute the information value of the reports, or in other words, how too much information can drown the value of it.

In order to understand this phenomenon the chapter first investigates rule-based reporting (i.e. when the government prescribes exact rules, such as a value threshold, as to when to report a transaction). Enforcing such a regulation can be investigated by a combination of the deterrence model in the style of Becker (1968) and costly state verification models. The government, who prefers to save on costs, wants to minimize the likelihood of (costly) investigations. Hence, the government can use very strong fines, so as to make sure even with little investigation that banks do not want to deviate from reporting transactions which are prescribed to be reported.

However, such rule-based reports cannot be effective, precisely because money launderers know them and can figure out how to avoid triggering a report. For instance, one known method is to break down larger transactions into smaller ones, so that the transactions would be under the reporting threshold.

The solution is one form of discretionary report (i.e. when the government tells the bank to find out on its own which transactions are suspicious). Here the government needs an optimal number of reports. Obviously, if the bank reports all transactions, then the government will not know which ones are truly suspicious. In other words, the increasing number of reports makes the government worse informed. In such a setting, excessively strong fines are harmful because they give incentives for banks to report too many transactions.

The chapter also shows that problems of excessive reporting are far from being only of theoretical interest. It shows that in the United States increasing numbers of reports have already started to erode the information provided to law enforcement agencies.

Chapter 7 investigates anti-money laundering from an international perspective. The chapter again captures anti-money-laundering problems as externalities. The most important one, the laundering externality, shows that governments, who do not internalize the harms of crime committed elsewhere, might want to turn a blind eye to laundering of foreign monies. The situation can also be analysed as a multi-country prisoner's dilemma, where individual countries might want to shirk their AML duties – to the eventual detriment of all countries. The chapter introduces the channels for international cooperation in order to avoid the non-cooperative equilibrium of the prisoner's dilemma.

The following points are still open for further research and discussion. First, terrorist financing entered the money laundering debate very late. Terrorist financing means a paradigm change in law (see Unger 2007, Chapter 2). Before, combating money laundering had to respect the privacy of the citizens. When terrorist financing is included in the money laundering definition, then the protection of national interest goes before privacy protection. With this, the opening of bank accounts is very much facilitated. Money laundering has become a much more important issue since terrorist financing was included in the money-laundering definition by the Financial Action Task Force, FATF. Are terrorist financing and money laundering the same?

We should stress that in terms of economic analysis the financing of terrorism (money dirtying) is a phenomenon conceptually different from the recycling of capital (money laundering).

The financing of terrorism resembles money laundering in some respects and differs from it in others. The objective of the activity is to channel funds of any origin to individuals or groups to enable acts of terrorism, and therefore crimes. Again in this case, an organization with such an objective must contend with potential transaction costs, since the financial flows may increase the probability that the crime of terrorism will be discovered, thus leading to incrimination. Therefore, an effective money-dirtying action, an activity of concealment designed to separate financial flows from their destination, can minimize the transaction costs. Money dirtying can also perform an illegal monetary function, responding to the demand for 'covertness' expressed by individuals or groups proposing to commit crimes of terrorism.

The main difference between money laundering and terrorism finance is in the origin of the financial flows. While in the money-laundering process the concealment regards capitals derived from illegal activity, the terrorist organizations use both legal and illegal fund for financing their action.

Money laundering and money dirtying may coexist when terrorism is financed through the use of funds originating from criminal activities. A typical example is the financing of terrorism with the proceeds from the production of narcotics. In those specific situations the importance of the transaction costs is greater, since the need to lower the probability of incrimination concerns both the crimes that generated the financial flows and the crimes for which they are intended. The value of a concealment operation is even more significant.

In summing up, one is prompted to think that the operational techniques of the two phenomena – the laundering of criminal capital and financing terrorism – are at least in part coincident. It is important, however, that the partial overlapping of money dirtying and money laundering remains a hypothesis to be tested from time to time rather than a thesis.

Empirical findings (from before September 11!) show that terrorism leads to a decline in per capita growth. If there were one terrorist event every year, this would lead to a 1.5% reduction of per capita income growth over the whole period of estimation, 1968-2000 (see Blomberg et al. 2004). It seems very likely that empirical estimates that include the effects of September 11 and of the Iraq war, will end up with a stronger decline in per capita growth.

Second, we would have to know more about the behaviour of money launderers. Are launderers rational? Do they behave economically? So far, we have to rely on case studies by Dutch criminologists, who analysed 52 big laundering cases in the Netherlands, each worth more than 400,000 euro, and some several hundred criminal cases. Both studies show that criminals in general and launderers in particular behave pretty much like normal people. They do not consume all their proceeds by buying big luxury cars, yachts, and fancy houses, but rather consume and invest like ordinary people. It would be very interesting to compare these findings of behaviour with other countries. At the moment, the studies made indicate that launderers do behave rationally.

Third, are international laundering transactions different from normal trade and financial flows? To what extent ? Do money launderers look for the same business opportunities than regular business and only consider the AML policy of a country as an additional constraint?

Case studies of internationally active launderers are necessary. The case of John Deuss, the seventeenth richest person in the Netherlands, with an estimated wealth of one billion euro, is being studied intensively at the moment in the Netherlands. He was jailed at his domicile in the Bermudas in October 2006. He owned several banks, including the First Curacao International Bank (FCIB), which attracted so many British customers that the British tax authorities became suspicious and found out that 2500 British citizens had committed value added tax fraud of about 7 billion euro through the bank. Many other accusations of money laundering are linked to his name. An intense study of international launderers such as the Colombian drug barons (Cuéllar 2003), is necessary in order to learn more about the behaviour of big international launderers. At the moment, it looks as if launderers are very much aware of AML policies and do consider them as additional constraints for their investment behaviour.

Fourth, it is important to work more on estimating money laundering. At the moment, the international community of laundering estimators seems to be split into two camps. One camp (to which our study belongs) thinks that money laundering is sizeable and a big problem. This view is supported by estimates from the IMF, Walker (1995).

The other camp criticizes these findings and thinks that the estimates are highly exaggerated. This view is supported by Reuter et al. (2004). Global estimates for money laundering range between 2.85 trillion US dollars and 200-500 billion US dollars. There is still some work necessary to back up the empirical estimates solidly and narrow down the range of the estimates.

Fifth, from our comparison of Europe and the US one also wonders whether money laundering is a US-made or a global problem? Especially, does money laundering fit European laws? Conforming to the international community, many countries have established legal paragraphs for money laundering. Some countries' law experts say they had to 'squeeze money laundering paragraphs in'. But do they truly fit into European laws? Many European legal constitutions do not allow double or accumulative punishment. Money laundering is precisely this. Somebody has committed a crime, for which he can be punished, plus launders the proceeds of this, for which he can again be punished. Many European legal systems have a problem with implementing this into their national law. The Austrian law for example, excludes self-laundering for this reason. It aims at punishing the source of money laundering, the crime itself, and tries to avoid double punishment, which would occur if self-laundering was part of money laundering. Double or accumulative punishment is no problem in the US legal system, where sentences can add up to several hundred years of jail. It will certainly be interesting for lawyers to study further the implications for the legal system of introducing money laundering and terrorist financing into national European laws.

There is still quite some work to be done for lawyers, criminologists, social scientists and political scientists. For economists we tried to establish a framework for further analysis of the demand and the supply of laundering, empirical work on laundering and questions of combating money laundering.

Given the increasing attention and size of the problem, and given the fact that the behaviour of launderers seems to fit economic theory or rational behaviour, it seems important to use this framework and to continue theoretical and empirical research on black finance, the economics of money laundering.

PART ONE

Money Laundering: Principles

1. Economics: The Demand Side

Donato Masciandaro

INTRODUCTION

Only in recent times has economic analysis developed a special, original focus on financial issues related to the study of criminal activity, thus far completely absent in the international literature. The basic theoretical reason lies in the absence of special treatment of monetary and financial aspects within the traditional Becker model. Furthermore the complexity of the topic also concerns the need to adopt a multidisciplinary approach, using cognitive instruments associated with different disciplines: economic, legal and social sciences.

In the first two chapters[1] of this book we propose a simple but hopefully useful framework to understand the mechanisms of the black finance markets, starting from the demand side.

The emphasis on the study of money laundering has progressively increased, recognizing its role in the development of any crime that generates revenues. In fact, the conduct of any illegal activity may be subject to a special category of transaction costs, linked to the fact that the use of the relative revenues increases the probability of discovery of the crime and therefore incrimination.

Those transaction costs can be minimized through an effective laundering action, a means of concealment that separates financial flows from their origin, an activity whose peculiar economic function is to transform potential wealth into effective purchasing power.

In this chapter we will show how, from a microeconomic point of view, money laundering performs an illegal monetary function, responding to the overall demand for black finance services, expressed by individuals or groups that have committed income-producing crimes.

---

[1] The author thanks Raffaella Barone for excellent research assistance.

1

The micro foundations of money laundering allow us to shed light on its macroeconomic effects. In fact, if at the micro level the demand should be matched by an effective supply – that we will analyse in Chapter 2 – it is possible to demonstrate that money laundering, in a given economy with legal and illegal sectors, can play the role of multiplier of the volume of the economic endowments that concerns to criminal and illegal agents.

In the following pages we will analyse in depth the study of money laundering of illegal capital, highlighting its crucial function, theoretical and practical, in the development of any crime that generates revenues.

In fact, any illegal activity must deal with a peculiar category of transaction costs, linked to the fact that the use of the relative revenues increases the possibility of detection of the crime itself and thus incrimination. These transaction costs can be minimized by effective laundering, an activity whose distinctive economic function is precisely to transform potential purchasing power into actual purchasing power. In this sense, money laundering performs a peculiar illegal monetary function.

The economic analysis of money laundering will necessarily start from its precise economic definition, which will stress the following characteristics:

Generality: money-laundering activity concerns any proceeds generated by criminal or illegal activities;
Peculiarity: the purpose of this activity is to reduce peculiar transaction costs, concealing the illicit origin of the proceeds.

Money laundering is an autonomous criminal economic activity whose essential economic function lies in the transformation of liquidity of illicit origin, or potential purchasing power, into actual purchasing power usable for consumption, saving, investment or reinvestment. The money-laundering phenomenon can then be studied through microeconomic analysis of the behaviour of the criminals, consistent with the Becker base model.

This approach, that will be illustrated in this chapter, proposes a model to study in general the choices of an economic agent who must decide whether and to what extent to launder the proceeds of a crime. It assumes that the economic agent (the 'criminal') derives a flow of income from an illicit activity. This illegal income represents potential purchasing power, in a specific sense: its direct use would increase the probability that the crimes committed by the agent will be discovered. More generally, a 'laundered' euro, or dollar, has greater value for the criminal agent than a 'dirty' euro, since the former can be invested with lower risks of incrimination. The criminal agent thus must decide, for each euro of illicit income, whether to launder it or not.

The criminal's utility is decreasing in the probability of detection of the crime and the severity of the sanction, while it is rising in the expected average return on the laundered cash. The criminal agent must therefore determine the optimal level of cash to launder, taking into account the maximum resources available to him. The optimal value represents the limit over which it is no longer advantageous to request money-laundering services: the damage deriving from detection of the crime and the relative sanction becomes so great as to make the expected utility negative.

The critical value can be interpreted as the propensity to launder, which depends on the model parameters: more effective and/or more severe anti-money-laundering policies reduce the propensity to launder; increasing the profitability of laundered cash and reducing the costs of money-laundering operations increase the propensity to launder.

Having defined a microeconomic approach to the money-laundering choices enables the formulation of a macroeconomic model of the relationship between development of the illegal markets and the laundering activity.

The macro analysis can be faced by using the traditional multiplier approach in a novel analytical framework. We will represent the multiplying effects of money laundering with respect to the criminal subject's economic endowment. Starting from the initial crime that produces some dirty revenues, the laundering process allows – given some laundering costs – such capitals to be re-invested in the legal and illegal sectors of the economy. The portion which is destined to the illegal sector will further produce some other dirty revenues to undergo the laundering process; the money-laundering cycle has therefore taken off and each step – provided that no obstacle hinders the process – contributes to strengthen the economic and financial power of criminal subjects.

The macro polluting effect of money laundering is higher: the lower is the opportunity cost; the bigger is the share of reinvestment in illegal activities, as well as the necessity of financing this reinvestment with clean liquidity; the bigger is the differential of the expected real return of the illegal activities; the lower is the expected riskiness of the illegal activities; the bigger is the initial volume of the revenues of the criminal sector.

In conclusion the chapter discusses similarities and differences between money-laundering and terrorism finance, or money-dirtying.

The goal of terrorism finance is to channel capitals of any origin to individuals or groups to enable acts of terrorism. As in the money-laundering activity, the financial flows may increase the probability that the crime of terrorism will be discovered, thus increasing the probability of incrimination. The main difference between money laundering and terrorism finance is in the origin of the financial flows. While in money laundering the concealment regards capitals derived from illegal activity, terrorist organizations use both legal and illegal funds for financing their action.

MONEY LAUNDERING: DEFINITION

First of all, we need a definition of money laundering, in terms of economic analysis, that points up its specificity with respect to other illegal or criminal economic activities, typically involving accumulation and/or reinvestment. It is the following: given that the conduct of any illegal activity may be subject to a special category of transaction costs, linked to the fact that the use of the relative revenues increases the probability of discovery of the crime and therefore incrimination, those transaction costs can be minimized through an effective laundering action, a means of concealment that separates financial flows from their origin.

In other words, whenever a given flow of purchasing power that is potential – since it cannot be used directly for consumption or investment as it is the result of illegal accumulation activity – is transformed into actual purchasing power, money laundering has occurred.

Focusing attention on the concept of incrimination costs enables us to grasp not only the distinctive nature of this illegal economic activity but also its general features. The definition we have adopted maintains basic unity among three aspects that, according to other points of view, represent three different objects of the anti-laundering action: the financial flows; the wealth and goods intended as terminal moments of those flows; the principal actors, or those who have that wealth and goods at their disposal.

In our scheme of analysis there will always be an agent who, having committed a crime that has generated accumulation of illicit proceeds, moves the flows to be laundered, so as to subsequently increase his financial assets, by investment in the legal sector or re-accumulation in the illegal sector.

The first crucial agent to place under observation is therefore the criminal organization. By criminal organization we mean a group of individuals and instrumental assets associated for the purpose of exclusively exchanging or producing services and goods of an illicit nature or services and goods of a licit nature with illicit means or of illicit origin.

The criminal organization accumulates resources through its activity in the illegal markets. The moment it accumulates illegal resources, however, a problem of laundering arises. The purpose of money-laundering activity is to transfer the 'dirty' liquidity coming from any criminal or illegal activity into funds that, since they are 'clean', i.e. devoid of traces that could connect them to the underlying crimes, can be allocated to consumption, savings, or investment in legal sectors or reinvestment in illegal markets. The phase of legal investment and illegal re-accumulation complete the model.

In general, following the classic intuition à la Becker, we can claim that the choices of an economic agent to invest his resources in illegal activities, thus becoming a criminal, will depend, ceteris paribus, on two peculiar magnitudes, given the possible returns: the probability of being incriminated and the punishment he will undergo if found guilty. An analysis of the choices of organized crime would undoubtedly follow the same approach.

This analysis of the conduct of criminal organizations in terms of rationality can certainly not be considered exhaustive. One cannot exclude, in fact, the possibility that criminals are constrained by forms of logic other than rationality. It should also be noted that the economic component has become the characterizing element, if not the predominant one, of the more recent type of criminal organizations.

Now, to undertake money-laundering activity, an organization possessing liquidity coming from illegal activity will decide whether to perform a further illicit act, in a given economic system – i.e. money laundering – assessing precisely the probability of detection and relative punishment and comparing that with the expected gains, net of the economic costs of this money-laundering activity.

The choice of the organization requires that the crime in question, and the relative production function, be basically autonomous with respect to other forms of crime, those that generated the revenues in the accumulation phase. Furthermore, the crucial role that money-laundering activity plays in the growth and profitability of the entire criminal industry suggests that it is central, qualitatively and quantitatively, to all criminal organizations.

Assigning a monetary utility to the crime of money laundering, by giving it a unitary expression, actually summarizes the value of a series of more general services that stimulate the growth of demand for money-laundering services on the part of criminal organizations that accumulate illegal resources. Money laundering, in fact, produces for its users:

1. the economic value, in the strict sense, of minimizing the expected incrimination costs, transforming into purchasing power the liquidity deriving from a wide range of criminal activities (transformation); transformation, in turn, produces two more utilities for the criminal agent;
2. the possibility of increasing his rate of penetration in the legal sectors of the economy through the successive phase of investment (pollution);
3. the possibility of increasing the degree to which the criminal actors and organizations are camouflaged in the system as a whole (camouflaging).

Having defined the problem in the most general terms possible, we can now investigate in detail and in depth the choices of a generic criminal organization that, having accumulated resources in the illegal markets, must decide whether, and to what extent, to launder the proceeds of a given crime. In other words, we shall analyse the determinants of the demand for money-laundering of a single criminal organization at the microeconomic level.

THE MICRO MODEL

Let us assume[2] that the agent – a criminal organization – derives a certain flow of income from illegal activity equal to W. This income cannot be spent immediately, since it would increase the probability that the crimes committed by the criminal organization are detected. This may seem a rather drastic assumption: in effect, we can imagine that some expenditures can be made without risk, others less, and others with a very high probability of incrimination. In any case, clean liquidity, unlike dirty fi-

---

[2] Donato and Masciandaro (2001).

nancial resources, permits the maximum freedom of allocation, given its smaller expected incrimination costs.

The general circumstance whereby not all the illegal revenues need necessarily be laundered, but that at the same time the clean liquidity has a competitive advantage over dirty funds, can be represented in a very simple way: a clean euro (or dollar) 'is worth more' – in the eyes of the Criminal Organization – than a dirty euro. The greater utility value of the clean euro is reflected in greater profitability, at least potentially. The illegal income W therefore represents only potential purchasing power; without laundering, it has less value. For each euro of illegal income, the Criminal Organization must first decide whether to launder it or not. A dirty euro is worth less than a laundered one.

If we consider that the clean euro can be used in a welfare-increasing manner or invested with profit and without risk of incrimination, activating the phase of investment and re-accumulation with the utmost effectiveness, and that therefore the dirty euro can be spent with less profit and/or greater risk of incrimination, for the sake of simplicity we can assume that the expected value of the dirty euro is zero: in fact, we could even assign it a smaller positive value, with respect to the cleaned euro, or a negative expected value, given the incrimination costs.

We shall adopt the zero value case, so by calling the utility function of the Criminal Organization U we shall be assuming that the expected utility of the unlaundered income is zero, whatever its amount:

$$U(W) = 0 \qquad (1.1)$$

If the decision to launder were cost-free, indicating with Y the amount of illegal income the Criminal Organization seeks to launder, it is trivial to deduce that we shall have $Y = W$. But money laundering is a crime, and as such it is characterized by a sanction T and a probability that the said crime will be detected, equal to p. The dilemma for the criminal is the following: if I have the liquidity laundered, and all goes well, I derive maximum benefit from the clean money in the investment and re-accumulation phase, net of the cost of the money-laundering operation. If all goes badly, I will not only lose the liquidity paid for the money-laundering operations but will also suffer the sanction of the law.

Now, let us define the hypotheses related to the monetary value of the benefit B of having laundered cash, the cost C of the money-laundering operation, and the damage T deriving from the law sanction.

Each laundered euro can be invested without restrictions and with profit in the reinvestment phase. The fact that the laundered cash Y has a positive expected profitability can be represented by imagining that the monetary value B of that benefit is equal to:

$$B = (1+r)Y = mY \qquad (1.2)$$

where r is the average rate of return expected from reinvestment – licit (investment) and/or illicit (re-accumulation) – of the laundered cash.

The cost C of the money-laundering operation will be proportional – according to a parameter c between 0 and 1 – to the amount of the liquidity that is laundered:

$$C = cY \qquad (1.3)$$

The monetary value of the damage of the sanctions T against money laundering must be, as an amount, at least equal to value Y of the laundered liquidity (due to seizure of the sum, for example). In reality, the damage of a sanction is undoubtedly a multiple, whether due to the monetary amount or to the value of the intangible damage of such a sanction. We can therefore hypothesize that the amount of the value of the sanction is a multiple of the detected 'laundry', the square of that sum for simplicity of calculation.

Furthermore, once the crime is discovered, the sanction can be applied with a variable degree of efficiency and/or severity. The rapidity and mode of execution of the punishment can be variables, affected by national or international institutional variables; the severity (or the laxity) of executing the sanctions can be represented by variations in the parameter t:

$$T = tY^2 \qquad (1.4)$$

Having defined the terms of the question, the Criminal Organization is faced with the problem of deciding whether and how much of the sums obtained in the accumulation phase to launder. The expected utility E of the Criminal Organization, previously expressed in generic terms, can now be better specified as:

$$E = u\big[(1-p)(B-C) + p(-C-T)\big]$$
$$E = u\big[(1-p)(my-cy) + p(-cy-ty^2)\big] \tag{1.5}$$

The linear specification of the utility function of the Criminal Organization shows us that it is risk-neutral. This utility function is consistent with the economic characteristics we requested and recalled earlier. In fact:

$$\frac{\partial E}{\partial p} = -uy(ty+m) < 0$$

$$\frac{\partial E}{\partial t} = -upy^2 < 0 \tag{1.6}$$

$$\frac{\partial E}{\partial m} = uy(1-p) > 0$$

The utility of the Criminal Organization is reduced to an increase in the probability of detection of the crime and the severity of the sanctions, while it increases as the expected return on the laundered liquidity, re-invested in the investment and re-accumulation phase, rises.

The alternatives for the Criminal Organization can thus be summarized in Figure 1.1.

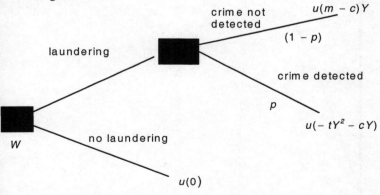

Figure 1.1 The alternatives for the criminal organization

The Criminal Organization must find the optimal level Y^* of liquidity to launder, bearing in mind that the maximum resources at its disposal, obtained in the accumulation phase, amount to W. Deriving (1.5) twice respect to that variable subject to decision of the Criminal Organization – in order to observe the conditions necessary and sufficient for a maximum – we find that:

$$\frac{dE}{dY} = -u\left[2\ pty + c - m(1 - p)\right]$$
$$\frac{d^2E}{dY} = -2\ upt$$

(1.7)

The function reaches its optimal point when:

$$Y^* = \frac{m(1 - p) - c}{2\ pt}$$

(1.8)

The expected utility of the Criminal Organization therefore depends on the level of liquidity laundered (Figure 1.2):

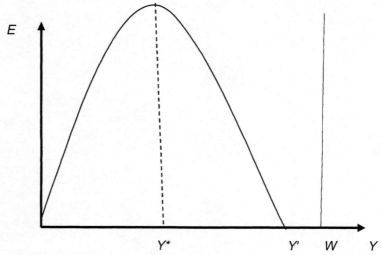

Figure 1.2 The expected utility of the criminal organization

First, let us observe that the value of this utility is positive for levels of laundered liquidity between 0 and:

$$Y' = \frac{m(1-p)-c}{pt} \tag{1.9}$$

The threshold value Y' tells us the limit over which it is undoubtedly optimal for the Criminal Organization to abstain from money-laundering activity. Above a certain amount, the damage associated with the risk of discovery and punishment is so high that the expected utility is negative, so it is best to hold onto the dirty money and invest it in those expenditures or uses where the expected value – as we said earlier – is less or, in the case of our model, zero. This result depends, all other conditions being equal, on the fact that the amount of the sanctions is a multiple of the liquidity to be laundered, so as that value rises the damage of crime detection rises more than proportionately.

The critical value Y' must obviously be compared with the level of the illegal resources available from the accumulation activity W.

If $Y' < W$ (as in Figure 1.2), the amount of resources $(W - Y')$ will be excluded a priori from any decision on laundering.

If, on the contrary, $Y' > W$, it is potentially advantageous to launder all the illegal resources available.

The threshold value Y' – or, if divided by W, the propensity to launder the accumulated illegal funds – will depend on the structural parameters of the model. In fact:

$$\frac{dY'}{dp} = \frac{c-m}{p^2 t}, \frac{dY'}{dt} = \frac{-m(1-p)+c}{pt^2}$$

$$\frac{dY'}{dm} = \frac{(1-p)}{pt}, \frac{dY'}{dc} = -\frac{1}{pt} \tag{1.10}$$

Regarding the reactivity of the propensity to launder compared to the probability of incrimination and the severity of the sanctions, it is crucial to assume that the profitability of each euro laundered is greater than the per-euro cost of money laundering. In this case, more effective policies (p rising) and/or greater severity (t rising) reduce the propensity to launder.

On the other hand, an increase in the profitability of the economic activities, which require clean liquidity in the investment phase (*m* rising), increases the propensity to launder. Finally, a drop in the costs of the money-laundering operation (*c* declining) increases it.

Having defined the framework of values in which the Criminal Organization can exercise its money-laundering choice, we must find the optimal level Y^* of that choice from (1.7):

$$Y^* = \frac{m(1-p)-c}{2pt} \qquad (1.11)$$

always below the constraint:

$$Y^* < W \qquad (1.12)$$

As for the potential propensity to launder, we can also identify the optimal level of laundering respect to the structural variables of the model. First, the liquidity to be laundered will be inversely proportional to the probability of detection of the crime (Figure 1.3).

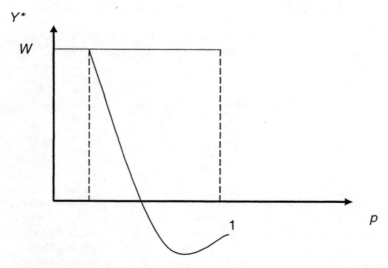

Figure 1.3 The optimal level of money laundering respect to the probability of detection

As we expected, as the probability of detection of the money-laundering crime increases, the level of that criminal activity declines. It is interesting to note that the liquidity to be laundered becomes zero when the probability of incrimination is high ($p = (m - c)/m$), but not maximum ($p = 1$).

This result depends on the fact that the money laundering operation has an economic cost that, when added to the costs associated with the risk of incrimination, makes the laundering activity not advantageous in the absolute sense, even when the probability of discovery of the crime is not maximum. In fact, only if money laundering cost nothing ($c = 0$) would this activity be zero only for $p = 1$.

Given the constraint on available illegal resources we can identity the minimum value of the probability of detection ($p = (m - c)/(m + 2tW)$); lower values of that probability have no effect on the level of money-laundering.

Secondly, money laundering is affected by the severity of the punishment (Figure 1.4): the more severe the law, the less advantageous it will be to attempt to launder dirty money. Again, given the constraint on available illegal resources, a minimum level also exists for the severity of the punishment ($t = [m(1 - p) - c]/(2pW)$). Overall, the incrimination costs matter.

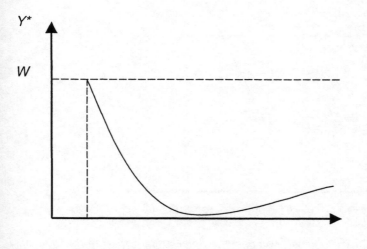

Figure 1.4 The optimal level of money laundering respect to the severity of the punishment

Money laundering will also depend on the profitability of the laundered money in the investment phase (Figure 1.5). We have seen that the Criminal Organization decides to launder depending on the profitability of the clean money with respect to dirty money. The more this profitability increases, the more advantageous it will be to invoke money-laundering services. On the other hand, if the profitability of clean money tends to decline – as when dirty money can be used for consumption or investment without risk of incrimination – the incentive to utilize laundering services also declines. More specifically, money laundering becomes zero if:

$$m = (1+r) \leq \frac{c}{(1-p)} \qquad (1.13)$$

Again, given the constraint on the available illegal resources, the maximum relevant value of profitability from the laundered liquidity ($m = (c + 2ptW)/(1 - p)$) is found.

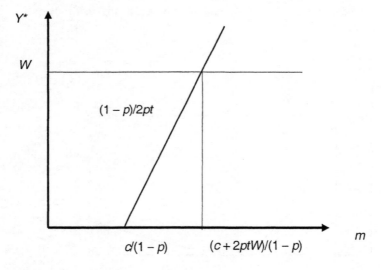

Figure 1.5 The optimal level of money laundering respect to the value of the profitability

Finally, it is possible to analyse the relationship between the cost of laundering operations and the amount of liquidity to be laundered, i.e. the demand for laundering in the strict sense, where the demanded good is precisely the laundering service and its price the cost (Figure 1.6).

The price-quantity relationship – as one might imagine – is an inverse one, and the sensitivity of the demand for money-laundering services compared to the their price (elasticity) is equal to:

$$\eta_{Y^* c} = \frac{c}{2ptY^*} \tag{1.14}$$

The elasticity of the demand for money laundering varies along a curve that rises as the cost rises (from zero to infinity) and is equal to one at point $Y^{**} = c/(2pt)$. Money laundering is zero with a price of $c = m(1 - p)$, while, on the contrary, with a price of zero the optimal level of money-laundering would be $Y^* = [m(1 - p)/(2pt)]$. In reality, the constraint of illegal resources must be taken into account, and when it hurts, the minimum value of the price is not zero but rather $c = m(1 - p) - 2ptW$.

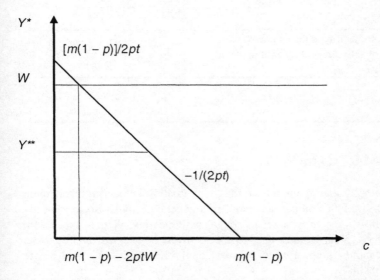

Figure 1.6 The optimal level of money laundering respect to the cost of laundering operations

As with elasticity, the position of the money-laundering demand curve also changes as the structural parameters of the model vary. An increase in the profitability of laundered liquidity causes an upward movement, while an increase in the probability of detection and the severity of the punishment produces a downward movement.

In conclusion, the choice of the Criminal Organization regarding the amount of liquidity to launder is influenced in certain directions by a series of key variables: the variables are summarized in Table 1.1, along with the extent of their influence on the 'laundering'.

Table 1.1 Money laundering: the determinants

Key Variables	Elasticity
W = amount of the proceeds of criminal activity related to the accumulation phase	$\eta_{Y^*,W} = \dfrac{W}{Y^*} > 0$
p = probability of detection of the crime in the money-laundering phase	$\eta_{Y^*,p} = -\dfrac{(m-c)}{2\,ptY^*} < 0$
T = severity of the sanctions in the money-laundering phase	$\eta_{Y^*,t} = \dfrac{-(1-p)m+c}{2\,ptY^*} < 0$
M = profitability of the laundered cash compared to that of dirty cash in the investment phase	$\eta_{Y^*,m} = \dfrac{(1-p)m}{2\,ptY^*} > 0$
c = cost of money-laundering operations	$\eta_{Y^*,c} = -\dfrac{c}{2\,ptY^*} < 0$

THE MACRO MODEL

To define a macro model of the accumulation-laundering-investment process, we focus on the behaviour of a general Criminal Sector that derives its income from a set of illegal activities and that, under certain conditions, must launder the income to invest it. We will highlight the role of money laundering as a overall multiplier of the Criminal Sector endowment.[3]

---

[3] Masciandaro (1998, 1999 and 2000).

Let us assume that in a given economic system there is a Criminal Sector that controls an initial volume of liquid funds *ACI,* fruit of illegal activities of accumulation. Let us further suppose that, at least for part of those funds, determined on the basis of the optimal microeconomic choices studied in the previous chapter, there is a need for money laundering. Without separating these funds from their illicit origin, given the expected burden of punishment, they have no value. Money-laundering activity is therefore required.

Incidentally, to underscore the general nature of the analysis, we can claim that the demand for money-laundering services could be expressed – distinguishing the different potential components of a criminal sector according to their primary illegal activity – by organized crime in the strict sense, by white collar crime, or by political corruption crime, also considering the relative cross-over and commingling.

Each laundering phase has a cost for the Criminal Sector, represented by the price of the money-laundering supply. The price of the money-laundering service, all other conditions being equal, will depend on the costs of the various money-laundering techniques. If we suppose, as in the previous chapter, that the Criminal Sector is price taker, i.e. the cost of money laundering cR is constantly proportional to the amount of the illicit funds, designating the costs c, both regulatory and technical, we can write:

$$cR = cACI \qquad (1.15)$$

If the first laundering phase is successful, the Criminal Sector that expressed the demand for this service may spend and invest the remaining liquid funds $(1 - c)yACI$ in both legal economic activities (investment) or illicit activities (re-accumulation).

The Criminal Sector will spend part of the laundered liquidity in consumer goods, equal to d, while a second portion will be invested in the legal sectors of the economy, for an amount of f, and then a third portion, equal to q, will be reinvested in illegal markets (giving, of course, $d + f + q = 1$).

If the Criminal Sector makes investment choices according to the classical principles of portfolio theory, indicating with $q(r, s)$ the amount of laundered funds reinvested in illegal activities, with r the differential between the actual expected return on the illegal re-accumulation and the actual expected return on the legal investment, and with s the relative risk of the two investments, we might think that the differential in return between illicit and legal activities is positive. We use this assumption if for no other reason than the presence of taxation in computing the return on legal economic activity, while the various assumptions on the relative risk are anything but certain. Furthermore, it should be noted that the relative risk of the illegal sector will depend in part on the effectiveness of the public action to combat it.

Finally, we can assume that the re-accumulation of funds in the illegal sector requires their laundering only in part, thus indicating with the positive parameter y the portion of illegal re-accumulation that requires laundered liquidity.

The Criminal Sector reinvests and a new flow of illegal liquidity will be created. The illegal revenues will be characterized again by incrimination costs, that will generate a new demand for money-laundering services. Obviously, the laundering will concern the overall proceeds of the new phase of investment in illicit activities, whether they have been financed, for a portion equal to a, with laundered cash, or have been financed, for a portion $(1 - a)$, with dirty cash. It will be therefore equal to:

$$(1 + r)(1 - c)^2 \, qy^2 ACI \tag{1.16}$$

The crucial assumption, in fact, is that both the lawful investment and part of the unlawful re-accumulation require financing with 'clean' cash. This assumption can be supported by the presence of rational, informed operators in the supply of services to the Criminal Sector for the illegal re-accumulation, or by rationality of the criminal himself, who wishes to minimize the probability of being discovered.

Repeating infinite times the demand for money-laundering services, which each time encounter a parallel supply, with the values of the parameters introduced remaining constant, the total amount of financial flows generated by money-laundering activity AFI will be equal to:

$$AFI = \frac{yACI(1 - c)}{1 - yq(1 - c)(1 + r)} = mACI \tag{1.17}$$

with $0 < c, q, y < 1$.

The flow AFI can represent the overall financial endowment generated by the money-laundering activity, and m can be defined as the multiplier of the model. Doing comparative static exercises, it is easy to show that the amount of liquidity laundered will increase as the price of the money-laundering service declines:

$$\frac{\partial AFI}{\partial c} = -\frac{ACIy}{\left[1 - qy\left(1 - c\right)\left(1 + r\right)\right]^2} < 0 \qquad (1.18)$$

the amount of re-accumulation of laundered cash in illegal activities increases, which in turn depends on expected profits, in terms of return and risk:

$$\frac{\partial AFI}{\partial q} = \frac{\left(1 - c\right)^2 \left(1 + r\right) ACIy^2}{\left[1 - qy\left(1 + r\right)\left(1 - c\right)\right]^2} > 0 \qquad (1.19)$$

the differential of expected actual return on the re-accumulation in illegal activities rises, given the return on legal investment:

$$\frac{\partial AFI}{\partial r} = \frac{\left(1 - c\right)^2 ACIqy^2}{\left[1 - qy\left(1 - c\right)\left(1 + r\right)\right]^2} > 0 \qquad (1.20)$$

the initial volume of illegal proceeds increases:

$$\frac{\partial AFI}{\partial ACI} = \frac{y\left(1 - c\right)}{\left[1 - qy\left(1 - c\right)\left(1 + r\right)\right]} > 0 \qquad (1.21)$$

the optimal share of the initial volume of illegal revenues requiring cleaning increases:

$$\frac{\partial AFI}{\partial y} = \frac{\left(1 - c\right) ACI}{\left[1 - qy\left(1 + r\right)\left(1 - c\right)\right]^2} > 0 \qquad (1.22)$$

As is evident, whatever the original crime, if failure to launder the proceeds implies greater probability of detection of the crime, then there is no need for additional or specific assumptions about the nature of that criminal activity. The only characteristic that it must satisfy is the ability to produce flows of income that cannot be reinvested without cancelling their origin, thus generating a demand for money-laundering services.

Therefore, the more effective the money-laundering action, the greater the cash flows available to the criminal organizations for reinvestment, illegal and legal, will be.

Now we look at the volume of investment in the legal sector. Also the legal investment may grow the more effective the money-laundering is. It helps camouflage the illegal organizations within the economic system. Using *ARL* to indicate the total flow of legal investments and r_l the average rate of return:

$$ARL = \frac{f(1-c)(1+r_l)yACI}{1-yq(1-c)(1+r)} \qquad (1.23)$$

So the total investment flow *ART* — illegal and legal — made possible by the money-laundering activity will be equal to:

$$ART = ARI + ARL = \frac{(1-c)[q+f(1+r_l)]yACI}{1-yq(1-c)(1+r)} \qquad (1.24)$$

where:

$$ARI = \frac{q(1-c)yACI}{1-yq(1-c)(1+r)} \qquad (1.25)$$

Expression (1.24) grasps the central role of money laundering in favouring the growth of revenues for the Criminal Sector. Thanks to laundering, the criminals are able not only to consume and spend but, more importantly, to input capital into the legal and illegal circuits of the economy. Furthermore, the more the investments are successful and profitable, the more the criminals increase their strength, raising the level of pollution in the overall economy.

Returning to the initial expression (1.17), if the money-laundering multiplier is stable, changes in the initial revenues from the criminal activities of accumulation will have a more-than-proportional effect on the volume of funds laundered. The maximum multiplying effect is obtained when the costs are negligible ($c = 0$), while at the same time all the proceeds from the criminal activities must be laundered ($y = 1$). In this case, the degree of expansion of the volume of activity *AFI* — which coincides with the maximum flow of liquidity available for reinvestment – produced by laundering is equal to:

$$AFI_{max} = \frac{ACI}{1 - q(1 + r)} \qquad (1.26)$$

The money laundering multiplier become more evident with a dynamic version of the model.[4] Let us assume that the initial criminal endowment is equal to I_0. For the sake of simplicity the criminal organization launders only the capital that will be used in legal transaction, equal to yI_0. The costs of the money-laundering services is a share c of the criminal proceeds. Therefore the laundered capital will be equal to:

$$R_0 = (1 - c)yI_0 \qquad (1.27)$$

The criminal organization will use for legal investment the amount fR_0, with a rate of return r_l, while the expenditure in goods and services is equal to $(1 - f) R_0$. After the first period the total legal endowment will be equal to:

$$L_1 = fR_0(1 + r_l) \qquad (1.28)$$

While the total illegal endowment, given a illegal rate of return r, will be equal to:

$$I_1 = (1 - y)I_0(1 + r_i) \qquad (1.29)$$

In the second period the total legal endowment will be equal to:

$$L_2 = f(1 + r_l)(L_1 + R_1) \qquad (1.30)$$

with

$$R_1 = (1 - c)yI_1 \qquad (1.31)$$

At the end of the days (period) the total legal amount will be:

---

[4] Barone (2004).

$$L_n = f(1 + r_l)(L_{n-1} + R_{n-1}) \tag{1.32}$$

with:

$$R_n = (1 - c)yI_n \tag{1.33}$$

and:

$$I_n = (1 - y)I_{n-1}(1 + r_i) \tag{1.34}$$

The equations from (1.32) to (1.34) define a recursive system, which can be solved starting from the initial condition I_0. From:

$$I_2 = (1 - y)I_1(1 + r_i)$$

Substituting the value of I_1:

$$I_2 = (1 - y)^2 I_0(1 + r_i)^2$$

In general terms:

$$I_n = (1 - y)^n I_0(1 + r_i)^n$$

In order to solve equation (1.32) we will use the iterative procedure, with $L_0 = 0$, given that we can rewrite:

$$
\begin{aligned}
L_n &= f(1 + r_l)(L_{n-1} + R_{n-1}) \\
&= f(1 + r_l)[L_{n-1} + (1 - c)yI_{n-1}] \\
&= f(1 + r_l)[L_{n-1} + (1 - c)y(1 - y)^{n-1}(1 + r_i)^{n-1} I_0]
\end{aligned}
$$

Given the general expression:

$$a_n = r(a_{n-1} + g_{n-1})$$

with:

$$a_1 = r\left(a_0 + g_0\right)$$

$$a_2 = r\left(a_1 + g_1\right) = r\left[\left(a_0 + g_0\right) + g_1\right] = r^2 a_0 + r^2 g_0 + rg_1$$

$$a_3 = r\left(a_2 + g_2\right) = r\left(r^2 a_0 + r^2 g_0 + rg_1 + g_2\right)$$
$$= r^3 a_0 + r^3 g_0 + r^2 g_1 + r g_2$$

....

$$a_n = r^n a_0 + r^n g_0 + r^{n-1} g_1 + \ldots + rg_{n-1}.$$

We can write:

$$a_n = L_n$$
$$r = f\left(1 + r_i\right)$$
$$g_{n-1} = R_{n-1} = \left(1 - c\right) y \left(1 - y\right)^{n-1} \left(1 + r_i\right)^{n-1} I_0$$
$$g_{n-1} = R_{n-1} = R_0 s^{n-1}$$

with:

$$s = \left(1 - y\right)\left(1 + r_i\right)$$

given:

$$a_0 = L_0 = 0$$
$$g_0 = R_0 = y\left(1 - c\right)I_0,$$

we will have:

$$L_n = r^n R_0 + r^{n-1} R_0 s + \ldots + r R_0 s^{n-1}$$
$$= r R_0 \left(r^{n-1} + r^{n-2} s + \ldots + s^{n-1} \right) \qquad (1.35)$$
$$= r R_0 \left(s^n - r^n \right) / (s - r)$$

If as usual $r_i \gg r_l$, $s > r$ holds. Furthermore we can write, with $q = r/s$:

$$L_n = r \cdot R_0 \cdot s^{n-1} \frac{\left[1 - q^n \right]}{\left[1 - q \right]} \qquad (1.36)$$

L_n is linked with a geometric process:

$$1 + q + q^2 + \ldots + q^{n-1} = \frac{1 - q^n}{1 - q}$$

And the equilibrium level is equal to:

$$L_n \cong r s^{n-1} R_0 \frac{1}{1 - q} = \frac{r}{s - r} s^n R_0 \qquad (1.37)$$

$$L_n \cong \frac{f(1 + r_l)}{(1 - y)(1 + r_i) - f(1 + r_l)} y(1 - c) I_0 \left[(1 - y)(1 + r_i) \right]^n \qquad (1.38)$$

We can therefore conclude that the volume derived from the money-laundering activity increases as the extent of the illegal economy increases and has a multiplying effect on it. The growth of the criminal industry in general, and that of money laundering in particular, increases the rate of pollution in the economic and financial system.

MONEY LAUNDERING AND TERRORISM FINANCE

From September 2001, financial systems have come increasingly into the sights of the state agencies appointed to combat terrorism. In that context, the need to increase the fight against the laundering of illicit capital was included in the agenda.

We should immediately stress that in terms of economic analysis the financing of terrorism (money dirtying) is a phenomenon conceptually different from the recycling of capital (money laundering).[5]

To understand the similarities and differences we must briefly review the economic peculiarities of the money-laundering phenomenon that we described in the previous pages. The conduct of any illegal activity may be subject to a special category of transaction costs, linked to the fact that the use of the relative revenues increases the probability of discovery of the crime and therefore incrimination.

Those transaction costs can be minimized through an effective laundering action, a means of concealment that separates financial flows from their origin. Money laundering performs an illegal monetary function, responding to the demand for black finance services expressed by individuals or groups that have committed income-producing crimes.

The financing of terrorism resembles money laundering in some respects and differs from it in others. The objective of the activity is to channel funds of any origin to individuals or groups to enable acts of terrorism, and therefore crimes. Again in this case, an organization with such an objective must contend with potential transaction costs, since the financial flows may increase the probability that the crime of terrorism will be discovered, thus leading to incrimination. Therefore, an effective money-dirtying action, an activity of concealment designed to separate financial flows from their destination, can minimize the transaction costs. Money dirtying can also perform an illegal monetary function, responding to the demand for 'covertness' expressed by individuals or groups proposing to commit crimes of terrorism.

The main difference between money laundering and terrorism finance is in the origin of the financial flows. While in the money-laundering process the concealment regards capitals derived from illegal activity, the terrorist organizations use both legal and illegal fund for financing their action.

Money laundering and money dirtying may coexist when terrorism is financed through the use of funds originating from criminal activities. A typical example is the financing of terrorism with the proceeds from the production of narcotics. In those specific situations the importance of the transaction costs is greater, since the need to lower the probability of

---

[5] Masciandaro (2004b).

incrimination concerns both the crimes that generated the financial flows and the crimes for which they are intended. The value of a concealment operation is even more significant.

In summing up, one is prompted to think that the operational techniques of the two phenomena – the laundering of criminal capital and financing terrorism – are at least in part coincident. It is important, however, that the partial overlapping of money dirtying and money laundering remains a hypothesis to be tested from time to time rather than a thesis.

2.   Economics: The Supply Side

Donato Masciandaro

INTRODUCTION

In this chapter we shed light on the supply side of black finance. When one wonders what procedures the crime of money laundering follows, and how important the banking and financial system is from this standpoint, the traditional approach to the analysis of illegal markets must be supplemented by considering the peculiarities of the financial markets.

In other words, the crucial question is: is there a specificity of banking and financial laundering that makes the activity of intermediaries subject – we shall see whether intentionally or not – to the risks of pollution caused by involvement in laundering transactions? To give a convincing answer to this question, we must explain the reasons why the topic of vulnerability of a country to money-laundering phenomena coincides more or less with an assessment of the vulnerability of its banking and financial sector.

The specificity of banking and financial laundering can be determined by considering, in turn, the peculiarities of the functions that intermediates perform within the economic system. This reflection is particularly necessary, since over the past decade evolution in the architectures of markets and the characteristics of intermediaries has blurred the differences between banks and non-banking financial firms, and this is inevitably reflected in the functioning of the various types of intermediation with respect to the capacity to match the demand of money laundering.

Through an analysis of the specificity of the function of intermediaries, we can therefore also derive useful indications about the specificity of the relative money-laundering activity. We must therefore start from a vision, albeit concise, of the peculiarities of the functions performed in general by financial intermediation with respect to other economic activities, and then go on to consider the differences between banks and other financial intermediaries.

In the traditional approach to the analysis of economic functions of financial intermediaries, these firms satisfy essentially three recurrent demands of heterogeneous economic agents: they reduce transaction costs and risk; coordinating the time preferences.

By reducing the overall transaction costs for the other economic agents, financial intermediaries improve those actors' ability to choose how to allocate their own purchasing power in terms of consumption, savings and investment. The intermediaries thus ultimately animate an industry in which the services offered and sold are intrinsically intangible, with an information content that is at the same time high and not uniformly distributed among all the market participants.

In this way, financial firms become familiar with and coordinate the diversity of the operators' characteristics through the offering and sale of their services, and each intermediary pursues the maximizing of its profit, precisely through the management and enhancement of its information assets, in a sector where information is not uniformly distributed. So financial firms are ultimately credited with having peculiar information assets greater than and different from all the others.

As a result, the financial industry ultimately distinguishes itself, with respect to the purpose of laundering money activity, by two crucial features:

- a higher-than-normal degree of what we can call opacity (a synthetic way to stress the role of asymmetric information), since the exchanges and flows of purchasing power are filtered, coordinated and managed by specialized operators;
- the privileged position of such operators.

It should be emphasized, in any case, that the characteristic of incomplete and asymmetrical distribution of information, between parties that stipulate the various forms of contract or agreement, is accentuated in the provision of financial services but is certainly not a prerogative of those markets: it manifests itself, for example, whenever the characteristics of professional services are examined.

In any case, the central role, quantitative and qualitative, of the financial industry within the overall economic system clearly evidences the features of opacity and centrality of the specialized operators.

The evolution of theoretical literature on financial intermediation has in recent times further accentuated the focus on the question of the distribution of information as the fundamental feature of financial activity. In markets where each agent, on the supply or demand side of funds or services, has a limited information base, financial intermediaries are ultimately characterized as operators who specialize in the handling of information.

The financial contracts can reach extremely high levels of sophistication and complications, because their outcome is ultimately determined or evaluated thanks to new information or events, and because the clients themselves can be absolutely heterogeneous. The relationship between intermediaries and its clients is conducted according to repeated and continuous exchanges, permitting them to extract information of a confidential nature.

Inside the financial sector, a special role is then played by the banks, intermediaries characterized by the simultaneous offering of deposit contracts, which can meet the needs of payments and cash, and loan contracts, which generally cannot be transformed into marketable assets. Banks thus emerge as special financial intermediaries, since both their deposit and loan contracts permit them considerable economies of scale and diversification in the management of information. Thus in markets 'opaque' by definition, they become endowments of confidential information on the beneficiaries of the loans and on the users of the payment services, or the services they provide in general.

The management of the payments system places banks in a crucial position with respect to the money-laundering activity. A payments system will be all the more efficient the more it minimizes the costs that operators sustain to transform their potential goals of allocation of purchasing power into actual choices. But if this is true, this system can be also a potentially optimal and efficient vehicle for transforming the potential purchasing power of illicit revenues into actual purchasing power. In other words, the management of the payments system has a positive value for the honest operator, as it facilitates resource allocation choices. At the same time, it may also prove crucial for criminal agents, who – as we pointed out in Chapter 1 – are seeking to reduce peculiar transactions, in order to minimize the risks of detection, and thus the costs of sanctions and punishment.

It is therefore evident that in markets like banking and lending, where information is neither complete nor readily available, the likelihood of concealing the purchasing power coming from illegal transactions and exchanges becomes greater, and a crucial role is assumed by the conduct of the firms – the banks – involved in those markets.

Banking and financial intermediaries thus stand at the centre of attention of both criminal organizations on the one side, and the law enforcement authorities, on the other side.

For criminals, the presence of collusive operators (criminal intermediaries) or operators ineffective in safeguarding their integrity (honest intermediaries) increases the possibility of utilizing the payment or credit systems, or the financial services system in general, for their illegal objectives. Likewise, for the investigative agencies, the information assets of those companies can be of essential value in revealing the identity and verifying the presence of criminal organizations.

To summarize, the peculiarity of banking and financial laundering is that it is conducted through markets dominated by asymmetric information. The effectiveness of law enforcement will crucially depend on the characteristics and conduct of the banking and financial operators.

This aspect differentiates banking and financial laundering from the forms of crime traditionally examined by economic analysis, where the public authority delegates enforcement to the police forces only. As we will discuss in the following pages, in the repression of banking and financial laundering the banks can play an important role. The banks can be an effective instrument of money-laundering activities, but the degree of involvement of the bank operators can be quite different.

We could have the case of collusion between the bank and the criminal organization, where one or more professionals known perfectly that the transaction is a laundering operation. But we could also have the case of an honest but ineffective bank, unable to detect suspicious transactions. But not every money-laundering operation produces suspicious transactions. If the money-laundering activity is perfectly camouflaged, the bank involved could be honest and normally effective too.

Therefore a criminal organization can implement a money-laundering operation using both criminal bankers and honest ones. At this stage of the analysis we will keep distinct the two possible configurations of banks, in order to shed light on their quite different objectives, incentives and features.

Furthermore, we shall anticipate that the theoretical distinction between honest bankers and criminal bankers is quite consistent with the actual design of money-laundering regulations over the world, which try to discourage the emergence of dishonest professionals and to realize an incentive alignment with the honest ones.

The chapter concludes the analysis of the supply side of the money-laundering markets focusing on the features of the regulator. Recently in several countries the design of the regulation against black finance has been characterized by the institution of specialized agencies: the financial intelligence units (FIUs). The authority with clear responsibilities in detecting money-laundering activities is assuming a precise identity worldwide. The objective of the last section is to analyze from an economic point of view the creation of a financial intelligence unit.

LAUNDERING AND THE ROLE OF BANKS

In this section we shall examine the problems that arise, in a given country and in terms of laundering money risk, from the presence of criminal bankers, i.e. those who knowingly perform laundering transactions. The picture is different with honest banks, through whose many transactions, on both the asset and liability sides, laundering manoeuvres may be attempted by third parties.

Money-laundering manoeuvres if the professionals are honest and proper, however, can leave traces and represent irregularities in the banking and financial accounts, so the authorities rightly find it efficient to request the cooperation of the operators. The more effective this cooperation, the lower the risk of money laundering will be. So while for the criminal professionals the central theme will be deterrence, the principal effects in terms of laundering risk, deriving from the existence of anti-laundering laws aimed at obtaining the cooperation of honest bankers, will depend on how acceptable the laws are to those intermediaries.[1]

The initial assumption is that each form of regulation tends to modify the structure of the incentives to the agents and therefore their conduct. The effectiveness of a regulatory regime therefore depends on its ability to influence the decisions of operators in the proper direction.

The term acceptability, in other words, may indicate a principle central to all banking and financial regulations, and therefore also to anti-money laundering: avoid generating ineffective, or even

---

[1] Masciandaro (2002).

counterproductive, behaviour on the part of intermediaries, by altering their incentives structure in the wrong way.

A drop in regulatory effectiveness will result in a rising risk of money laundering. The possibility that regulation may generate counterproductive effects, deriving from the degree to which it is accepted by the regulated firms, is a general phenomenon, given the existence at least of regulatory compliance costs.

As the costs of regulation rise, the level of regulation acceptability to operators declines: this implies a change in the structure of incentives, and thus conduct, that may become inconsistent respect to the objectives of the regulatory effort. As a result, each regulatory system, to be effective, must be sufficiently acceptable to the firms being regulated.

The costs of money-laundering regulation must be offset by the expected gains of regulation, so that the final net result is a lowering of laundering risk. A distinction must be made between earnings expected at the industry level and gains expected for the individual banks, for both the rules of law aimed at regulating honest bankers and those designed to deter criminal professionals. At the aggregate level, the banking industry obviously encourages all the market participants to accept rules favourably that represent an obstacle to the diffusion of money-laundering phenomena.

Less obvious, however, is the design of anti-money laundering regulations with net expected gains at an individual level. We have seen on the previous pages that the banking and financial industry can play a pivotal role in the development of the criminal sector, as a preferential vehicle for money laundering. Banking and financial laundering performs an essential function in the overall growth of criminal activity by separating the liquid funds from their illicit origin, whatever it might be, and thus permitting their reinvestment in licit or illegal activities. The more the risk return encourages reinvestment in illicit activities, the more the demand for money laundering will increase, exalting the role of laundering as a multiplier of criminal activity. This process can be hindered if the money laundering activity involves costs for the criminals: all other conditions being equal, the costs will rise as the anti-money laundering regulations become more effective.

It is worth noting that the cooperation requested of banks in terms of reporting and monitoring has gradually become more demanding as money laundering techniques have advanced. Let us reconsider the definition of money laundering with respect to any financial transaction: this transaction not only has an economic function of its own but, if adopted for money-laundering purposes, it will also fulfil an illegal function.

Now the assumption is that, precisely because the transaction in question is responding to an unusual (and illegal) purpose, it will be distinguished by elements of irregularity with respect to its normal, physiological features. What will the sources of the irregularity be? They could result from at least one of the base elements of the definition of money laundering, in which an agent activates a procedure for transforming a given amount of potential purchasing power into actual purchasing power, in order to minimize the incrimination risks. Thus the irregularity could refer to at least one of the three elements – the agent, the procedure or the amount – of a given banking transaction.

The evolution in money-laundering procedures has made its detection and monitoring more difficult, precisely because it has made the concealment and separation of the three components of the laundering transaction increasingly effective. Compare, for example, a traditional money-laundering operation – the 'smuggler' – with a more sophisticated version – the offshore and/or on-line financial money-laundering operation.

A first important point, therefore, is the growing difficulty of recognizing the money-laundering irregularity. A second important point is to reflect on the fact that a banking transaction may present forms of irregularity but still not involve attempted money-laundering: the irregularity can therefore be regarded as neither a necessary nor sufficient condition for detecting money laundering.

Therefore what role can banks play in reducing the vulnerability of the legal markets to attempts at criminal pollution? The answer, as we shall seek to demonstrate in the following paragraph, must be sought using economic analysis and inserting two keywords into the reality of the banking and financial industry: information and incentives.

The effectiveness of anti-money laundering regulation, and therefore the greater impermeability of the banking and financial system, depends on the first of the keywords: information. One must consider, as we began to do on the previous pages, that the peculiarity of the criminal activity in question is that it is conducted in markets dominated by various forms of asymmetric information. The banks, by virtue of their information assets, are therefore in a position where it is efficient to delegate them an agency function, as actually occurs, to detect and report criminal instances of money-laundering.

Given that the banks, the public authorities and clients face a series of situations where information is incomplete – nature of the client, nature of the intermediary, his diligence in performing the agent function, environmental factors independent of the conduct of either client or intermediary – the central problem of anti-money-laundering regulation will be to design a system of procedures and incentives that will induce the banking agent to act effectively with respect to the necessary supply of information. In other words, the regulation must influence the choices of banks in the right direction. The risk of misconduct is not just theoretical: as stressed earlier, one general problem of regulation is precisely to minimize the expected costs from exceeding the expected benefits, thus encouraging the agents who do not accept this system of rules to conduct themselves in a elusive manner.

We must again emphasize that it is not sufficient for the regulatory regime to appear effective at the aggregate level, and perhaps formally accepted at the industry level. The macroeconomic advantages of money-laundering regulation, represented by greater stability and efficiency in a safe and sound financial system, do not automatically guarantee effective behaviour at the level of the individual bank, which could, on the contrary, act as a free-rider.

For the individual bank there is a concrete trade-off between the function of agent and the relative costs, linked, on the one hand, to the management and transmission of information and, on the other, to the partial or complete loss of a traditional asset like confidentiality. The less the definition of the role and obligations of intermediaries in the anti-money laundering function affects their incentives in the right way, the greater the risk that each of them will find it optimal to expend the minimum effort, counting on the fact that the others are producing the necessary effort or even on the competitive advantages of not producing it. But if it is optimal for each one not to exert an effort, no one will.

The design of an effective regulatory architecture must therefore take the second keyword into consideration: the incentives. Banks must find it optimal to perform their function of agent effectively. But, given the complex nature of a banking organization – as analysed in the following pages – and the plurality of relationships with the various law enforcement authorities, the system of rules must have a positive effect on the resources deemed important by intermediaries.

Among these, we will consider the possible role of reputation: if a bank operates in markets that assign value to endowments, as reputation, the regulatory system must take that into account. It will then be the banks themselves that are endogenously driven to ensure that the structure of internal incentives in each individual role (from top manager to teller) moves toward conduct of business consistent with the fight against money laundering.

HONEST BANKS

The intuitions described in the previous section can now be organized and examined through a simple model[2]. In defining the characteristics of money-laundering regulation, the behaviour of at least two agents must be taken into account: on the one hand we have the regulator-supervisor, on the other the honest bank. The task of the former is to pursue financial integrity, designing an effective anti-money-laundering rule and monitor its effects in terms of lowering the laundering risk.

Let us remember that in the real word the responsibilities of regulator and supervisor can be not only separate but also much more complex and diversified. In general, we claim that the principal-agent theory is the appropriate general analytical framework to analyse the design of a money-laundering regulation framework. Society is the main principal with an interest in the financial integrity of individual banks and the banking system as a whole and the regulatory authority is the agent of the government. But the question is not so simple.

In addition to the principal-agent approach to the explicit contract between society (taxpayers), and the regulator (social contract), two implicit contracts, with associated risks of capture, could be identified. These are the government-driven and the industry-driven contracts.

An implicit contract between the government and the regulator could exist within the framework of the grabbing hand theory. According to this theory, the contract would be designed to extract short-term political rent from regulators. For example, a corrupt government may put pressure on the regulator not to implement an effective anti-money laundering policy, given its relationship with organized crime.

Another implicit contract may exist between the banking industry – as a vested interest group – or even between individual banks and the regulator. This implicit contract would serve the specific interests of the regulated firm(s), for example by minimizing the compliance costs,

---

[2] Donato and Masciandaro (2001).

whatever should be the negative consequences on the effectiveness of the fight against the illegal capitals.

Last but not least, there is the risk that the regulator will pursue its self interest, which may not be consistent with social welfare. This self interest may be its financial revenues, if the regulator is corrupt. Obviously the interests of the government and/or the banking firms can capture the supervisor through the influence on its self interest, for example its career and financial reward. Alternatively, the banking industry capture could be an indirect case of political capture, or vice versa. In other words, the grabbing hand theory, the capture theory and the career concern theory can be deeply intertwined. Finally, more than one authority can be involved in anti-money laundering responsibilities, notwithstanding – as we will discuss in the last paragraph – the actual trend is toward the creation of specialized agencies.

For the sake of simplicity in our analysis we will use always a single figure of public agency – the Authority – whose objective function is perfectly coincident with the social welfare function. We do not consider any delegation problem between the public agent and the society, nor the existence of capture risks.

The second agent, the Honest Bank, is an economic organization oriented toward maximizing profit, characterized by the fact that because of its banking activity it has private information assets on the economic agents operating in a given geographical area. The bank is viewed as an economic unit with the sole objective of seeking profit (maximizing shareholder value), without considering other possible purposes (maximizing stakeholder value). This assumption does not categorically exclude the possibility that the conduct of banking and financial operators is sensitive to considerations of an ethical nature; it is only to work with the more general assumption of behaviour.

Furthermore, banks are viewed as special firms, in the sense specified in the preceding pages: the characteristics of their assets and/or liabilities identify information assets, actual and potential, greater than those of the customers or other operators in contact with the financial industry.

The rationale of conduct of banks is thus reflected in their attempt to maximize the difference between expected revenues and costs. Any form of money-laundering rule, to influence the conduct of the banking operators, must therefore start from the knowledge that regulation must have a balanced impact on the structure of revenues and/or costs, since in any case it affects costs.

For banks, monitoring and reporting the flow of suspicious liquidity implies the assumption of costs of two types: investments in capital, physical and human, and diminished secrecy with respect to clients. These two types of costs for banks, deriving from anti-money-laundering activity, will be called simply economic costs and secrecy or reputation costs.

Information is the crucial theme in correctly addressing the nature of the relationships between the Authority and the Honest Bank. This theme presents itself in at least three fundamental points. The first point is the difference in information assets between the individual banks and the Authority. Because of this difference, it is rational for the Authority to identify in the banking operators the parties that should be empowered to carry out the anti-money-laundering monitoring and reporting action, to lower the laundering risk. Therefore it is rational for the Authority to ask the bankers for cooperation in identify money-laundering operations.

The second point derives from the fact that the effectiveness of the anti-money-laundering action depends on the effort the intermediaries spend in that action, an effort that the Authority cannot observe and that is costly for the banks. The difficulty in observing the intermediaries' effort associated with the obligation of cooperation typical of the anti-laundering laws is that the intermediaries are asked to produce a good – information useful for anti-money laundering purposes – whose characteristics are difficult to recognize either ex ante or, often, ex post.

The third point is the fact that the effectiveness of anti-money laundering depends not only on the effort of the intermediaries but also on factors independent of them: changes in the level of criminal pollution of the geographical area in which the intermediaries operate; changes in the level of sophistication of the techniques used by the launderers, and so forth. On those factors the Authority and the intermediaries can have only partial information and therefore must conjecture. As a whole, these variables are termed the environmental factor, which makes the performance of anti-money-laundering tasks more or less difficult.

This means that the performance of the regulation not only cannot be totally attributed to the efforts, strong or weak, of the operators but also that the relative role played by external factors cannot be measured with certainty, not even ex post. An example could be a little town with only one bank, where the total absence of money-laundering reporting from the bank to the law enforcement agency might be the epiphenomenon of two diametrically opposed situations: the complete absence of money-laundering activity, or the total indolence of the local intermediary.

The design of anti-money laundering regulations must therefore take four fundamental aspects into account: the information assets, the non-verifiability of bankers' efforts, the costliness of that effort for the intermediaries, and the non-verifiability of the influences of the different factors (agent effort, environment) on the performances (success rather than failure) of the regulation.

The overall framework can be summarized as follows. To contrast the criminal organizations the Authority faces a situation in which it utilizes banks because of their specific information assets, delegating the anti-money-laundering reporting action to them. The intermediaries perform the reporting function with an effort, and the level of effectiveness of the anti-money laundering depends on either this effort and other environmental factors. The Authority cannot observe the banker effort nor its relative effectiveness in combating money laundering.

Regarding the features of the intermediaries' effort, the first issue to discuss is the content of the reporting function, which describes the duties assigned by the anti-laundering rules. The key elements are transparency and consistency of the banker responsibilities.

First, the regulation must minimize ambiguity in defining the purposes and procedures that characterize the bankers' anti-money-laundering function, considering that greater ambiguity increases the expected compliance costs to the agent (inefficiency factor) and consequently increase the temptation to elude.

Similar reasoning applies to the consistency of the mandate: the definition of purposes and procedures of the money-laundering reporting must maximize the consistency between them, so as to avoid the undesirable chain of higher compliance costs – greater temptation to elude.

Since the bankers' effort is unobservable and costly, the anti-money-laundering framework must be designed in such a way that it produces not only expected compliance costs but also expected benefits for the intermediaries. In other words, the regulatory system should provide incentives for the banks involved in the anti-money-laundering function, so that their conduct will be consistent with its goals.

It is important to stress that the concept of incentives is of a different nature and broader scope than that of sanctions: of a different nature, since incentives affect directly the economic sphere of the banks; of a broader scope, since even sanctions, if appropriately designed, can represent a special case of incentive. If the sanctions influence the economic dimension of the intermediaries' activity, given its probability of being applied, it becomes a possible cost item, and avoiding it is consistent with rational behaviour.

Ceteris paribus the difference in effectiveness between a sanction incentive and a compensation incentive depends on the probability that the sanction will be applied. In a world dominated by asymmetric information – the financial markets – it is less likely that the probability of sanction should be a sufficient condition for achieving an effective anti-money-laundering policy. Therefore a well designed anti-money-laundering regulation should contemplate expected benefits as well as costs. The collective gains of the fight against criminal capitals must be internalized in some way, creating individual benefits.

The positive incentives will be indicated simply as economic and/or reputational benefits. If the regulatory system is properly balanced between economic costs and economic benefits, the conduct of intermediaries will be influenced in the proper direction, and they will cooperate; otherwise, they will tend to produce a less-than-optimal effort, eluding regulation. The banks' effort therefore depends on how the system of sanctions and incentives affecting them is formed.

Finally, once the anti-money laundering rules have been defined, and the banks have selected their individual levels of effort, the final outcome in terms of effectiveness of regulation will also be affected by external elements, independent from the goal of the Authority and the intermediaries, which we can call the environment factor. As the technology employed by the launderers changes, for example, the difficulty banking professionals have in understanding that they are instruments of a laundering transaction may change.

The Model

We can start from the fact that the effort of the banks, which we indicate with the variable I, is not observable by the Authority. The difficulty derives precisely from the fact that the regulation cannot define directly the level of effort of the banking operators in their anti-money-laundering duties, which cannot be observed and therefore cannot be objectively on empirically, continuously measured over time.

The consequence of the impossibility of observing the bankers' effort is that the regulatory design must give up seeking to oblige them to expend an effort that cannot be verified but must endeavour to formulate rules that induce them to apply the effort necessary for an effective anti-money-laundering action.

The objective of the Authority will be to make the anti-money-laundering action as effective as possible. We can assume that, in a country where money-laundering activity is possible, one variable that might capture that effectiveness is the number of significant reports, which we shall indicate with variable X.

Qualifying this crucial variable with the adjective 'significant' is a way of emphasizing that the effectiveness of an anti-money-laundering regime can be measured through a two-stage process: it is not enough for the number of reports to increase, since they must also regard financial phenomena that are actually irregular.

It goes without saying that nothing can be said a priori about the relationship between the number of the reports and their significance. But we might also advance the assumption that, ceteris paribus, this relationship will depend on the effectiveness of the rules in influencing bankers in the right direction. If the regulation design produces an alignment of interest between public authorities and individual banks, it is likely that there will be a direct relationship between the number of reports and their significance.

On the other hand, an ineffective but still binding regulatory regime might even push intermediaries toward elusive conduct, in which the anti-money-laundering duties would be fulfilled in form but with little or no effort, perhaps with an increase in the number of reports, but certainly not in their significance. The objective of the Authority is therefore to maximize the number of significant anti-money-laundering reports but with an awareness that this goal is not without costs for the Authority itself.

The objective of the banks, on the other hand, is to select the optimal level of effort in their anti-money-laundering signalling action. The situation of asymmetric information derives precisely from the fact that intermediaries are perfectly aware of their effort in reporting and monitoring, unlike the public Authority. The effort of the intermediaries is reflected, however, in the effectiveness of the anti-money-laundering action, which the Authority can observe ex post.

In an ideal world, if the effort of professionals were the only determinant of the number of significant reports, the level of effort expended by intermediaries could be inferred from the number and the relative sanction/benefit applied to them. The difficulty, however, is that the number of significant reports is also affected by other factors, outside the control of both Authority and intermediaries, which we shall indicate with the general term Environment and represent with the changes in a stochastic variable A.

One might, for example, assume that the effectiveness of anti-money laundering depends on the degree of sophistication – economic and legal – of the money-laundering techniques used by the agents involved in criminal or illegal activity. In this case, the variable A may reflect the level of technology of the launderer. To simplify the analysis, we assume that the variable representing the technology of money-laundering can assume only two values: if $A = A1$, the money-laundering is rudimental, while if $A = A2$, the money laundering is sophisticated.

This means that in the first case the environmental factors are favourable to an effective anti-money-laundering action: the number of significant reports is likely to rise, for a given level of intermediary effort, given that the money-laundering operations are carried out with rudimentary techniques and thus more easy to detect.

In the second case the environmental conditions are adverse: the number of reports, again with a given level of intermediary effort, tends to decline, given that the attempts at money laundering are carried out using refined procedures and thus not easy to detect.

Furthermore, both the Authority and the Honest Bank seek to foresee what money-laundering techniques will be used. Our assumption is that both have the same information and therefore formulate the same conjectures on the probability that the technology is rudimental or sophisticated: these probabilities are expressed by $p1$, for environment $A1$ and $p2$ for environment $A2$.

This assumption may seem restrictive, since the banks are likely to be more familiar with the territory than the Authority; nonetheless, let us imagine that all the agents have the same knowledge about the potential rate of criminal presence in the territory, which is reflected in the characteristics of the money laundering. We can then say that the number of significant anti-money-laundering reports will depend on the effort of the Bank and the technology of the launderers:

$$X = X\left(i, A\right)$$

$$\frac{dX}{di} > 0, \frac{d^2 X}{di} < 0, \frac{dX}{dA} > 0 \qquad (2.1)$$

The first and second derivatives of effort level i of the Bank indicate that the number of significant reports increases as the level of effort increases. The first derivative indicates that the marginal product of the effort is positive, while the second derivative tells us that this product is declining: as the Bank's effort level rises, the effect of regulation on the effectiveness is still positive, but decreasingly so.

The derivative of environment factor A indicates that the more this variable increases, the more the money-laundering technology is rudimental, with positive effects on the number of significant reports.

The objective function of the Authority will be to maximize the social utility of the anti-money-laundering rules, which coincides with its effectiveness in terms of significant reports. We also consider that motivating the Bank with an incentive whose monetary value is equal to Y, is costly:

$$U\left[X-Y\right]$$
$$U_x > 0, U_{xx} \leq 0 \tag{2.2}$$

Given the first derivative, the utility U of the Authority increases as the difference between regulatory effectiveness and the cost that that level of effectiveness has in terms of incentives to the Bank increase. The second derivative tells us that the Authority is risk adverse.

The Bank maximizes its utility V, which will increase as the monetary value corresponding to the incentives increases and as the effort expended in anti-money-laundering activity decreases. If we consider that the Bank is risk adverse, we shall have:

$$V = v\left[Y, i\right]$$
$$\frac{dV}{dY} > 0, \frac{d^2V}{dY} < 0, \frac{dV}{di} < 0, \frac{d^2V}{di} > 0 \tag{2.3}$$

Let us also stress that the regulatory design cannot weigh excessively on the choices of the Bank. In other words, if the anti-money-laundering responsibilities require an effort that is too burdensome relative to the incentives, the Bank will ultimately stop cooperating. The phenomenon of elusion can be gauged, in this model, by assuming that the utility of the intermediaries cannot drop below a minimum level, or reserve utility, which we shall indicate as $V0$. If the incentives are too low, the Bank will take no concrete anti-money-laundering action.

Having defined all the necessary assumptions, we can seek to identify the optimal incentive scheme, starting from the standpoint of the Authority. The Authority must consider that its goal of effectiveness of the anti-money-laundering regulation depends crucially, though not exclusively, on the conduct of the Bank, who must therefore be given incentives. To make the terms of the Authority's problem homogeneous, we must be able to express the social value of an effective money-laundering regulation in monetary terms, as a monetary value can also be assigned to the incentives system, which we shall indicate with the variable Y.

The Authority, in other words, must select an incentives scheme Y: if it had all the necessary information, it could define an incentive scheme dependant on all the relevant variables, i.e. the effectiveness X achieved by the anti-money laundering action, the effort i of the intermediary, and the level A of money-laundering technology, however sophisticated:

$$Y = Y(X, i, A) \qquad (2.4)$$

To be effective, the system of incentives must be correlated to the results, but the responsibilities of the Bank must be distinguished from the effects of factors outside the control of the Bank itself. If there were perfect information we could easily define an optimal design of incentives. It is worthwhile to start from this situation, because it enables us to define the ideal regulatory scheme.

Let us consider that in implementing the money-laundering detection action the Bank has only technical costs, which we assume to be perfectly observable by the Authority.

If the Authority is perfectly informed of the actions the Bank performs in implementing the anti-laundering laws, one of the sources of uncertainty is eliminated, leaving only the question of money-laundering techniques. If the level of effort of the Bank can be observed at all times, and at zero cost, the necessary effort will be ensured with the minimum possible incentive to avoid elusion, while each incentive additional to that minimum will depend on the degree of sophistication of the money-laundering techniques, which will determine whether the regulation is successful.

Note that uncertainly about the effectiveness of the anti-money-laundering action implies that in all cases someone must assume the implicit risk of regulatory success or failure. The propensity of the Bank to assume this risk can vary. The definition of the incentives Y must, therefore, take this element into account if the cooperation of the Bank is to be optimal; otherwise there is the risk of scant collaboration, or even elusion, that can take various forms, including, for example, the formal rejection of the regulatory system by all the intermediaries.

Let us start from a situation in which not only does perfect information exist between Authority and Bank but the level of effort that can be required of them is also a constant, such that $i = i^0$. In other words, the anti-money-laundering duties are reflected in an observable effort that carries measurable costs (investment in information technology, reorganization and training of personnel).

In this first scenario, the task of the Authority seems to be relatively simple, but there are two caveats: first, the effort produces costs for the bank, so a positive incentive must be defined; secondly, considering that in any case the anti-money-laundering effectiveness depends also on environmental factors, the outcome in terms of number of significant reports is uncertain. The probability that the anti-money-laundering action could prove unsuccessful is still different from zero.

This statement prompts a question: who assumes the risk of failure? In other words: must the incentive to the Bank be designed in such a way that it depends on the success or failure of the anti-money-laundering action?

The Authority must define a system of incentives Y^* that maximizes the effectiveness of the anti-money-laundering action and at the same time ensures that the intermediaries actually cooperate (participation constraint):

$$
\begin{aligned}
max_{y(A1),y(A2)} &p1 U\left[X\left(i^0,A1\right)-Y(A1)\right]+ \\
&p2 U\left[X\left(i^0,A2\right)-Y(A2)\right]
\end{aligned}
\tag{2.5}
$$

under the constraint:

$$
p1V\left[Y(A1),i^0\right]+p2V\left[Y(A2),i^0\right]\geq V_0
$$

The conditions necessary for the Authority to obtain the optimal value of the incentive are:

$$
\begin{aligned}
-p1\left\{u'(A1)\left[X(A1)-y^*\right]+\lambda v_y(A1)\right\}&=0 \\
-p2\left\{u'(A2)\left[X(A2)-y^*\right]+\lambda v_y(A2)\right\}&=0
\end{aligned}
\tag{2.6}
$$

If the Bank is equally likely to find itself in a favourable or unfavourable situation, regarding the possibility of performing its anti-money-laundering responsibilities, we can write:

$$\lambda = \frac{u'(A1)}{u'(A2)} = \frac{v_y(A1)}{v_y(A2)} \tag{2.7}$$

Equation (2.7) tells us that in equilibrium the relative welfare procured for the community as a whole – in terms of the fight against criminality – by changes in the incentives must be equal to that procured for the Bank in terms of individual benefits. Or, expressing (2.7) as:

$$\lambda = \frac{u'(A1)}{v_y(A1)} = \frac{u'(A2)}{v_y(A2)} \tag{2.8}$$

The parameter λ can be interpreted as an indicator of the sensitivity of the Authority to the Bank participation constraint. Note that in equilibrium equation (2.8) implies that the Authority sensitivity is higher when the social utility of the anti-money laundering is higher (U') and lower, in turn, when the Bank is sensitive in terms of incentives (Vy). The more the Bank is reactive in terms of effort, for a given change in incentives, the less difficult it will be for the Authorities to match the participation constraint.

The social utility the Authority attributes to an anti-money-laundering regulation depends on how strong the pursuit of financial integrity – i.e. the financial war against criminal organization – is in the country in question at a given time. The sensitivity of the Bank to the incentives tells us how difficult it is to internalize the financial integrity goal.

In this sense, we could also include the ethics rate present in the banking and financial system into the analysis. In fact, the more ethical the Bank, the more sensitive it will be to changes in incentives. This implies that changes, even small ones, in the level of those incentives will cause large increases in the effort expended by the Bank. In other words it will be increasingly easy to satisfy the participation constraint.

Returning to the analysis, it can be represented graphically (Figure 2.1) with an Edgeworth box, in which the relationship between utility and anti-money-laundering reports can be represented simultaneously, in the two environmental states, for both the Authority and the Bank.

From the utility function of the Authority we can derive indifference curves in terms of numbers of reports in the two environmental states. The indifference curves will be linear, since the Authority is risk-neutral. The utility due to the anti-money-laundering action grows from the bottom up.

At the same time from the utility function of the Bank we obtain indifference curves in the two different states that cause – via the incentives scheme – changes in its individual welfare, this time from the top down.

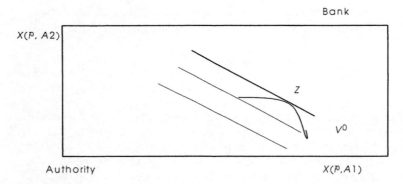

Figure 2.1 The Authority and the Bank: the optimal choice

Equilibrium is reached at point Z, where the participation constraint of the Bank meets with the higher curve (indifference line) of the Authority.

To obtain the value Y^* of the incentive, remembering that the effort of the Bank is fixed, observable and influenced by environmental conditions, deriving (2.6) with respect to A, we find:

$$
-u'\left(\frac{dX}{dA} - \frac{dY^*}{dA}\right) + \lambda v_{yy}\frac{dY}{dA} = 0
$$
$$
-u'\left(\frac{dX}{dA} - \frac{dY^*}{dA}\right) + \frac{u'}{v_y}v_{yy}\frac{dY}{dA} = 0
$$

$$(2.9)$$

Using r to indicate the risk aversion of each of the players – recalling that it is measured, à la Arrow-Pratt, as the relationship between the second derivative and first derivative of the given utility function – we can write:

$$\frac{dY^*}{dA} = \frac{r_A}{r_A + r_I} \frac{dX}{dA} \tag{2.10}$$

where r_A and r_I are the risk aversion of the Authority and the Bank.

The incentive scheme depends on the sensitivity of the effectiveness of the regulatory regime to the characteristics of the money-laundering phenomenon (i.e. how much the number of reports depend on the money-laundering technologies) and on the risk aversion of the two parties.

Two consequences follow. First of all, if the Authority is able to observe without costs the effort expended by the Bank in the anti-money-laundering action, the incentive system, given the participation constraint, should consider that the actual effectiveness of the regulatory regime depends on factors outside the control of the Bank. Furthermore, to ensure optimal cooperation, the risk aversion (or propensity) of the intermediaries involved in the anti-money-laundering action must be taken into consideration. A wrong assessment implies non-optimal cooperation.

Secondly equation (2.10) implies:

$$\frac{dY^*}{dA} \leq \frac{dX}{dA} \tag{2.11}$$

Condition (2.11) tells us that the social welfare gains, in terms of greater financial integrity, that derive from a more favourable environment generally do not translate entirely into private benefits for the Bank. Consequently, obtaining the optimal level of the incentive as the solution to the differential equation (2.10):

$$Y^* = \frac{r_A}{r_A + r_I} x\left(i^0, A\right) + k \tag{2.12}$$

We highlight an interesting result: in general, the optimal incentive consists of two parts, one constant and the other variable with environmental factors. We observe that, if the Authority is risk-neutral ($r_A = 0$), the compensation is fixed, and uncertainty about the degree of success of the anti-money-laundering regulation all accrues to the Authority. If, on the contrary, it is the Bank who are risk-neutral, the compensation will totally absorb the advantages linked to changes in the efficiency of the anti-money-laundering action.

In conclusion, when the compliance costs of anti-money laundering are observable and fixed, if the Authority is risk-neutral, the optimal incentives will be a fixed amount; for example, monetary incentives (or fines) for all the intermediaries that incur (do not incur) those costs.

Let us not examine the case where the Authority is not perfectly informed on the environment situation. The compliance costs, which were fixed before, become variable: the extent and quality of personnel training, as well as the degree of sophistication of the IT products for money-laundering detections may require a variable investment; the larger the investment, the higher the effort of the Bank will be. It is natural to think that now the fixed incentive is no longer sufficient to obtain the optimal effort from the Bank.

The Authority is faced with the problem of designing an incentive scheme that ensures not only that the Bank will cooperate but also that it will produce the best effort. In the previous case, since the effort was fixed, the cooperation alone ensured an optimal level of effort.

The Authority's maximization problem becomes:

$$\max{}_{y(A1),y(A2),i} \; p1U\big[X(i,A)-Y(A)\big] + p2U\big[X(i,A)-Y(A)\big] \tag{2.13}$$

under the constraint:

$$p1V\big[Y(A),i\big] + p2V\big[Y(A),i\big] \geq V_0 \tag{2.14}$$

From the standpoint of timing, we assume that the Authority defines the incentive scheme before it is known in what money-laundering environment (favourable or unfavourable) the Bank will operate. The Bank, knowing the risk level of money-laundering risks, will produce its effort, which will not necessarily be the optimal, if the incentives are not well designed.

The optimization of equation (2.13) under the constraint of (2.14) produces the following first order conditions:

$$\lambda = \frac{u'(A)}{v_y(A)} \tag{2.15a}$$

$$E\left(u'x_i + \lambda v_i\right) = 0 \tag{2.15b}$$

if the first condition is well known from the previous discussion, the second derives precisely from the need of influencing the level of Bank effort in the right direction. Recalling that the Authority is risk-neutral, and substituting (2.15a) into (2.15b), we can write:

$$E\left(u'x_i + u'\frac{v_i}{v_y}\right) = 0 \tag{2.16}$$

$$E\left(x_i\right) = -\frac{v_i}{v_y}$$

The Authority must determine an incentive Y^* that will confirm equations (2.16). In other words, the marginal increase in effectiveness of the anti-money-laundering signalling must be equal to the marginal effort of the Bank, net of its remuneration. The greater the effort of the Bank, the greater the success of the anti-money-laundering action will be, and the optimal level of effort is obtained paying just the necessary remuneration.

A graphic representation of the equilibrium (Figure 2.2) may be useful for highlighting three interesting features.

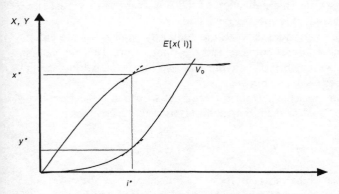

Figure 2.2 The optimal choice with asymmetric information

The Figure represents, on the one side, the expected pattern of the number of money-laundering reports as a function of the Bank effort (a demand for anti-money-laundering effort). On the other side the objective function of the Bank $V(y, i)$ gives the curve of the participation constraint V_0, which may indicate the supply of anti-money laundering effort.

The optimal level of incentive Y^* – and therefore of effort i^* and the number of reports X^* – is obtained when the slopes of the two curves are equal, thus satisfying equations (2.16).

First of all, the optimal incentive is such that the benefit increases with the effort of the Bank, observable in terms of sustained costs. The incentive must therefore be variable, like the effort. Secondly, note how the equilibrium point is such that maximizes the distance between the social welfare related to the number of reports and that of the incentive provided to the Bank. The design of the regulation extracts the maximum rent from the Bank effort.

In fact another equilibrium could be obtained by matching the demand and supply of anti-money-laundering effort. The Bank will still be on its participation constraint, but the remuneration value should be equal to the social value of the number of reports. For the social welfare point of view the first equilibrium is better.

Thirdly, it is interesting to stress that both increases in the sensitivity of the Bank to the costs of signaling (V_A) and reductions in the sensitivity to the incentive (V_i) shift upward the supply of anti-money-laundering effort, producing an increase in the remuneration necessary to obtain the same effort. Any change that reduces the incidence of the compliance costs, or increases the internalization of the financial integrity goal (i.e. more ethics in banking) is socially desirable.

The last case to consider is when the Authority cannot observe either the money-laundering technologies and the Bank effort. The regulators simply known the number of banking reports. The incentive alignment problem becomes more complicated.

Let us assume that the Authority continues to propose the incentive scheme Y^*. The Bank will calibrate their effort to that incentive:

$$\max_i \ p1V\left[Y^*\left(A,i\right),i\right] + p2V\left[Y^*\left(A,i\right),i\right] \tag{2.17}$$

The difference is that now the Bank, as it cannot longer be observed, will have more degree of freedom to chose the effort level consistent with incentive Y^*. From the Bank point of view, the optimal effort is the result of the following condition:

$$E\left[v_i\left(\frac{dY^*}{dX}x_i + \frac{v_i}{v_y}\right)\right] = 0 \qquad (2.18)$$

While in perfect information from the Authority point of view the optimal effort is the result of the condition:

$$E\left(u'x_i + u'\frac{v_i}{v_y}\right) = 0 \qquad (2.19)$$

Nothing guarantees that the optimal level of effort will coincide in the two cases. Other things being equal, in the case of perfect information the optimal effort depends on the social welfare produced by a greater number of reports, caused in turn by greater effort ($U'X_i$), while with asymmetric information the Bank benefits produced by more effective signalling action [$Vp(dP^*/dX\, X_i)$] become crucial.

We will demonstrate that in asymmetric information the Authority must correlate the incentives on the banking performances in the anti-money-laundering action, but with different values for the same incentives compared to the case with perfect information.

Let us start by considering the utility function of the Bank, which is assumed to be separable and additive:

$$V(Y,i) = v(y) - w(i) \qquad (2.20)$$

Knowing that a correlation exists, though imperfect, between the effectiveness x of the anti-money laundering action and the Bank effort, we define the remuneration for a given number of reports x_n and the relative level of utility as $y = y(x_n)$ and $Z_n = v[y(x_n)]$. Introducing a function t as the inverse function of v, we can write:

$$\begin{aligned} t[v(y)] &= y \\ y(x_n) &= t(z_n) \end{aligned} \qquad (2.21)$$

To compute the optimal incentive, the Authority must first consider that each action by the Bank – precisely because it is not observable – may result in various outcomes, in terms of anti-money-laundering effectiveness. Indicating, for each action i_m, the probability that success is equal to x_n with p_{mn}, the expected level of the incentive corresponding to that action will be:

$$\sum_{n=1}^{N} p_{mn} t(z_n) \qquad (2.22)$$

Now the Authority must not only satisfy the usual participation constraint of the Bank:

$$\sum_{n=1}^{N} p_{mn} z_n - w(i_m) \geq v^0 \qquad (2.23)$$

but also consider that among the actions that satisfy condition (2.24) the Bank will choose the most convenient (incentive constraint):

$$\sum_{n=1}^{N} p_{mn} z_n - w(i_m) \geq \sum_{n=1}^{N} p_{m'n} z_n - w(i_{m'}) \qquad (2.24)$$

$$m' \neq m$$

Optimizing (2.22), under constraints (2.23) and (2.24), from the first order conditions, letting λ stand for the Lagrange multiplier relative to constraint (2.23) and β the multipliers relative to (2.24), we find:

$$y'(x_n) = t'(z_n) = \lambda + \sum_{m'=1}^{M} \beta_m \left(1 - \frac{p_{m'n}}{p_{mn}}\right) \qquad (2.25)$$

The equilibrium condition (2.25) tells us that the optimal level of incentive will depend on how consistent the Bank's choices are with the Authority's. The same level of anti-money-laundering effectiveness (x_n) can be achieved with effort m consistent with the social welfare, or with a different level of effort m'.

If the socially desirable effort is also the most efficient ($p_{mn} > p_{m'n}$), we shall have that the incentive is greater than the corresponding level with symmetric information (λ). The society must be willing to pay more for the Bank' effort, if it wishes the Bank to follow and cooperate in the financial war against organized crime.

CRIMINAL BANKS

In the previous section we discussed how to design regulation when honest banks are unconsciously used in money-laundering processes. But it could be also the case of collusion between the bank and the criminal organization, where one or more banking operators knows perfectly that the transaction implemented is a laundering operation (criminal bank).

The criminal bank is an intermediary owned or controlled by criminals which, among its activities, conceals the origins of capitals generated by illegal activities. The money-laundering activity of a criminal bank consists of a process of transformation, in which the financial input is the liquidity to be cleaned and the financial output is cleaned money.

A criminal bank can be interpreted as a special type of legal firm whose ownership or control relates to criminals. More precisely, we can say that a criminal intermediary represents the typical example of a legal company involved in a specific illegal activity.

The reasons why a criminal organization decides to control a banking firm can be classified in two categories: one the one hand, the general reasons why a criminal organization decides to be involved in legal activity; on the other, the specific functionality of the banking sector with regard to money laundering. We have already discussed how the supply of banking services can be useful for money-laundering activities.

In order to analyse how to design the regulation in order to prevent and combat the criminal bank we shall focus on two agents: the public Authority and the criminal bank.

The Authority is focused on the social losses deriving from the existence of a criminal bank. It has been demonstrated in the preceding pages that the more effective the money-laundering action, the greater the economic weight of criminal organizations. The social welfare is improved when the Authority pursues financial integrity.

The Model

We might assume[3] that the presence of criminal banks produces social losses. The social loss D grows linearly with the level of money-laundering activity R. The parameter d can be considered the weight assigned to the financial integrity in the behaviour of the Authority.

Therefore:

---

[3] Masciandaro (1996).

$$D = dR$$

$$d = \frac{dD}{dR} > 0 \qquad (2.26)$$

Money-laundering activity can be approximated by the values of a continuous variable ranging from 0 (no money laundering) to 1 (maximum money laundering). We can also consider that this variable represents the probability that a criminal bank will carry out a money-laundering operation.

The most natural assumption is to consider that money laundering causes net social losses, due to the effect of pollution in the financial, economic and social system. We should also mention the possibility that for some countries or some policymakers the money-laundering activity can cause both losses and benefits. The possibilities of benefits is paradigmatic in the case of the offshore centres (OFCs).[4]

The major industrialized countries view as vulnerable those countries and territories whose regulations are relatively accommodating compared to their own, in the sense that greater risks exist that money laundering or terrorism financing transactions can be concealed.

But why do the offshore financial centres possess these lax regulations? To answer, the key concept is the surplus of economic benefits that the OFCs receive by having lax regulations. Thanks to theoretical and empirical analyses it was demonstrated that the OFCs display relatively uniform structural characteristics, economic and institutional: they are countries and territories of modest wealth, poor in natural resources, with a strong dependence on the income produced by their banking and financial services, devoid of particular problems associated with terrorism risk and organized crime risk.

Therefore the laxity of their financial regulation ultimately becomes a case of free lunch for the OFCs: the anticipated benefits of laxity, in terms of increasing the value produced by the financial industry, are evident, while they do not perceive the anticipated costs, represented by greater risks of increasing terrorism and organized crime.

However, we shall assume that the net social loss of money laundering is positive, i.e. that this crime is considered politically 'bad'. We can take into account the possible presence of benefits from money laundering by considering the costs of anti-money laundering.

---

[4] Masciandaro (2004a) and (2005a).

The Authority must consider not only the net social loss of money-laundering but also the social costs that the community sustains for its anti-money-laundering action. The Authority must take into account the resources necessary for an effective anti-money-laundering policy, evaluating both the widespread costs to the community – linked to both enforcement and sanctions – and the specific compliance costs for the financial sector, discussed in the previous section.

The Authority decides to undertake an activity A to combat and prevent the money laundering. If we assume that the social costs are related to the intensity of the anti-laundering activity A, we may write:

$$C = cA$$

$$c = \frac{dC}{dA} > 0 \tag{2.27}$$

The parameter c can be interpreted as the cost inefficiency factor. This assumption, as we shall see, is crucial for determining whether an anti-money-laundering policy is effective or not. If the actions taken by the Authority to increase the probability of discovery of the crime are conducted according to procedures that have an effect on the costs, the risk is that it will produce unsatisfactory results in terms of both efficiency and effectiveness.

How intense should the activity to combat and prevent the phenomenon be? If we assume that it increases as the perceived results of the war against crime worsen, we can suppose that the level of anti-laundering activity will rise the more unsatisfactory the results achieved, R, become in terms of crimes detected, given the probability p that the crimes are detected:

$$A = a(1 - p)R \tag{2.28}$$

Finally it should be noted that the anti-money-laundering sanctions T that the Authority may decide to apply to the individual criminal banks may be reflected in costs for the financial system as a whole. The punishment inflicted in the case of flagrant money-laundering crime can have widespread costs, involving, for example, the overall reputation of the banking and financial system. Let us assume that the social costs S of the existence of a scheme of anti-money laundering sanctions depend –

according to a parameter q, the reputation inefficiency factor – on the extent of the sanction, as well as the probability it will be inflicted:

$$S = qpT \qquad (2.29)$$

Criminal banks that offer laundering services are faced with the problem of generating the profits related to money-laundering activity without incurring the sanctions contemplated for that crime. The expected utility *EU* deriving to criminal intermediaries from money-laundering activity *R* can be expressed as:

$$EU_R = pU(Y-T)+(1-p)U(Y) \qquad (2.30)$$

where *p* is the probability of being detected and incriminated for the crime of money-laundering, *U* is a parameter that represents a linear utility function, *Y* the income deriving from the laundering activity, and *T* the sanctions, whose value – whatever their nature – is always expressed in monetary terms, for the sake of simplicity.

The behaviour of the Criminal bank depends on the two classical law enforcement variables à la Becker: probability of incrimination and level of sanction. Any cost (pecuniary, personal, reputational, etc.) is translated into a monetary value which anti-money-laundering regulation can inflict on those convicted of that crime. This is an important point, since in our analysis the sanction has a dual characteristic: it is any measure whatsoever but one that actually affects the objective function of the intermediary. Consequently, when we go on to consider the concrete institutional and juridical structures, we must ask ourselves which of the various possible sanctions actually hurts in that specific context. Both an increase in the sanctions and an increase in the probability of being incriminated reduce the utility of undertaking money-laundering activity:

$$EU_P = -UT < 0$$
$$EU_T = -pU < 0$$

(2.31)

We can also wonder if the deterrent effect is stronger with intensified anti-laundering action (increase in p) or with harsher sanctions (increase in T). The answer generally depends on the risk propensity of the criminal bank: the less the risk aversion, the more effective the anti-laundering action will be with respect to the extent of punishment. In our case, having assumed a linear utility function, the banks are risk neutral, so the sensitivity (or elasticity) of criminal banks to the risk of detection s_p and to the risk of sanctions s_T are equal:

$$s_p = \frac{dEU}{dp} \frac{p}{EU} = \frac{-Tp}{Y - pT}$$

(2.32)

$$s_T = \frac{dEU}{dT} \frac{T}{EU} = \frac{-Tp}{Y - pT}$$

(2.33)

$$s_p = s_T$$

(2.34)

Finally we have to describe our assumptions on the determinants of money-laundering activity. Let us to define a linear relationship between the number of money-laundering operations, the two law enforcement variables and volume of the legal activity of the criminal Bank, the later summarized with a variable W:

$$R = R(p, T, W) = fW - x(p + T)$$

(2.35)

Given the utility function of the Criminal Bank, the number of money-laundering crimes will be negatively correlated to the incrimination risk and to the relative sanction trough the same parameter x (punishment effect):

$$R_p = \frac{dR}{dp} = -x < 0$$

$$R_T = \frac{dR}{dT} = -x < 0 \qquad (2.36)$$

The relationship between the criminal activity R and the legal banking activity W captures the assumption that money laundering is more likely if it is muddled and concealed through an increasing number of legal transactions. In this way, the corrupt intermediaries are able to enjoy economies of scale and range in the conduct of their activity.

The Authority defines the optimal values of the law enforcement variables, taking in account the costs to implement money-laundering policy. The Authority faces a trade off between financial integrity and efficiency. If we wish to completely eliminate the risk that a money-laundering crime can be committed using the banking system, the costs, in terms of well-being for the legal operators – households, firms and banks – would probably be relevant and must be considered. We can define the social cost function V in the following way:

$$V = D(R) + C(p,R) + S(p,T)$$
$$V = dR + caR(1-p) + qpT \qquad (2.37)$$
$$V = d(fW - xp - xT) + ca(1-p)(fW - xp - xT) + qpT$$

The Authority obtains the equilibrium values of p and T by differentiating (2.37):

$$P = \frac{x(d+ca)}{cax+q}$$

$$T = \frac{2cax}{(cax+q)}\left[\frac{dx+cafW+cax}{2cax} - \frac{x(d+ca)}{(cax+q)}\right] \qquad (2.38)$$

The Authority derives the optimal law enforcement policy, depending on the structural variables of the model, such as the relative value of integrity and efficiency (the values of d, on the one hand, and c and q, on the other) as well as the crime attitude among the banking operators (the value of x):

$$\frac{dP}{dc} = \frac{ax(q - dx)}{(acx + q)^2} \tag{2.39}$$

$$\frac{dP}{dd} = \frac{x}{acx + q} \tag{2.40}$$

$$\frac{dP}{dq} = -\frac{(d + ac)x}{(acx + q)^2} \tag{2.41}$$

$$\frac{dP}{dx} = \frac{(d + ac)q}{(acx + q)^2} \tag{2.42}$$

$$\frac{dT}{dc} = \frac{qafW(acx + q) + q^2 ax + da^2 cx^3 - 3qax^2(ac + d)}{(acx + q)^3} \tag{2.43}$$

$$\frac{dT}{dd} = \frac{x(q - acx)}{(acx + q)^2} \tag{2.44}$$

$$\frac{dT}{dq} = -\frac{1}{(acx + q)}\left[T - \frac{2acx^2(d + ac)}{(acx + q)^2}\right] \tag{2.45}$$

$$\frac{dT}{dx} = \frac{-c^2 a^2 fW(acx + q) - q(d + ac)(3acx - q)}{(acx + q)^3} \tag{2.46}$$

$$\frac{dT}{df} = \frac{acW}{acx + q}$$ (2.47)

First, an increase in sensitivity toward the cost of money laundering –
the integrity factor – increases the optimal level of both the law
enforcement variables. Vice versa the sanction policy is better than the
incrimination policy when the weight of anti-laundering action on the
cost allocation – the cost-inefficiency factor – increases.

Furthermore if the country becomes more sensitive to the risks of anti-
money-laundering sanctions – the reputation-inefficiency factor – both
the policies shift toward laxity. Finally greater sensitivity of criminal
bankers to the risks of detection and sanctions – the punishment factor –
encourages the Authority to make its prevention and control action more
aggressive, while the effect on sanction policy is uncertain.

In conclusion the optimal anti-money-laundering policy, which
determines the level of money laundering tolerated in a given country –
how true *pecunia non olet* is – will be influenced by the structural factors
and by the actual attitudes of the different actors involved.

THE AUTHORITY: DESIGNING A FINANCIAL INTELLIGENCE UNIT

In recent years the design of the regulation against money laundering has
been influenced by an interesting phenomenon: to ensure economic and
financial integrity, financial intelligence units (FIUs) have been instituted
in several countries, to make the national and international fight against
organized crime and terrorism more effective. In other words the
Authority, with clear responsibilities to detect money-laundering
activities, is assuming a precise identity worldwide. The objective of this
section is to analyze from an economic point of view the creation of a
financial intelligence unit.

To evaluate the phenomenon of the creation of financial intelligence
units (FIUs), it is appropriate to begin with a model of economic
analysis. In general, an FIU stands between the lawmaker (or

policymaker) and the banks. To study this situation the most natural scheme of analysis is a hierarchical principal-agent model.[5]

We must consider simultaneously the choices of the lawmaker, the FIU and the bank. The lawmaker works in the public interest, optimizing the social objective function; the FIU, thanks to the information advantages obtained through the relationship with the banking system, acts as an agent of the lawmaker, with the task of collecting and processing relevant information. The banks, because of their activities in the markets and their systematic, privileged relations with the business community, can become agents of the FIU, with the task of providing useful information.

The time sequence is the following. The bank perceives the general environmental conditions (money-laundering technologies, market characteristics) that reflect on the degree of difficulty in fulfilling the duties of anti-money laundering. The lawmaker must determine the characteristics of anti-money-laundering regulations, knowing well, however, that the way he designs the incentives of the banks and the compensation scheme of the FIU will determine their behaviour.

The goal of the lawmaker is to maximize the flow of information from the banks useful for combating money laundering. In other words he must minimize the vulnerability of the banking system through the action of each intermediary.

The level of vulnerability can be verified ex-post. Using c to indicate the level of vulnerability, intuition suggests that the more effective the action of the bank and the FIU, the lower this level will be.

Let us assume that level c of vulnerability can drop from a higher level $c2$ (risks of money laundering) to a lower level $c1$ (no risks of money laundering). To achieve his result, the lawmaker must design an incentives scheme for the bank, with a value Y.

The bank can provide some degree of information, according to his commitment i, and the financial environmental situation, summarized by the variable A, where the environment can be favourable ($A1$) or unfavourable ($A2$) with respect to the money-laundering reporting activity, with $A2 > A1$. Unlike the lawmaker and the FIU, the bank is familiar with the environment in which it operates. The probability that vulnerability c will decline is therefore a function $f(i, A)$ of the commitment and the environment, with the following properties:

---

[5] Masciandaro (2005b).

$$1 > f(i/A1) > f(i/A2) > 0$$
$$f_i(i/A1) > f_i(i/A2) > 0$$
$$f_{ii}(i/A1) < 0, f_{ii}(i/A2) < 0$$

The bank is faced with the classic dilemma: on the one hand, the objective of financial integrity, on the other the fact that reporting and monitoring irregular financial flows is costly. Thus the function of total cost will be equal to:

$$C_T = c + V(i) \qquad (2.48)$$

where the function $V(i)$ has the usual features:

$$\frac{dV}{di} > 0, \frac{d^2V}{di} < 0$$

The bank transmits his report to the FIU. Let us assume that the FIU can do its task with constant effort k – not observable by the lawmaker – that enables it to understand, at least partially, the nature of the banking information. If the FIU increases the effort, it can understand, though not perfectly, in which financial environmental situations the intermediary had to perform his monitoring task. We assume that the FIU, monitoring and interacting with the banks, gains the information flow s, transmitted as a report to the lawmaker, that can assume one of two values, $s1$ or $s2$, with the hypothesis that :

$$\frac{\varphi_{ii}}{\varphi_{i1} + \varphi_{i2}} > \frac{\varphi_{ji}}{\varphi_{j1} + \varphi_{j2}} \qquad (2.49)$$

where φ_{ij} represents the joint probability that $s = si$ and $A = Aj$.

The expression (2.49) tells us that if the FIU's information indicates a favourable environmental situation, it is more probably, but not certainly, true rather than false.

The lawmaker will design the incentives Y for the bank and the remuneration G for the FIU, basing his choices on the report of the FIU. The incentives and the remuneration will be of the type Y_{ij} and G_{ij} . The lawmaker optimization problem is the following:

$$\min_{Y,G,i} \sum_{i=1}^{2} \sum_{j=1}^{2} \left[\varphi_{ij} \left\{ \begin{array}{l} f\left(i_{ij}/A_j\right)\left(G_{i1} + Y_{i1}\right) + \\ \left[1 - f\left(i_{ij}/A_j\right)\right]\left(G_{i2} + Y_{i2}\right) \end{array} \right\} \right] \tag{2.50}$$

under the bank participation constraint:

$$\left[\begin{array}{l} f\left(i_{ij}/A_j\right)\left(G_{i1} - C_1\right) + \left[1 - f\left(i_{ij}/A_j\right)\right]\left(G_{i2} + C_2\right) \\ -V\left(i_{ij}\right) \end{array} \right] \geq 0, \tag{2.51}$$

$$\forall i,j = 1,2$$

$$a_{ij} \in \operatorname{argmax} \left[\begin{array}{l} f\left(i/A_j\right)\left(G_{i1} - C_1\right) + \\ + \left[1 - f\left(i/A_j\right)\right]\left(G_{i2} + C_2\right) - V(i) \end{array} \right] \tag{2.52}$$

and the FIU participation constraint:

$$U^{FIU} = \sum_{i=1}^{2} \sum_{j=1}^{2} \left[\varphi_{ij} \left\{ \begin{array}{l} f\left(i_{ij}/A_j\right)Y_{i1} + \\ + \left[1 - f\left(i_{ij}/A_j\right)\right]Y_{i2} \end{array} \right\} - k \right] \geq U^* \tag{2.53}$$

$$U^{FIU} \geq \sum_{i=1}^{2} \sum_{j=1}^{2} \left[\varphi_{ij} \left\{ \begin{array}{l} f\left(i_{hj}/A_j\right)Y_{h1} + \\ + \left[1 - f\left(i_{hj}/A_j\right)\right]Y_{h2} \end{array} \right\} \right] \tag{2.54}$$

$$\sum_{j=1}^{2} \frac{\varphi_{ij}}{\varphi_{i1} + \varphi_{i2}} f\left(i_{ij}/A_j\right)Y_{i1} + \left[1 - f\left(i_{ij}/A_j\right)\right]Y_{i2} \geq$$

$$\geq \sum_{j=1}^{2} \frac{\varphi_{ij}}{\varphi_{i1} + \varphi_{i2}} f\left(i_{hj}/A_j\right)Y_{h1} + \left[1 - f\left(i_{hj}/A_j\right)\right]Y_{h2} \tag{2.55}$$

$$h \neq i, i, h = 1,2$$

$$G_{ij} \geq \overline{G} \tag{2.56}$$

Condition (2.55) ensures us that the FIU will communicate all the information gathered, excluding the case of regulatory capture, while condition (2.56) guarantees that the FIU has a level of reputation at least equal to its minimum level. The conduct of the FIU is socially optimal when the condition (2.57) holds:

$$\overline{G} \leq \overline{V} - \omega k \tag{2.57}$$

where:

$$\omega = \frac{\left[\begin{array}{l} ((\varphi_{11}+\varphi_{21})f^*_{11}+(\varphi_{12}+\varphi_{22})f^*_{12})(\varphi_{11}(1-f^*_{21})+ \\ \varphi_{12}(1-f^*_{22})(\varphi_{21}(1-f^*_{21}+f^*_{11})+\varphi_{22}(1-f^*_{22}+f^*_{12}) \end{array} \right]}{(\varphi_{11}\varphi_{22}-\varphi_{12}\varphi_{21})(f^*_{11}(1-f^*_{22})-f^*_{12}(1-f^*_{21})(\varphi_{21}f^*_{11}+\varphi_{22}f^*_{12})}$$

with f^* that corresponds in every state of the world to the optimal level of commitment i^*.

The FIU optimal behaviour is more likely (a) the higher the FIU reputation costs and (b) the lower the FIU required effort. We have therefore derived two desirable features for the FIU.

On the one hand, the utility of the FIU must be strongly dependent on the effort expended in that specific function. Failure to conduct the anti-money-laundering action has an opportunity cost that depends on whether the regulator has other sources of remuneration. The less it has, the more its reputation and therefore its utility are linked to the outcome of the anti-money laundering. We can claim that the more the FIU is specialized in anti-money laundering, the more effective it will be.

On the other hand, it is crucial that the FIU will perform its information research, collection and processing function in a relatively easy way. The broader and more detailed its information assets, the more effective its action will be. The economic model stresses the gains of a FIU as an agent characterized by two features: institutional specialization, in order to maximize the reputational advantages, and financial nature, in order to increase the information advantages.

The model helped us to explain the reasons for instituting an agency specialized in the collection and analysis of information useful for combating money laundering and the financing of terrorism. Over the past years, specialized government agencies have been created as countries develop systems to deal with the problem of money laundering.

These entities are commonly referred to as 'financial intelligence units' or 'FIUs'.

Based upon the work of the Legal Working Group, Egmont approved the following definition of a FIU in 1996:

> A central, national agency responsible for receiving (and, as permitted, requesting), analyzing and disseminating to the competent authorities, disclosures of financial information: (i) concerning suspected proceeds of crime, or (ii) required by national legislation or regulation, in order to counter money-laundering.

FIUs have attracted increasing attention with their ever more important role in anti-money-laundering programmes in exchanging and processing relevant information between financial institutions and law enforcement/prosecutorial authorities, as well as between national jurisdictions.

Two major influences shape the creation of the FIUs: implementing anti-money-laundering departments or offices, alongside already existing law enforcement systems (the Judicial, Law Enforcement and Hybrid models) or providing a single agency for centralizing the receipt and assessment of financial information and sending the resulting disclosures to competent authorities (the Administrative Model). Using the above economic model, the four institutional models can be interpreted as different designs of the principal-agent scheme:

- The Judicial Unit is established within the judicial branch of government wherein disclosures of suspicious financial activity are received by the investigative agencies of a country from its financial sector such that the judiciary powers can be brought into play e.g. seizing funds, freezing accounts, conducting interrogations, detaining people, conducting searches, etc.
- The Law Enforcement Unit implements anti-money-laundering measures alongside already existing law enforcement systems, supporting the efforts of multiple law enforcement or judicial authorities with concurrent or sometimes competing jurisdictional authority to investigate money laundering;
- The Administrative Unit is a centralized, independent, administrative authority, which receives and processes information from the financial sector and transmits disclosures to judicial or law enforcement authorities for prosecution. It

functions as a buffer between the financial and the law enforcement institutions;

- The Hybrid Unit serves as a disclosure intermediary and a link to both judicial and law enforcement authorities. It combines elements of at least two of the FIU models.

In 2005 there were 94 countries with recognized operational FIUs. Table 2.1 reports the 61 FIUs existing in our 68 countries sample. The Administrative Model is adopted in 38 countries (62% of the sample). The Administrative Model is the more frequent one. More importantly, this institutional framework is the closest to the specialized agency setting, highlighted in the economic analysis.

Furthermore, we note that FIUs subordinated to the Minister of Finance, to the Central Bank, or to the Banking Supervisory Authority – that we can label 'insider' FIU – are present in 29 countries (47%). Among the different governance settings, the insider FIU is the more frequent one. From the economic point of view the insider FIU setting is particularly interesting, given that its peculiar financial nature can maximize the expected information gains in implementing the anti-money-laundering activities.

In conclusion, our findings can be summarized as follows. First we demonstrated that, from an economic point of view, the more specialized and financially characterized the anti-money laundering agency is, the more useful it will be. And, in effect, several countries have created specialized agencies, in the form of FIUs, with different institutional forms.

Table 2.1 Financial intelligence units: institutional models, agents and principals

Countries	Institutional Models	Agents: the FIUs	Principals
Albania	Administrative	Drejtoria e Bashkerendimitte Luftes Kunder Pastrimitte Parave (DBLKPP)	Minister of Finance
Argentina	Judicial	Unidad de Información Financiera (UIF)	Minister of Justice
Australia	Administrative	AUSTRAC	Minister of Justice
Austria	Law enforcement	Bundeskriminalamt (A-FIU)	Minister of Interior
Belgium	Administrative	Cellule de Traitement des Informations Financières/ (CTIF- CFI)	Mixed Governance: Minister of Finance, Minister of Justice
Brazil	Administrative	Conselho de Controle de Atividades Financeira (COAF)	Minister of Finance
Bulgaria	Administrative	Bulgaria – Financial Intelligence Agency (FIA)	Minister of Finance
Canada	Administrative	Financial Transactions and Reports Analysis Centre of Canada (FINTRAC)	Minister of Finance
Chile	Administrative	Unitad de Analisis Financiero (UAF)	Minister of Finance
Colombia	Administrative	Unidad de Informaciony Análisis Financiero (UIAF)	Mixed Governance: Minister of Finance, Public Prosecutor Office

continued

Table 2.1 continued

Countries	Institutional Models	Agents: the FIUs	Principals
Croatia	Administrative	Financijska Policija/Uredza Sprjecavanje Pranja Novca/Money Laundering Prevention Bureau	Minister of Finance
Cyprus	Judicial	MO.K.A.S. Unit for Combating Money Laundering	Public Prosecutor Office
Czech Republic	Administrative	Financní analytický útvar (FAU-CR)	Minister of Finance
Denmark	Judicial	SØK/Hvidvasksekretariatet (HVIDVASK)	Public Prosecutor Office
Ecuador *	Administrative	Financial Intelligence Unit	Banking Supervision Authority
Egypt	Administrative	Egyptian Money Laundering Combating Unit (EMLCU)	Central Bank
Estonia	Law enforcement	Rahapesu Andmeburoo	Police
Finland	Law enforcement	Keskusrikospoliisi/ Rahanpesun selvittelykeskus (RAP)	Police
France	Administrative	Traitement du renseignement et action contre les circuits financiers clandestins (TRACFIN)	Minister of Finance
Georgia	Hybrid	Saqartvelos Finansuri Monitoringis Samsaxuri/ Financial Monitoring Service (FMS)	Central Bank
Germany	Law enforcement	Zentralstelle für Verdachtsan-zeigen-Financial Intelligence Unit	Police

continued

Table 2.1 continued

Countries	Institutional Models	Agents: the FIUs	Principals
Greece	Hybrid	Committee of Financial and Criminal Investigation (CFCI)	Mixed Governance: Minister of Interior, Minister of Finance, Minister of Public Administration Minister of Development, Central Bank, Stock Market Commission
Hong Kong	Law enforcement	Joint Financial Intelligence Unit (JFIU)	Police
Hungary	Law enforcement	Orszagos Rendorfkapitany-sag Pénzmosás Elleni Alosztály (ORFK)	Minister of Interior
Iceland	Law enforcement	Ríkisssaksóknari (RLS)	Police
India *	Administrative	Financial Intelligence Unit	Minister of Finance
Ireland	Administrative	Irish Financial Services Regulatory Authority (IFSRA)	Central Bank
Israel	Administrative	Israel Money Laundering Prohibition Authority (IMPA)	Minister of Justice
Italy	Administrative	Ufficio Italiano dei Cambi (UIC)	Central Bank
Jamaica *	Administrative	Financial Intelligence Unit	Central Bank

continued

Table 2.1 continued

Countries	Institutional Models	Agents: the FIUs	Principals
Japan	Administrative	Japan Financial Intelligence Office (JAFIO)	Financial Supervision Authority
Latvia	Judicial	Kontroles dienests, Noziedzīgiiegūtu līdzeklu legalizācijas novērsanas dienests (KD)	Public Prosecutor Office
Lituania	Law enforcement	Mokesčiu policijos departamentas prie Lietuvos Respublikos Vidaus reikalu ministerijos/Financial Crime Investigation Services	Minister of Interior
Luxembourg	Law enforcement	Cellule de Renseignement Financier (FIU-LUX)	Public Prosecutor Office
Macedonia	Administrative	Ministerstvo za Finansii-Direkcija za Sprecuvanje na Perenje Pari/Money Laundering Prevention Directorate (MLPD)	Minister of Finance
Malaysia	Administrative	Unit Perisikan Kewangan, Bank Negara Malaysia (UPW)	Central Bank
Malta	Administrative	Financial Intelligence Analysis Unit (FIAU)	Mixed Governance: Central Bank, Financial Services Authority, Police, Public Prosecutor Office
Mauritius	Administrative	Mauritius – Financial Intelligence Unit (FIU)	Minister of Finance

continued

Table 2.1 continued

Countries	Institutional Models	Agents: the FIUs	Principals
Mexico	Administrative	Dirección General Adjunta de Investigación de Operaciones/Unidad de Inteligencia Financiera (DGAIO/UIF)	Minister of Finance
Netherlands	Hybrid	Meldpunt Ongebruikelijke Transacties Ministerie van Justitie (MOT) Office for the Disclosure of Unusual Transaction	Mixed Governance: Minister of Justice, Minister of Finance
New Zealand	Law enforcement	NZ Police Financial Intelligence Unit	Police
Norway	Hybrid	Hvitvaskingsenheten (ØKOKRIM) Norwegian National Authority for Investigation and Prosecution of Economic Crime	Mixed Governance: Minister of Justice, Minister of Finance
Perù *	Administrative	Unitad de Intelligencia Financiera (UIF)	Minister of Finance
Philippines*	Administrative	Anti-Money-Laundering Council (AMLC)	Central Bank
Poland	Administrative	Generalny Inspektor Informacji Finansowej (GIIF)	Minister of Finance
Portugal	Law enforcement	Brigada de Investigacao Branqueamento	Police

continued

Table 2.1 continued

Countries	Institutional Models	Agents: the FIUs	Principals
Romania	Hybrid	Oficiul Nacional de Prevenire si combattere a Spalaari Banilor (ONPCSB)	Mixed Governance: Minister of Interior, Minister of Finance, Minister of Justice, Public Prosecutor Office Central Bank
Russia	Administrative	Financial Monitoring Committee of the Russian Federation (FMC)	Minister of Finance
Slovak Republic	Law enforcement	Odbor financného spravodajstva (OFiS ÚFP)	Minister of Interior
Slovenia	Administrative	Urad RS za Preprecevanje Pranza Denarja Ministrstvo za Finance (MF-UPPD)	Minister of Finance
South Africa	Administrative	South Africa – Financial Intelligence Centre (FIC)	Minister of Finance
South Korea	Administrative	Korea Financial Intelligence Unit (KoFIU)	Minister of Finance
Spain	Administrative	Servicio Ejecutivo de la Comisión de Prevención de Blanqueo de Capitales e Infracciones Monetarias (SEPBLAC)	Mixed Governance: Government Central Bank
Sweden	Law enforcement	Finansplisen/ Rikspolisstyrelsen (NFIS)	Police
Switzerland	Judicial	Money-laundering Reporting Office-Switzerland (MROS)	Minister of Justice

continued

Table 2.1 continued

Countries	Institutional Models	Agents: the FIUs	Principals
Thailand	Judicial	Taiwan – Money Laundering Prevention Center (MLPC)	Minister of Justice
Trinidad and Tobago*	Administrative	Criminal Investigation Bureau	Minister of Finance
Turkey	Administrative	Mali Suçlari Arastirma Kurulu (MASAK)	Minister of Finance
UK	Administrative	National Criminal Intelligence Service/ Financial Intelligence Division (NCIS/FID)	Home Secretary
Ukraine	Administrative	Держфінмоніторинг, Державний департамент фінансового моніторингу/ State Department for Financial Monitoring (SDFM)	Minister of Finance
USA	Administrative	Financial Crimes Enforcement Network (FinCEN)	Mixed Governance: Central Bank, Minister of Finance, Other Federal Agencies

* = non Egmont
   Member

3. International Economics

Brigitte Unger

INTRODUCTION

Money-laundering profits from the liberalization of capital and open borders. It is much easier to disguise the origins of criminal money by making use of global markets than by using only national ones. Money laundering is, therefore, very often an international phenomenon of the flow of money, funds or assets circulating all over the globe. What can international economic theory contribute to the understanding of this international phenomenon?

The following chapter shows how traditional international economics can be applied to money-laundering questions. It is sketchy and the main goal is to give some hints and ideas regarding further modelling of money laundering in international economics.

The first section shows how international trade theory can be used to model and measure illegal flows of funds streaming into and out of a country. With this theory, it is possible to determine the most important countries of origin of illegal funds, and the principal destination of illegal funds. Furthermore, it allows the calculation of what part of the global illegal money or funds is attracted by a specific country with specific economic, political and social characteristics.

The second section uses a model of international tax competition to address the question whether or not it pays for countries to compete for criminal money. Criminal funds can mean additional finance for business and additional income for the government. Under which conditions will countries have an incentive to compete for criminal money and to be lax with regard to anti-money-laundering policies and under which conditions will they be willing to sign international AML policy agreements and stick to them?

International economics seems to be an attractive and prosperous field for further investigation and modelling of money-laundering issues.

THE ALLOCATION OF MONEY LAUNDERING AROUND THE GLOBE

Using the Gravity Model

In order to model the allocation of global money laundering, one can make use of the gravity model of international trade theory and modify it where necessary. Since the gravity equation of international trade theory itself has been borrowed from physics, why not borrow it from traditional economics and apply it to black finance matters?

A look at the gravity models used in international trade theory reveals that they resemble Newton's Apple. In 1687, Newton proposed the 'Law of Universal Gravity', which stated that the attractive force between two objects i and j depends on their masses, the square distance between these objects and a gravitational constant which depends on the units of measurement for mass and attractive force (see Head 2003).

$$\text{Attractive Force } F_{ij} = G * M_i * M_j / (D_{ij})^2$$

F_{ij} = Attractive Force between object i and j
M_i = Mass of object i
M_j = Mass of object j
D_{ij} = Distance between object i and object j
G = Gravitational constant

In 1962, the Dutch Nobel Prize winner Tinbergen transformed the understanding of the newly established economics of international trade by applying Newton's formula to bilateral trade flows. The trade from country i to country j depends on the economic mass of the two countries (measured by GDP) and the distance between the two locations (see Head 2003).

$$F_{ij} = G * M_i^{\alpha} * M_j^{\beta} / (D_{ij})^{\theta}$$

The export flows from country i to country j depend on the GDP of both the exporting and importing country and the distance between them.

Note that if α, $\beta = 1$ and $\theta = 2$, then this is the same as the original Newton formula.

For a long time, this formula was criticized as being a theoretical and ad hoc (see Gauws 2005, Chapter 6). Despite its use in many early studies regarding international trade, the equation was particularly suspect because of the fact that it could not easily be shown to be consistent with the dominant paradigm of international trade theory, the Heckscher-Ohlin model which explained net trade flows in terms of differential factor endowments (see Head 2003). According to the predominant economic paradigm, it was the amounts of labour and capital that determined the comparative advantage of countries that in turn determined which goods countries traded with each other.

Tinbergen's formula, however, had one convincing advantage: it predicted international trade flows very well (Head 2003: 9, Anderson and van Wincoop 2003). 'Measurement without theory' turned out to perform better than measuring from existing trade theories. Tinbergen's use of Newton's model of physics in economics has been applied to other fields, such as migration, tourism and foreign direct investment (FDI). Migration flows can be seen as the product of the population between two countries divided by distance. Inflows of tourists can be seen as the product of the GDP or population of two countries divided by distance. Foreign Direct Investment can be seen as the product of the GDP or GDP per capita of two countries divided by distance. The Tinbergen gravity model can therefore be applied to a whole range of social interactions, such as trade, the inflow of migrants, the inflow of tourists, and FDI. So why not apply it to money-laundering flows as well?

Theoretical Foundation of the Gravity Model

Since the Tinbergen formula worked so well but lacked theoretical justification, many scholars attempted to develop an adequate economic theory that was commensurate with the gravity formula. The first to develop such a theory was Anderson (1979), who showed that the gravity model was evident in expenditure share equations assuming commodities to be distinguished by place of production. Anderson also included remoteness measures in order to be fully consistent with the generalized expenditure share model. Helpman (1984) and Bergstrand (1985) demonstrated that the gravity model could also be derived from models of trade in differentiated products. Deardorff (1998) showed that a suitable modelling of transport costs produces the gravity equation, as estimation even for the

Heckscher-Ohlin model (for an overview see Helliwell 2000). Deardorff (1998) derived this gravity equation in a model with homogenous goods and a complete absence of trade frictions, so that countries are indifferent with regard to consuming domestic or foreign goods. The gravity equation was originally not implied by a plausible many-country Heckscher-Ohlin model, which did not address bilateral trade flows.

The theoretical approaches for the Tinbergen formula as applied to trade have been summarized and synthesized by Head (2003: 4).

The trade flows from country i to country j

$$F_{ij} = s_{ij} * M_j$$

where s_{ij} is the expenditure share of country j's income spent for goods from country i. This share lies between 0 and 1, increases if country i produces a greater variety of goods (n_i) or a higher quality of goods (larger m_i). This share also should decrease due to trade barriers such as distance. One can write this as:

$$s_{ij} = g(m_i, n_i, D_{ij})/\Sigma \ g(m_1, n_1, D_{1j})$$

Depending on the trade theory used, either $m_i = 1$ (which means all products from a country have the same average quality) or $n_i = 1$ (each country exports only one single good).

Under the assumption that $m_i = 1$ and that all firms q are of the same size, the number of products $n_i = M_i/q$. The higher the income of the country, the more products will be produced, and the larger the size of the country's firms, the less variety will be produced (this follows from monopolistic trade models à la Dixit-Stiglitz), which show that monopolists produce less variety than firms under perfect competition (see Head 2003: 4f).

From these assumptions and after some modification, it follows that

$$s_{ij} = M_i \, D_{ij}^{-\theta} R_j \quad \text{where } R_j = 1/\Sigma_1 \, (M_1, D_{1j}^{-\theta})$$

From this follows Tinbergen's Newtonian formula

$$F_{ij} = R_j * M_i * M_j/D_{ij}^{\theta}$$

Now, R_j has replaced the constant factor G of the old gravity formula. For a long time it was interpreted as a constant across countries. In more recent literature, the remoteness factor R_j stands for each importer's set of alternatives. Countries that have many nearby sources of goods themselves will have a low value of R_j and, therefore, import less. This factor of 'remoteness' explains why country groups that have the same distance from each other might still have different trade flows. The remoteness measure also includes M_i/D_{ii}, the distance of the country from itself. Head (2003) suggests taking the square root of the country's area multiplied by about 0.4 as an approximation for this internal distance. Other authors (Helliwell 2000) just use a value of 1 instead.

If one takes the logarithm of the newly derived economic Newton equation, one finds a linear reduced form equation that can be estimated with ordinary regression if the left-hand variable is observable or a proxy that can be observed.

$$\ln F_{ij} = a_0 + a_1\ln M_i + a_2\ln M_j - a_3\ln(DIST_{ij}) + a_4\ln R_J + e_{ij}$$

where F_{ij} is some measure of transaction between i and j, with any movement being from i to j, M_i and M_j are the masses of units i and j, $DIST_{ij}$ is the distance between them, R_j is a remoteness variable and e_{ij} is a random error term usually taken to be normally distributed.

Using the Gravity Model to Estimate Money Laundering

As I showed in Unger (2007, Chapter 3), Walker, in his seminal 1995 paper on how to measure global money-laundering, presented a formula which looks quite similar to the gravity model. In his seminal and in later papers (see Walker 1995, 1998, 1999 and 2003) Walker tried to measure how much money to be laundered will flow into and out of specific countries. To give an example, he found that US\$2.8 trillion are laundered worldwide and that 46% of this dirty money stems from the United States. From a sort of gravity model he calculated that two thirds of the world's laundered money is sent to 20 top laundering countries. The number one launderer in the world is, according to these findings, the United States. They are not only the largest producer of criminal proceeds, but also the most important destination for those launderers who have realized their criminal proceeds abroad. Of the money to be laundered worldwide, 18.9% is sent to the United States, followed by the Cayman Islands, Russia, China and Italy. Columns one and two in Table 3.1 show the original findings of Walker (1998). The last column shows the volumes of money sent to these countries when one adopts the more moderate estimate for global laundering done by the IMF (see Unger 2007).

Note that most of the countries listed in Table 3.1 are well-established, well developed, and quite sizeable countries. According to these findings, the top 20 countries receiving dirty money are mainly large, developed countries, not small islands and offshore centres. There are only a few microstate offshore centres and tax havens amongst them (the Cayman Islands, Vatican City, Bermuda and Liechtenstein). Countries of the European Union are represented prominently in this list as well. Italy, Luxembourg, France, Germany, the Netherlands, Austria, the UK and Spain can be found in this list of the top 20 laundering countries.

How did Walker arrive at these percentages? In order to calculate the percentage of total dirty money which flows into each country for laundering, he referred – consciously or not – to the gravity model. He claims that one has to understand how attractive each country appears for money launderers and how accessible it is. For the calculation of cross-border flows of laundered money, Walker introduced two indices: the attractiveness and distance deterrence indicator and defined the proportions of money laundered being sent from one country i to another country by attractiveness of country j divided by the square distance between the two countries.

Walker's gravity formula, therefore, assumes the following:

$$F_{ij}/M_i = \text{Attractiveness}_j / \text{Distance}_{ij}^2$$

where

$$F_{ij}/M_i = (GNP/capita)_j * (3BS_j + GA_j + SWIFT_j - 3CF_jCR_j + 15)/Distance_{ij}^2$$

where $GNP/capita$ is GNP per capita, BS is Banking Secrecy, GA is Government Attitude, $SWIFT$ is SWIFT member, CF is Conflict, CR is Corruption.

If one compares this to the original gravity model, Walker assumes,

$$R_j = (3BS_j + GA_j + SWIFT_j - 3CF - CR_j + 15)$$

and

$$M_j = (GNP/capita)_j$$

Table 3.1 Top 20 destinations of laundered money

Rank	Destination	% of worldwide money-laundering	Using Walker's original estimate of US$2.85 trillion Amount in million US$	Using IMF estimate of US$1.5 trillion worldwide Amount in million US$
1	United States	18.9	538,145	283,500
2	Cayman Islands	4.9	138,329	73,500
3	Russia	4.2	120,493	63,000
4	Italy	3.7	105,688	55,500
5	China	3.3	94,726	49,500
6	Romania	3.1	89,595	46,500
7	Canada	3.0	85,444	45,000
8	Vatican City	2.8	80,596	42,000
9	Luxembourg	2.8	78,468	42,000
10	France	2.4	68,471	36,000
11	Bahamas	2.3	66,398	34,500
12	Germany	2.2	61,315	33,000
13	Switzerland	2.1	58,993	31,500
14	Bermuda	1.9	52,887	28,500
15	Netherlands	1.7	49,591	25,500
16	Liechtenstein	1.7	48,949	25,500
17	Austria	1.7	48,376	25,500
18	Hong Kong	1.6	44,519	24,000
19	United Kingdom	1.6	44,478	24,000
20	Spain	1.2	35,461	18,000

Source: Walker (1998) and Unger (2007)

He has divided the flow formula by M_i. The GNP per capita of the sending country is not included in the percentages of laundering flows that he calculates. (It is included later, when the percentages are multiplied by the total amount of money that each country launders.) M_i represents the proceeds of crime multiplied by crime multiplied by the percentage that is laundered. It is the total money generated for laundering in the sending country. The 'mass' indicator between the sending and receiving country varies and this variation accounts for the economic and criminal size of countries. All the variables relevant for money laundering have been captured in the remoteness variable. The gravitational 'masses' of the two objects country i and country j have been assumed to be GNP per capita and money generated for laundering, respectively.

Unger (2007) modified the attractiveness indicator of Walker. The revised model takes into account that the size of the financial market might be an important factor for attracting money for laundering in rich countries. Furthermore, I included an additional variable to take combating money laundering into account explicitly, namely, whether or not the country is a member of the Egmont group, a group of countries that devote themselves to money laundering. Leaving the index j out for the moment, the formula used in our empirical part for attractiveness becomes:

Revised Attractiveness = $(GDP/capita)*(3BS + GA + SWIFT + FD - 3CF - CR - EG + 10)$

where *GDP/capita* is gross domestic product per capita, *BS* is Banking Secrecy, *GA* is Government Attitude towards money-laundering, *SWIFT* is being a SWIFT member or not, *FD* is Financial Deposits, *CF* is Conflict, *CR* is Corruption, and *EG* is Egmont Group membership.

The model used in Unger (2007) is thus very similar to the original Walker model and also assumes a remoteness variable that includes all kinds of variables relevant for money laundering such as the size of financial markets and being a member of the Egmont group.

Both approaches still share the same weaknesses. Compared to the, by now, sophisticated theoretical underpinning of the gravity model in international trade theory, the money-laundering gravity model is still quite simple. In order to justify the variables included in the attractiveness indicator, Walker makes the following assumptions:

- Foreign countries with a tolerant attitude towards money-laundering will attract a greater proportion of the money than more intolerant countries: tolerant countries are those with banking secrecy laws or uncooperative government attitudes towards money-laundering.
- High levels of corruption and/or conflict in a country will deter money launderers from laundering money in that country because of the added risk of losing their funds.
- Countries with high levels of GNP per capita will be preferred by money launderers, since it is easier to "hide" their transactions (Walker 1998).
- It is not only the attractiveness of a country but also the distance between the sending and receiving country that affects money laundering. Distance can be a barrier to trade flows as well as money-laundering flows. The closer the countries, the higher the proportion of money laundered.

In the original Walker model, distance deterrence is measured as the square of the physical distance between countries' capitals (see Walker 1998). In a more recent modification of this indicator, Unger (2007) followed Walker's proposal for further research and assumed that:

- All other things being equal, geographic distance, linguistic and cultural differences are deterrents to money launderers.
- Being a top trading partner of a country makes a country more likely to engage in money laundering (Walker 1998: 15).

Distance = language + 3 trade + 3 colonial background + physical distance (see Unger 2007)

Distance deterrence assigns a value to countries in relation to their relative distance from other countries depending on language, colonial background, trade and geographical distance. Countries have more distance between them if they speak different languages, have different historical backgrounds, do not trade with each other and/or have a large geographical distance separating them.

With regard to the distance deterrence index, Unger (2007) assumes $\Theta = 1$, using linear and not squared distance. This is supported by the fact that many trade gravity equations come up with this coefficient as well (Helliwell 2000).[1] For estimating the proportions of hot money sent from each country i to country j, one can either divide the two indicators by each other, as Walker suggests, or take the logarithmic form, used more often in international trade theory:

$$\ln F_{ij} = a_0 + a_1 \ln M_i + a_2 \ln M_j - a_3 \ln(DIST_{ij}) + a_4 \ln R_j + e_{ij}$$

Since our $\ln M_i = \ln 1 =$ the constant e, one can include $a_1 \ln M_i$ in the constant term a_0 of the equation and call it $c_0 = a_0 + a_1 \ln M_i$.

$$\ln F_{ij} = c_0 + a_2 \ln M_j - a_3 \ln(DIST_{ij}) + a_4 \ln R_j + e_{ij}$$

where $\ln M_j$ is the logarithm of the per capita GDP of country j, $\ln DIST$ is the logarithm of the distance deterrence indicator plus the attractiveness index (without GDP per capita), hence plus $(3BS + GA + SWIFT + FD - 3CF - CR - EF + 10)$.

Adding the indicators (due to the lack of knowledge about the coefficients) means to assume that $c_0 = e_{ij} = 0$ and that the coefficients a_2, a_3, and $a_4 = 1$.

$$\ln F_{ij} = \ln(GNP/capita)_j + \ln R_j - \ln DIST_{ij}$$

$$\ln F_{ij} = \ln(GNP/capita)_j + \ln(3BS + GA + SWIFT + FD - 3CF - CR - EF + 10) - \ln(language + 3*colonialbackground + 3*trade + physicaldistance)_{ij}$$

Besides modifying the attractiveness index and incorporating cultural distance into the distance deterrence index, Unger (2007) also revised the formula for calculating the percentages. In the original model, Walker used the following formula to calculate the proportion of laundered money flowing from one country to another:

$$P(X, Y) = \text{Attractiveness Score } Y/(\text{Distance } X \text{ to } Y)^2$$

There is nothing built into this model to ensure that the values of the proportions of money flowing from the country to other countries and to

---

[1] I owe this point to Thijs Knaap.

itself (money laundered locally) do not exceed 1, or 100%. For this reason, it seems important to calibrate part of the formula to ensure that values do not exceed 1. The formula that follows seems to be a better choice:

$$P(X, y_i) = \frac{1}{\sum_{i=1}^{n} \left[\dfrac{attractiveness(y_i)}{dist(X, y_i)} \right]} \times \frac{attractiveness(y_i)}{dist(X, y_i)}$$

where P is the proportion of money flowing from country X to country y_i.

For example, X is a specific country (the Netherlands), y_i is another country (Aruba). Then, the proportion of money flowing from country X (Netherlands) to country y_i (Aruba) equals the attractiveness of Aruba, weighted by the distance between the Netherlands and Aruba. In order to make sure that shares add up to 1, this weighted attractiveness for money laundering is corrected for the total weighted attractiveness scores throughout all countries.

The results of the gravity model calculated in this way are shown in Table 3.2 for the Netherlands in 2004.

The figures provided here in Table 3.2 are based on the original 'generated' money that Walker (1999) estimated, multiplied by revised proportions of money for laundering that flows into the Netherlands. Our own estimated data have been filled in for the Netherlands. The countries in Table 3.2 are the top 20 originators of laundered money and comprise about 90% of the world's total money generated for laundering. Although only 0.8% of the total money generated in the US flows to the Netherlands, it is, for the Netherlands, the largest amount of incoming funds ($11 billion) for laundering purposes. The last two columns show the results of Ferwerda (in Unger 2007), who has recalculated the model. He has improved the distance indicator. In Unger et al. (2006), Siegel had calculated distance by world regions. For this she had attributed numbers between 0 and 7 depending on how far one country was from the other. Ferwerda used distances between capitals in kilometres. Another improvement was that Ferwerda used, per country, the percentage of its total exports sent to its top trading partners. Siegel did feature top import and export partners as defined by the CIA World Factbook, but only as dummy variables. Further improvements will necessitate a look at the percentages imported from the top import partners. Once the 220 times 220 matrices are established for all countries for each variable (exports, imports, language, colonial background etc.), the model allows

Table 3.2 Inflows of money and domestic laundering in the Netherlands in million US$

Country	Walker (1999) Total generated money for laundering per country	Siegel in Unger et al. (2006) percentage and amount of each country's money for laundering flowing to the Netherlands		Ferwerda in Unger (2007) percentage and amount of each country's money for laundering flowing to the Netherlands	
	amount	%	amount	%	amount
Germany	128,266	1.6	2,113	0.8	1,027
Austria	20,231	0.9	187	0.7	149
Spain	56,287	1.1	617	1.0	542
UK	68,740	1.6	1,127	0.8	584
Romania	115,585	1.3	1,461	1.3	1,472
Italy	150,054	1.1	1,580	0.9	1,286
Poland	19,714	2.0	399	1.2	238
France	124,748	1.0	1,267	0.8	1,050
US	1,320,228	0.8	11,099	0.7	9,271
Mexico	21,119	1.1	228	1.0	205
Canada	82,374	0.8	650	0.6	503
Russia	147,187	1.5	2,179	1.2	1,788
China	131,360	1.0	1,367	1.1	1,447
HongKong	62,856	1.0	630	0.5	302
Thailand	32,834	0.9	307	0.9	292
Japan	21,240	0.8	143	0.7	139
Philipines	18,867	1.3	242	0.9	166
South Korea	21,240	0.9	189	0.7	156
Brazil	16,786	1.4	229	1.0	164
Flowing to NL			26,014		20,779
Netherlands	10,750	44.2	4,750	37.0	3,978
Total			**30,764**		**24,757**

Source: Unger (2007)

the calculation of the percentage of money for laundering flowing into and out of each country within the world.

Parallels and Differences between Regular Trade Flows and Money Laundering Flows

While international trade theory has experienced almost a proliferation of the micro-foundations of the gravity model, money-laundering modelling is still fairly young. 'Previous authors have shown that the gravity equation can be derived from any number of underlying models, so simply adding another model to the list is of limited consequence' (Haveman and Hummels 2001: 19). This might hold true for empirical research in a field with established theories such as international trade theory, but not for a new field. At the moment, we would be happy to derive one single gravity equation for money laundering which is micro-founded.

One way of trying to adapt international trade theory and to modify it for criminal behaviour of launderers is to look carefully at the parallels and differences between the behaviour of regular importers and exporters and the behaviour of launderers.

Trade flows versus laundering flows

Exporters and importers are trading goods and services. The expenditures and the proceeds from imports and exports are flows of money across borders. Launderers are shifting the proceeds from crime. Both groups are sending and receiving money, which is related to some kind of real sector activity. The behaviour of launderers is similar to that of exporters and importers in that it also includes some cost-benefit calculation. With regard to costs, Anderson and van Wincoop (2001) distinguish between border-related and trade-related and between rent-bearing and non-rent-bearing costs for importers and exporters. Border-related costs depend on regulation, product standards, language and cultural differences. Trade-related costs depend on distance and other variables that are distance related (see below). Rent-bearing costs are transfers between rent payers and receivers, non-rent-bearing costs are real resources used, such as for gathering information about foreign regulations, hiring lawyers familiar with foreign laws, and learning foreign languages. Many of the above issues also apply to launderers. Whether or not launderers decide to put their money across borders will depend on the strictness of anti-money-laundering regulation, on the language and on cultural differences. The product standards could be interpreted as the possible ways in which laundering can take place, for example due to the development and size of financial markets in the country in question. They could also be interpreted as the probability of getting caught or as the amount of fine or jail time a launderer has to expect when getting caught laundering in this country. Also, the distinction between rent-bearing and non-rent-bearing trade costs seems meaningful for laundering matters. Non-rent-bearing costs could include information about the probability of getting caught and the strictness of prosecution. In addition to trade costs, launderers face the threat of losing all of their fortune once they get caught. This threat of losing it all distinguishes their calculus from ordinary traders. But traditional international trade theory certainly poses a good point of departure for developing a micro-foundation of the gravity equation for money laundering.

The role of distance
In international trade theory, the role of distance is characterized in the following way:

- it is a proxy for transport costs
- it indicates the time elapsed between shipment and...
  - damage or loss of the goods (ship sinks in the storm)
  - spoiling of the goods
  - loss of the market (purchaser unable to pay once it arrives)
- communication costs, proxy for the possibilities of personal contact between managers, customers, i.e. for informal contacts which cannot be established over a wire
- transaction costs (searching for trading opportunities, establishment of trust between partners)
- cultural distance (clashes in negotiation style, language) (Head 2003: 8)

The distance indicator used by Walker (1998) assumes a similar importance for money laundering flows. Though physical distance is less important for money flows, since money cannot perish, and transporttation costs are negligible given that money can be sent around the globe at the click of a mouse, the communication costs, transaction costs and cultural barriers might still be important.

Income per capita

The gravity model has been augmented by income per capita. This takes into account that richer countries tend to trade more. Walker (1995, 1998 and 1999) assumes the same for money laundering. Richer countries attract more money laundering funds from poorer countries, because it is easier to hide large amounts of money in a rich country than in a poor country, where huge and sudden wealth will be more conspicuous. Money will, however, also be more conspicuous when laundered in a country with a very small population. If large amounts are invested into some microstates or offshore centres, it can happen that the GDP per capita or wealth per capita gets so high that this is conspicuous as well. To give an example, every resident of the Cayman Islands owns, on average, US$20 million (see Sikka 2003 quoted in Unger and Rawlings 2005).

Borders

McCallum (1995) claimed in his seminal paper in the *American Economic Review* that borders still matter as far as trade is concerned. He compared trade between two Canadian provinces to trade between Canadian provinces and US states and showed that borders are a barrier to trade.

Countries trade more if they have no border than if they have one. But when borders exist, it is better for trade to share a border than to be further apart. Trade is about 65% higher if countries share the same border than if they do not have a common border (Head 2003). So the Netherlands, for example, will trade more with Belgium than with Austria, even if one corrected for the difference in distance, just because they share a border. This means that if one takes coordinates of capitals and calculates their distance to each other (as Walker and I do), one might overestimate the effective distance, because neighbouring countries often engage in large volume border trade.[2]

Borders can also be a factor for specific laundering techniques and methods. Smuggling cash within the European Union is certainly easier within the Schengen countries that have abandoned border controls than when there are actual borders with the risk of getting caught to overcome. On the other hand, once the money is within the financial circuit

---

[2] I owe this point to Thijs Knaap.

and can be transferred via wire transfers all over the globe, borders will matter less for money laundering than for trade.

Common language and colonial links

Speaking a common language and sharing a common history and cultural background can lower transaction costs. 'Two countries that speak the same language will trade twice to three times as much as pairs that do not share a common language' (Head 2003, see especially the works of Helliwell, e.g. Helliwell 2000).

Something similar might hold true for launderers, at least when it comes to the first phase of bringing the money to a bank or financial institution and to the last phase of integrating the money in the real sector, for example by buying real estate, ships or cars. The middle phase of money laundering, however, might be different. Whether launderers do speak the language of Vanuatu or not will not be very important if some financial experts take care of international sophisticated transactions in order to make the original source of the money untraceable.

To summarize, the gravity type of money-laundering models share the beginner's fate, namely, to be called ad hoc and a theoretical. International trade theory, from the Heckscher-Ohlin to the Dixit-Stiglitz model, shares important theoretical synergies with the Walker model. One can also hope that the theoretical underpinning of the Walker model will not take as long as the microeconomic theoretical underpinning of the gravity formula by international trade theory. While the Tinbergen formula could always take the credit for predicting trade flows so accurately, the Walker model has, thus far, not received the same degree of acknowledgement. This is for the simple reason that, contrary to trade flows, the flows of money laundering stay in the dark and are unobservable. This means that it is not possible to assess the quality of the formula, the effectiveness of the fit and of forecasting. However, there are many parallels between flows of laundered money and FDI and the gravity model has been shown to be valid and theoretically sound in these contexts.

The three modifications to the Walker model and incorporating international trade theory have to be seen as a first step to open up the Walker model and identify its theoretical underpinning. As the next step, the assumptions of international trade theory shown above have to be compared to the assumptions of money laundering more carefully in order to derive a micro-foundation of the Walker model. There is still some modelling necessary in order to move from the gravity model to a money-laundering model, but given the progress that international trade theory has made, there is optimism that this can happen soon. The money-laundering debate can draw on a long history of developments and findings in economic trade theory.

What is still not captured in gravity model types of money laundering is the full layering phase of money laundering (money laundering is measured at the first phase, at placement, when it is generated and invested domestically or sent abroad). Although the second phase of money laundering, wherein money is transferred all over the world in order to hide its origin, is much higher in volume and much more prone to all kinds of financial tricks and sophisticated constructions, it is only sporadically treated. This second phase will be discussed in more detail in Chapter 4 regarding the implementation and techniques of money laundering. The third phase of laundering, the reintegration phase, where money is invested in real estate, diamonds or assets for fixed periods of accumulation is also not accounted for in this model. This phase will be discussed in Chapter 5 which examines the effects of money laundering on the economy.

The following section will show other types of models, which can be used for money-laundering issues, taken from international economics and public sector economics.

INTERNATIONAL COMPETITION FOR DIRTY MONEY

In the above example, the US and the Netherlands were shown to be attractive countries for money laundering. How do they get in the list of the top 20 laundering countries in the world? Do they, maybe even deliberately, compete for this dirty money? Do they try to attract foreign money no matter what its origins are? Or is the run to these countries just an unwanted side effect of other economic policies chosen?

To compete for criminal money by means of low bank secrecy seems a tempting strategy for countries in order to attract additional funds. *Pecunia non olet*, money does not stink. And as soon as it is diluted in the financial sector it is as good as any other money. So why not try to attract these huge and ever-increasing amounts of international criminal money? Unger and Rawlings (2005) called the strategy to deliberately compete for criminal funds the 'Seychelles strategy' after the Seychelles, an island state of some 80,000 people in the Indian Ocean which in 1995 invited international capital by guaranteeing immunity from prosecution, no matter where the funds came from, as long as somebody invested at least US$10 million (see Unger and Rawlings 2005: 4).

Laundered money does not only require the services of countries like the Seychelles. It is attracted to major industrialized economies such as the US, the Netherlands, the UK, France and Germany. 'The Seychelles was one extreme example of a pattern of countries seeking to attractively invite globally mobile capital. Small island states and enclaves with open capital markets, strict bank secrecy, a lack of transparency and anonymous bank accounts are the most likely candidates to arouse suspicion in cases of money-laundering' (Unger and Rawlings 2005). But big countries launder more, or to put it metaphorically, 'giants wash more' (Unger 2007).

Competing for criminal money by taking the proceeds from criminal activities in other countries and using them in legal business in your own country looks like a national election winner. The drug problem stays in Morocco, the money from it goes to the Netherlands where it is nicely laundered and may be reinvested in real estate or real business.

Welfare Gains from Criminal Money

We will show that a country following the Seychelles strategy can have efficiency gains. For this we use a model developed by Sinn (2003) for tax competition and reinterpret his variables in terms of money laundering.

Let us assume a small open economy that produces a homogenous output using labour L and capital K. Let $f(L, K)$ be a linear homogenous production function. The amount of labour employed is provided by domestic residents and is fixed. The amount of capital K used can vary. Capital is perfectly mobile and is available at the exogenously given world interest rate r.

The marginal product of capital, i.e. the additional output of one extra unit of capital, is positive but diminishes the more capital is being used: $df/dK > 0, (df/dK)/dK < 0$

Firms will invest up to the point where the marginal product of capital equals the world interest rate: $df/dK = r$.

If in this small open economy, the government would try to tax the mobile factor, it would fail, according to the standard argument of taxation. The standard argument of taxation says that you cannot tax a mobile factor, because you would burden the immobile factor by even more than the tax. If, for example, the government imposes a tax on capital, capital will withdraw from this country and go to a more attractive country with lower taxes. The small country is left with less capital, less output, and a higher tax burden on the immobile factor, which in our case is labour. The tax is shifted completely to the immobile factor. This argument is shown graphically in Figure 3.1 (see Sinn 2003: 29).

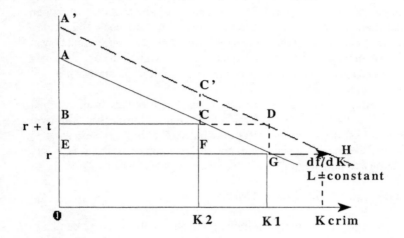

Figure 3.1 Criminal money instead of raising taxes

If the government levies a tax $t = BE$ on capital, capital will move to another country. The amount of capital used in the country will fall from $K1$ to $K2$, where the marginal product of capital minus the tax equals r:

$$df/dK - t = r$$

The tax is shifted completely to the immobile factor labour. Before the introduction of the tax, the income of capital is $E0K1G$ and the income of labour is AEG. When the tax t is introduced, capital leaves the country and labour income falls from AEG to ABC. The tax revenue of the government is $BEFC$. Even if the government were to give all the tax revenue to labour, labour would have a dead weight loss of CFG.

Now, consider the effect of criminal money entering the country. Criminals who invest in the country do not try to maximize their profits by investing up to the point where the marginal product of capital equals the interest rate plus the tax rate ($K2$). They are willing to pay a higher price if the chance of being detected is sufficiently small. For the sake of simplicity let us assume that the amount x, that criminals are willing to pay above the profit maximizing honest calculus, just amounts to the tax rate, GD. Or, to interpret the graph horizontally, assume that at the given world interest rate r criminals are willing to invest additional capital from G to H. If a tax $x = t$ is introduced, the small open economy will end up with capital $K1$ in the country, output will not shrink and labour will not be overburdened. The government's tax revenue is $EBGD$. If the government gives this revenue to labour, labour will earn $A'EGD$, which is a higher income by a factor two times CGD than before the introduction of the tax.

With criminal money and capital it is possible for a small open economy to tax the mobile factor. The gain in output is $CK2K1G$, plus an additional income from the overpaying two times CGD.

As Unger and Rawlings (2005) showed, at first glance the Seychelles strategy seems a tempting way indeed for small countries to attract additional capital, for which people are even willing to pay a higher price than in the case of honest capital.

If Other Countries also Compete for Criminal Money

The Seychelles strategy can be seen as the free rider position of small countries, which works only as long as other countries do not sanction it or try to do the same. Unger and Rawlings (2005) analyse whether it would still pay for a country A to follow the Seychelles strategy if another country, B, decided to do the same.

Starting from a monopoly model with a linear falling demand function, the situation of country A is described as follows. (The following model is an adaptation of Sinn's (2003, Chapter 8) model on the application of competition rules to money laundering).

The demand for laundering by criminals is a linear function of the form

$$P(X) = b\,(K{-}X) + c \quad \text{where } b, K, c > 0 \tag{3.1}$$

The slope of this demand function is $-b$, K is the quantity of laundering opportunities offered under perfect competition, X is the amount of laundering opportunities actually supplied and c is the marginal costs of supplying laundering facilities. In this form of writing, one can see the price as the marginal costs c the monopolist faces plus a mark-up $K - X$ depending on the degree of market concentration. (Under perfect competition $K = X$ and there would be no mark-up. We will see that under monopolistic competition $K/2 = X$, i.e. only half of the quantity sold under perfect competition is being supplied.)

The entrance of new nations as competitors in the money-laundering market is explained in Figure 3.2. If there is not just one country but two competing with each other for criminal funds, wherein each country takes the amount of money laundered in the other country as a given, these countries behave like Cournot-Nash followers.

If all countries have the same costs of providing laundering facilities and get symmetric shares of the world money-laundering volume one can write this as ±

$$X = \sum x_i = nx_i \qquad i = 1,...,n \text{ countries}$$

By maximizing profit for each country and filling this into the linear demand function, one arrives at the Amoroso-Robinson expression for Cournot oligopolies:

$$X = [1/(1/n) + 1] K \qquad \text{(Cournot solution)}$$

The Amoroso-Robinson formula allows us to see the quantity sold as a function of the market share $1/n$ a country has. If there is only one country ($n = 1$, a monopolist) it will supply only half of the competitive quantity K. If there are two countries ($n = 2$) they will supply two thirds of K. If there is an infinite number of countries (perfect competition among countries, $n = \infty$, $1/n$ approaches zero), they will supply K, the perfect competition output.

So each country will still profit from inviting dirty money, though the more countries that participate, the less the gain will be from following such a strategy.

Unger and Rawlings (2005) show that if country A decides instead to become a Stackelberg leader and the other countries are Cournot followers, then country A will choose the same amount as in the monopolistic situation. The other countries will take this amount as a given and adjust their share accordingly.

But what if the other countries try also to become a Stackelberg leader and want to get the largest market share? As Sinn (2003) shows in a recursive game – though not for money laundering but for deregulation – there will be an incentive for the second country to loosen its money-laundering policy as well. The third country will also follow, etc.

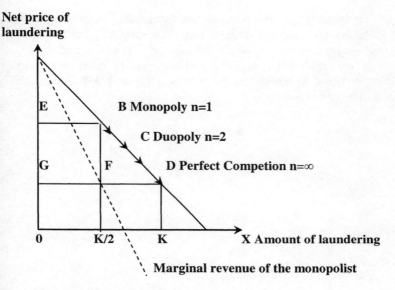

Figure 3.2 Countries competing for criminal money

Only for the very last country is there no more gain from engaging in the money-laundering race. It pays, therefore, for a country to be the first to abandon bank secrecy and to engage in competition for criminal money.

There can, thus, be a race to the bottom with regard to competing for criminal money. But there are two objections to be made. First, the above models are economic models and assume that countries make a deliberate choice whether to engage in letting money-laundering activities happen or not. Empirically, one sometimes gets the impression that some countries are surprised that they attract criminal money and have not made a deliberate choice. As Masciandaro (2000) pointed out, some countries tried to establish big functioning financial markets, which attracted all kinds of capital, criminal money being amongst these. They then started fighting money laundering in order to keep up their reputation as solid financial centres. This would go against the profit maximizing behaviour of countries with regard to money laundering.

On the other hand, there are also some countries who deliberately try to get a free ride on others and who seem to take such a Stackelberg position quite consciously. Tax havens and offshore centres seem to fit the model quite well.

The model only showed potential gains from money laundering without including the potential dangers and costs involved. For example, criminal money can lead to speculation in some sectors and lead to high volatility, for example with regard to real estate prices. It can undermine politics, and lead to corruption and bribery. Chapter 5 will discuss the effects of money laundering.

References

Anderson, J. (1979), 'A Theoretical Foundation for the Gravity Equation', *American Economic Review,* 69 (1), 106-116.

Anderson, J. and Eric van Wincoop (2003), 'Gravity with Gravitas: a Solution to the Border Puzzle', *American Economic Review,* 93, 170-192.

Barone, R. (2004), 'Riciclaggio Finanziario e Credito d'Usura: Un Modello di Analisi Economica, *Rivista Internazionale di Scienze Sociali,* (2), 119-135.

Bergstrand, J.H. (1985), 'The Gravity Equation in International Trade: Some Microeconomic Foundations and Empirical Evidence', *Review of Economics and Statistics,* 67, 474-481.

Deardorff, Alan V. (1998), 'Determinants of Bilateral Trade: Does Gravity Work in a Neoclassical World?', in Jeffrey A. Frankel (ed.), *The Regionalization of the World Economy,* Chicago: University Press, 7-22.

Donato, L. and D. Masciandaro (2001), *Moneta, Banca e Finanza. Gli abusi del mercato,* Milano: Hoepli.

Feenstra, Robert C., James A. Markusen and Andrew K. Rose (1998), 'Understanding the Home Market Effect and the Gravity Equation: The Role of Differentiating Goods', NBER Working Paper no. 6804, November.

Feenstra, Robert C., James A. Markusen, and Andrew K. Rose (1999), 'Using the Gravity Equation to Differentiate among Alternative Theories of Trade', http://www.econ.ucdavis.edu/faculty/fzfeens/pdf/ FMR new.pdf# search

Gauws, A.R. (2005), 'The Determinants of South African Exports', PhD University of Pretoria, South Africa, February, http://upetd.up.ac.za/ thesis/available/etd-04182005-141139/unrestricted/06chapter6.pdf

Haveman, J. and D. Hummels (2001), 'Alternative Hypotheses and the Volume of Trade: the Gravity Equation and the Extent of Specialization', *Federal Trade Commission Purdue University,* February http://www.mgmt.purdue.edu/centers/ciber/publications/pdf/00-

Head, K. (2003), 'Gravity for Beginners', version prepared for UBC Econ 590a students, Faculty of Commerce, University of British Columbia, Vancouver, Canada, February 5.

Head, K. and J. Ries (1999), 'Armington vs. Krugman: An Empirical Test', University of British Columbia, February.

Helliwell, J.F. (2000), 'Language and Trade, Gravity Modelling of Trade Flows and the Role of Language', The Department of Canadian Heritage, http://www.pch.gc.ca/progs/lo-ol/perspectives/english/explorer/page_01.html

Helpman, E. (1984), ´A Simple Theory of International Trade with Multinational Corporations', *Journal of Political Economy*, 92 (3), 451-471.

Hummels, D. and J. Levinsohn, (1995), 'Monopolistic Competition and International Trade: Reconsidering the Evidence', *Quarterly Journal of Economics*, 110, 799-836.

Knaap, T. (2006), 'Distances Between Countries'. Internet, http://knaap.com/data/location06.xls

Masciandaro, D. (1996), 'Pecunia Olet? Microeconomics of Banking and Financial Laundering', *International Review of Economics and Business*, October, 817-844.

Masciandaro, D. (1998), 'Money Laundering Regulation: The Micro economics', *Journal of Money Laundering Control*, 2 (1), 49-58.

Masciandaro, D. (1999), 'Money Laundering: The Economics of Regulation', *European Journal of Law and Economics*, (3), 245-240.

Masciandaro, D. (2000), 'The Illegal Sector, Money Laundering and Legal Economy: A Macroeconomic Analysis', *Journal of Financial Crime*, November (2), 103-112.

Masciandaro, D. (2002), 'What Do Your Customers Really Know? Bank Managers and Compliance Costs Perceptions', *Journal of Financial Transformation*, 1 (5), 37-42.

Masciandaro, D. (ed.) (2004a), *Global Financial Crime*, Aldershot: Ashgate.

Masciandaro, D. (2004b), 'Migration and Illegal Finance', *Journal of Money Laundering Control*, 7 (3), 264-271.

Masciandaro, D. (2005a), 'False and Reluctant Friends? National Money Laundering Regulation, International Compliance and Non-Cooperative Countries', *European Journal of Law and Economics*, (20), 17-30.

Masciandaro D. (2005b), 'Financial Supervision Unification and Financial Intelligence Units: a Trade Off?', *Journal of Money Laundering Control*, 354-370.

McCallum, J. (1995), 'National Borders Matter: Canada-U.S. Regional Trade Patterns', *American Economic Review*, 85, June, 615- 623.

Sikka, Prem (2003), 'The Role of Offshore Financial Centres in Globalization', *Accounting Forum*, 27, 365-399.

Sinn, H.W. (2003), *The New Systems Competition*, Blackwell Publishing, Oxford

Unger, B. and G. Rawlings (2005), 'Competing for Criminal Money', paper prepared for the Working Paper series of the Tjalings Koopmans Institute Utrecht School of Economics, Utrecht, 6.18.2005

Unger, B, J. Ferwerda, W. de Kruijf, G. Rawlings, M. Siegel, K. Wokke (2006), The Amounts and the Effects of Money Laundering, Report. for the Dutch Ministry of Finance, February 2006, http://www.minfin.nl/binaries/minfin/assets/pdf/old/06_011a.pdf

Unger, B. (2007), *The Scale and Impacts of Money Laundering*, Edward Elgar: UK

Van Wincoop, E. (2002), 'Borders, Trade and Welfare', Brookings Trade Forum 2001, Dani Rodrik and Susan Collins (eds), Washington: Brookings Institution.

Walker, J. (1995), 'Estimates of the Extent of Money Laundering in and through Australia', paper prepared for the Australian Transaction Reports and Analysis Centre, Queanbeyan: Jonh Walker Consulting, September.

Walker, J. (1998), 'How Big is Global Money Laundering?', *Journal of Money Laundering Control*, 3 (1).

Walker, J. (1999), 'Measuring the Extent of International Crime and Money Laundering', paper prepared for KriminálExpo, Budapest, June 9th.

Walker, J. (2002), 'Just How Big is Money Laundering?', Australian Institute of Criminology Seminar, Sydney.

Walker, J. (2003), Lecture in Bangkok, Thailand, http:// members. ozemail.com.au/~john.walker/crimetrendsanalysis/THAILAND%20MONEY%20LAUNDERING_files/frame.htm

PART TWO

Applied Money Laundering

4.   Implementing Money Laundering

Brigitte Unger

INTRODUCTION

How is money being laundered? How are the proceeds from criminal activities put into and through the financial system? Before describing how money laundering actually takes place, the techniques used by launderers and to what extent, it might be helpful to carefully filter out what money laundering is precisely, and what it is not. For applied research the challenge lies in the details. This chapter first gives an overview of potential definitions of money laundering, their common features and their most striking differences (first section). It then tries to locate money laundering within the framework of other definitions of illegal, criminal or black activities such as the shadow economy and the underground economy (second section). The next step shows national differences of money-laundering definitions and EU harmonization efforts (third section). The different national definitions will be applied and used in order to judge whether some recent events suspect of laundering have, indeed, been laundering under different jurisdiction, or just some other fraudulent behaviour (fourth section). In the fifth section we will discuss diverse money-laundering techniques, at which stage of laundering they are used and – as far as is known – by which types of criminals they are used.

WHAT IS MONEY LAUNDERING?

The term 'money laundering' is derived from the habit of the gangster Al Capone of funnelling his ill-gotten gains through launderettes to construct the pretence of a legitimate income (van Duyneet al. 2003, p. 73). This metaphor of dirty money, income, proceeds or other monetary gains

being washed in order to become white or clean is still adequate for all
definitions of money laundering. However, the definition of money laundering is more ambiguous than one would expect it to be. What precisely
is being laundered, and how? Here experts from law, economics and political or international organizations seem to present different views. This
makes the debate on money laundering more cumbersome than it needs
to be and encourages the shedding of some light on the subject by point-
ing out the common traits and differences between money-laundering
definitions.

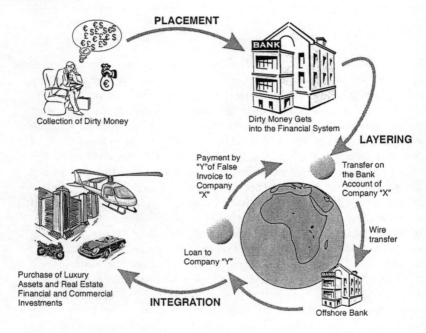

Source: Unger (2007), for a very similar graph see UNODC (2006),
http://www.unodc.org/unodc/money_laundering_cycle.html

Figure 4.1 The three phases of money laundering

Money laundering takes place in three phases, as illustrated in Figure
4.1. In the first phase, the placement or pre-wash phase, the money from
drugs or other crime is collected and brought to a bank or other financial
institution. It is at this stage that it is still the most easy to detect the dirty
money. The more it gets integrated into the financial system, the more

difficult this will become. In the second phase, the layering or main-wash phase, the money is sent around the globe in order to disguise its illegal origin. The launderer can make a money transfer from his bank to the bank of company X. By means of wire transfer the money is forwarded to an offshore bank, say on the Cayman Islands, which has less strict banking secrecy laws. The offshore bank gives a loan to company Y, which then pays a fake invoice to company X. Now company X, which can be the launderer himself or a straw man, has received money from company Y (again the launderer or a straw man) whose origin is almost untraceable. The layering phase can be very complicated and money can circle the globe many times in a couple of hours. As soon as the money appears safe from prosecution, the launderer will try to permanently park it. This third phase, the integration or after-wash phase, consists of purchases of luxury assets such as ships and expensive cars, diamonds, real estate or investments in real business or in the financial sector.

So when is something being laundered and when is it not? In Chapter 1 (p. 2) we defined money laundering as 'an autonomous criminal economic activity whose essential economic function lies in the transformation of liquidity of illicit origin, or potential purchasing power, into actual purchasing power usable for consumption, saving, investment or reinvestment'. The assumption of 'generality' refers to the fact that money laundering can concern any proceeds generated by criminal or illegal activities. The assumption of peculiarity refers to the purpose of laundering so as to reduce special transaction costs, namely concealing the illicit origin of the proceeds.

In Chapter 7 we will talk about money laundering as transactions which transfer illicit funds from their present form or place to somewhere them else, either to use there or to conceal their origins. Money laundering entails transferring illegally obtained funds to conceal their origins and make them appear legal. Furthermore, we will add terrorism. In this regard, Chapter 7 follows the FATF's definition of money laundering, a definition which has its origins in the US and its legal system.

For economic modelling purposes the definitions we chose are sufficiently encompassing. Not so, however, when we want to empirically find out how much money is being laundered in which country and whether specific events have to be classified under laundering or not. When somebody pays his gardener for illegal work, and the gardener spends his ill-gotten proceeds in the supermarket for a crate of beer, is the gardener or the supermarket laundering money (Dutch journalist Janssen in NRC 2006)? The gardener has illegally obtained proceeds, he transfers potential purchasing power into actual purchasing power when buying the beer, he transfers illegally obtained funds from their present form (cash in his pocket) to somewhere else (the supermarket) in order to use it there (for beer). Whether the gardener (or the supermarket) is a launderer or not depends on the definition of what money laundering is precisely. Most people would not call this laundering, but for different reasons. Economists might prefer to put this under the shadow economy and not under money laundering (see the third section), lawyers would call this laundering only if illegal work is a predicate crime for laundering (see the second section). Furthermore, they might argue that the supermarket has no reason to suspect that the money for the crate of beer stems from an illegal activity, and, therefore, find the supermarket not guilty of laundering. Some national laws and some academic studies will not consider the gardener's purchase of a crate of beer money laundering, because of bagatelle amounts, while others will. In the US the gardener is definitely a launderer if he is an illegal immigrant, since the US money-laundering definition lists work from illegal immigrants as a predicate crime for laundering (some more sophisticated examples and techniques of laundering will be studied in more detail under the fourth and fifth sections).

In order to construct a universal definition of money laundering, Ferwerda (in Unger et al. 2006, Chapter 1) collected the definitions used by different scientists, (international) organizations and legislations and compared them with one another. Table 4.1 presents his findings and adds to the Dutch definition the legal definitions of Austria, Germany, Switzerland and the US (respectively number 1a-1e). Apart from the national legal definitions, it includes the legislations of the European Union and the United Nations, definitions by international organizations such as the FATF, IMF and World Bank, Interpol, IOSCO, IFAC and the Australian Institute of Criminology Research and Public Policy Series and some scientists' research. Further included were definitions from the Conference on Global Drugs Law (1997) and the Council of Europe Convention on Laundering, Search, Seizure and Confiscation of the Proceeds from Crime (1990).[1] Finally, a definition found in a Reagan Administration report (number 18) was included, because of its early appearance in 1984.

---

[1] The definition of money laundering was not changed in the Council of Europe Convention on Laundering, Search, Seizure and Confiscation of the Proceeds from Crime in 2005.

1a. He is guilty of money laundering who conceals or disguises the true origin, the source, the alienation, the movement or the place where an object can be found, or hides or disguises who is the rightful claimant of an object or has it available, while he knows/should have known that the object is – directly or indirectly – derived from a crime. (Objects are all means and property rights.) (Dutch Penal Code)[2]

1b. Who hides, or disguises the origin of parts of wealth, which result from somebody else's crime, especially if he makes wrong statements in legal procedures about the origin, the true condition of these parts of wealth, their ownership or other rights to them, the authority of disposal over them or about where they are... (Austrian Penal Code)[3]

1c. Who conceals or disguises the origin of an object which is due to an illegal offence listed under the second paragraph, who prevents or endangers the investigation about the origin, the finding, the decay, the confiscation or seizure of such an object... (German Penal Code)[4]

1d. Who takes an action which is appropriate to prevent the investigation of the origin, the finding or the confiscation of assets, which as he knows or has to assume, result from a crime... (Swiss Penal Code)[5]

---

[2] Translated from: Schuldig aan witwassen is 'hij die van een voorwerp de werkelijke aard, de herkomst, de vindplaats, de vervreemding of de verplaatsing verbergt of verhult, dan wel verbergt of verhult wie de rechthebbende op een voorwerp is of het voorhanden heeft, terwijl hij weet/redelijkerwijs moet vermoeden dat het voorwerp – onmiddellijk of middellijk – afkomstig is uit enig misdrijf.' (Voorwerpen zijn alle zaken en vermogensrechten). Source: Dutch penal code (Nederlands Wetboek van Strafrecht) article 420bis, 420quater en 420ter at 18 October 2004.

[3] Translated from: Austrian Penal Code, StGB § 165 (1) Wer Vermögensbestandteile, die aus einem Verbrechen eines anderen herrühren, verbirgt oder ihre Herkunft verschleiert, insbesondere, indem er im Rechtsverkehr über den Ursprung oder die wahreBeschaffenheit dieser Vermögensbestandteile, das Eigentum oder sonstige Rechte an ihnen, die Verfügungsbefugnis über sie, ihre Übertragung oder darüber, wo sie sich befinden, falsche Angabenmacht...

[4] Translated from the German Penal Code StGB § 261 – Geldwäsche; Verschleierung unrechtmäßig erlangter Vermögenswerte (1) Wer einen Gegenstand, der aus einer in Satz 2 genannten rechtswidrigen Tat herrührt, verbirgt, dessen Herkunft verschleiert oder die Ermittlung der Herkunft, das Auffinden, den Verfall, die Einziehung oder die Sicherstellung eines solchen Gegenstandes vereitelt oder gefährdet, wird mit Freiheitsstrafe von drei Monaten bis zu fünf Jahren bestraft.

[5] Translated from the Swiss Penal Code StBG Art.305bis – Geldwäscherei 1. Wer eine Handlung vornimmt, die geeignet ist, die Ermittlung der Herkunft, die Auffindung oder die Einziehung von Vermögenswerten zu vereiteln, die, wie er

1e. Whoever, knowing that the property involved in a financial transaction represents the proceeds of some form of unlawful activity, con-
ducts or attempts to conduct such a financial transaction which in fact
involves the proceeds of specified unlawful activity

(A)
(i) with the intent to promote the carrying on of specified unlawful activity; or
(ii) with intent to engage in conduct constituting a violation of section 7201 or
7206 of the Internal Revenue Code of 1986; or

(B) knowing that the transaction is designed in whole or in part -
(i) to conceal or disguise the nature, the location, the source, the ownership,
or the control of the proceeds of specified unlawful activity; or
(ii) to avoid a transaction reporting requirement under State or Federal
law,...
(US Penal Code § 1956 – Laundering of Monetary Instruments, a (1))

2. When the following conduct is committed intentionally it is money
    laundering:

- the conversion or transfer of property derived from criminal activity for the purpose of concealing or disguising the illicit origin of
  the property or of assisting any person who is involved in the
  commission of such activity in evading the legal consequences of
  his action;
- the concealment or disguise of the true nature, source, location,
  disposition, movement or rights with respect to, or ownership of,
  property, knowing that such property is derived from criminal activity or from an active participation in such activity;
- the acquisition, possession or use of property, knowing, at the time
  of receipt, that such property was derived from criminal activity
  or from an active participation in such activity;
- participation in, association to commit, attempts to commit and
  aiding, abetting, facilitating and counseling the commission of
  such actions. (European Council Directive)[6]

---

weiß oder annehmen muß, aus einem Verbrechen herrühren, wird mit Gefängnis
oder Busse bestraft.
[6] Council Directive 91/308/EEC of 10 June 1991 on prevention of the use of the
financial system for the purpose of Money Laundering [Official Journal L 166 of

3.   A person commits the offence of money-laundering if:

- the person acquires, possesses or uses property, knowing or having reason to believe that it is derived directly or indirectly from acts or omissions which constitute an offence against any law punishable by imprisonment for not less than 12 months;
- or renders assistance to another person for the conversion or transfer of property derived directly or indirectly from those acts or omissions, with the aim of concealing or disguising the illicit origin of that property, or of aiding any person involved in the commission of the offence to evade the legal consequences thereof; or concealing or disguising the true nature, origin, location, disposition, movement or ownership of the property derived directly or indirectly from those acts or omissions. (UNODC 2003)[7]

4.   Money laundering is the processing of criminal proceeds to disguise their illegal origin. (FATF 2003, p. 1)[8]
5.   Money laundering is a process in which assets obtained or generated by criminal activity are moved or concealed to obscure their link with the crime. (IMF 2004)[9]
6.   Money laundering is any act or attempted act to conceal or disguise the identity of illegally obtained proceeds so that they appear to have originated from legitimate sources. (Interpol 1995)
7.   Money laundering is a wide range of activities and processes intended to obscure the source of illegally obtained money and to create the appearance that it has originated from a legitimate source. (IOSCO 1992)
8.   Money laundering is the process by which criminals attempt to conceal the true origin and ownership of their criminal activities. (IFAC)
9.   Money laundering is the process by which the proceeds of crime ('dirty money') are put through a series of transactions, which dis-

---

28.06.1991]. Amended by: European Parliament and Council Directive 2001/97/EC of 4 December 2001 [Official Journal L 344 of 28.12.2001].

[7] United Nations Office on Drugs and Crime (UNODC), UNODC model money laundering, proceeds of crime and terrorist financing bill, 2003.

[8] Financial Action Task Force (FATF) on Money Laundering, The Forty Recommendations, 1996 (these recommendations were revised in June 2003, but this revised version did not present a (new) definition).

[9] The IMF worked with the World Bank on this; the World Bank adopted the same definition.

guise their illicit origins, and make them appear to have come from a legitimate source ('clean money'). (Australian Institute of Criminology)

10. Money laundering is all acts that are needed to give money from criminality an apparent legal source. (WODC, Dutch Ministry of Justice 2002)[10]

11. Money laundering is an activity aimed at concealing the unlawful source of sums of money. (Savona 1997, p. 3)

12. Money laundering is the process by which the proceeds of crime are converted into assets which appear to have a legitimate origin, so that they can be retained permanently or recycled into further criminal enterprises. (Graham 2003, p. 1)

13. Money laundering is falsely claiming a legitimate source for an il legally acquired advantage. (van Duyne et al. 2003, p. 69)

14. Money laundering is the process by which illicit source moneys are introduced into an economy and used for legitimate purposes. (Walker 1995)

15. Money laundering is a process whereby money from crime is rendered more useful by two means: converting it into a desirable medium (i.e. a bank balance or equity in a company) and erasing its more obvious links to crimes. (Cuéllar 2003)

16. Money laundering is the process of converting cash, or other property, which is derived from criminal activity, so as to give it the appearance of having been obtained from a legitimate source. (McDonell 1997)

17. The conversion or transfer of property, knowing that such property is derived from serious crime, for the purpose of concealing or disguising the illicit origin of the property or of assisting any person who is involved in committing such an offence or offences to evade the legal consequences of his action, and the concealment or disguise of the true nature, source, location, disposition, movement, rights with respect to, or ownership of property, knowing that such property is derived from serious crime. (EC Convention on Laundering)[11]

---

[10] Translated from: 'Witwassen is het geheel van handelingen dat nodig is om gelden die afkomstig zijn van criminaliteit een ogenschijnlijke legale herkomst te geven.' Source: Kleemans et al. (2002, p. 127).

[11] Article 1 of the 1990 European Communities (EC) Convention on Laundering, Search, Seizure and Confiscation of the Proceeds from Crime (http://www.ex.ac.uk/politics/pol_data/undergrad/ron/ index.htm).

18. Money laundering is the process by which one conceals the existence, illegal source, or illegal application of income, and then disguises that income to make it appear legitimate. (Reagan Administration Report 1984)[12]

Table 4.1 gives an overview of the common features of all of these definitions. Columns 2-4 list the subject of laundering quoted in the definitions. For economists, the fact that money laundering is sometimes defined as a stock and sometimes as a flow is important. Some legal definitions make it impossible to distinguish. Some talk about 'money' which
can be both a stock and a flow. If money is interpreted as a flow, then
one can see from Table 4.1 that the majority of definitions view the subject of money laundering as a flow rather than a stock. With this, most
definitions are in line or follow the US Penal Code, which very clearly
has a flow in mind, which can be proceeds, transactions, income or
money flows. With regard to the source of the subject, some definitions
refer only to (serious) criminal acts, whereas others also include other
illegal activities, such as tax evasion, illegal copying, illegal gambling
and illegal prostitution. Some definitions stress that money laundering
endeavours to try to hide the source, while others chose the more active
approach of making it appear legal. Those activities especially that involve the layering phase of laundering, which necessitates active steps to
make the illegal proceeds appear legal, are better captured in the latter
definitions. To keep money under one's pillow or hide it in the roof of
one's house would, according to all legal national definitions listed in
Table 4.1 (first rows), then be money laundering as well. However, this
does not necessitate bringing money into the financial circuit.

The Swiss Penal Code is the only definition that does not fit into our
scheme. The Swiss define money laundering as trying to prevent investigations about the origin of an object.

What is still missing in the definitions presented thus far, is the concrete crimes to which money laundering refers. Busuioc (2007, p. 22)
sees the definition of predicate offences as the most important legal problem of money-laundering definitions:

---

[12] President's Commission on Organized Crime, Interim Report to the President
and Attorney General, The Cash Connection: Organized Crime, Financial Insti
tutions, and Money Laundering 7, a Reagan Administration Report, 1984.

Table 4.1 Money laundering definitions: their subject and laundering purpose

Money Laundering Definition	Subject			Source of Subject		Purpose	
	Stock	Flow	Stock or flow	Illegal	Criminal	Hide the source	Make it appear legal
1a Dutch Penal Code (2004)			Objects, all means and property rights		Criminal	Hide the source	
1b Austrian Penal Code	Parts of Wealth				Criminal	Hide the source	
1c German Penal Code			Object	Illegal		Hide the source	
1d Swiss Penal Code	Assets				Criminal	Prevent the investigation	
1e US Penal Code		Proceeds, Financial Transactions		Illegal		Hide the source	
2 Council Directive (1991)	Property				Criminal	Hide the source	
3 United Nations law model for money laundering (2003)	Property				Criminal	Hide the source	

continued

Table 4.1 continued

Money Laundering Definition	Subject			Source of Subject		Purpose	
	Stock	Flow	Stock or flow	Illegal	Criminal	Hide the source	Make it appear legal
4 FATF (1996)		Proceeds			Criminal	Hide the source	
5 IMF and World Bank (2004)	Assets				Criminal	Hide the source	
6 Interpol (1995)	Assets			Illegal		Hide the source	Make it appear legal
7 IOSCO (1992)			Money	Illegal		Hide the source	Make it appear legal
8 IFAC (2001)		Criminal activities			Criminal	Hide the source	
9 Australian Institute of Criminology Research and Public Policy Series (1996)		Proceeds			Criminal	Hide the source	Make it appear legal
10 Kleemans et al.(2002)			Money		Criminal		Make it appear legal
11 Savona (1997)			Money	Illegal		Hide the source	
12 Graham (2003)		Proceeds			Criminal		Make it appear legal

continued

Table 4.1 continued

Money Laundering Definition	Subject		Source of Subject			Purpose	
	Stock	Flow	Stock or flow	Illegal	Criminal	Hide the source	Make it appear legal
13 Duyne, van et al. (2003)			Advantages	Illegal			Make it appear legal
14 Walker (1995)			Money	Illegal			Ambiguous
15 Cuéllar (2003)			Money		Criminal	Hide the source	Make it appear legal
16 International Conference on Global Drugs (1997)	Property		Money		Criminal		Make it appear legal
17 European Communities Convention (1990)	Property				Criminal	Hide the source	
18 President's Commission on Organized Crime (1984)		Income		Illegal		Hide the source	Make it appear legal

Source: Unger et al. (2005, Appendix IV p.16, Table done by J. Ferwerda) plus some modifications

From a legal point of view, the Achilles' heel in defining and criminalizing money-laundering relates to the so-called 'predicate offences' understood as the criminal offences which generated the proceeds thus making laundering necessary.

Hiding or disguising the source of certain proceeds will, of course, not amount to money laundering *unless* these proceeds were obtained from a criminal activity (i.e. predicate crime). Therefore, what exactly amounts to money-laundering, which actions and who can be prosecuted is largely dependent on what constitutes a predicate crime for the purpose of money laundering.

Despite harmonization efforts at both the European and international level, national legislations criminalizing money laundering continue to differ. Member States of the European Union applied the Money Laundering EU Directives (see below), but 'Given that it was left open to states to decide exactly which crimes would qualify as predicate offences to money-laundering, a veritable patchwork of national lists of predicate offences has resulted' (Busuioc 2007, p. 23). Most countries have listed serious offences as predicate crimes but have nevertheless adopted different approaches to what exactly constitutes a serious crime for the purpose of money laundering. Thus, the predicate offences vary from one country to the other as follows.

In Austria, with the 1993 Amendment to the Penal Code, money laundering was criminalized and penalties were introduced for the commission of such crimes ranging from six months to five years. However, the scope of money laundering was extended only to offences of a minimum penalty threshold of three years (Silberbauer and Krilyszyn, 2003, p. 179). In addition, a list with predicate offences such as document forgery or custom fraud was added. Furthermore, the Austrian Money Laundering Definition excludes self-laundering. Only if the crime has been committed by somebody else does one speak of laundering (§ 165 StGB (1)). A fraudster or a drug dealer who launders his own illicit proceeds could not be prosecuted for money laundering. The Austrian Penal Code for money laundering differentiates between simple crime and gainful and organized crime. The law foresees two years maximum sentence for simple crime and higher sentences between six months and five years of prison for the latter (§ 165 Abs.3 StGB). Organized crime faces a much higher penalty, ten years of prison, in the neighbouring country Germany ((§ 261 Abs.4 StGB). Hufnagel (2003, p. 50) criticizes the big differences between the two countries. Austria's Penal Code does not foresee punishment of simple offences from narcotics and does not include all hard narcotic offences as predicate crimes for money laundering. This means that parts of organized drug crime cannot be prosecuted.

The United Kingdom, through the 2002 Proceeds of Crime Act, introduced an 'all crimes' approach to predicate offences to money-laundering. Section 334 sets out the penalties. A person convicted of an offence under ss327-329 is liable on conviction on indictment to imprisonment for a maximum of 14 years or a fine or both. A person guilty of an offence under ss330-333 is liable on conviction on indictment to imprisonment for a maximum of five years or a fine or both. This will include nominated officers who are guilty of failing to make required disclosures (Mitchell 2002). On 1 March 2004, the Money Laundering Regulations 2003 were added and orders amending the Proceeds of Crime Act 2002 and the Terrorism Act 2001 came into force. The 2003 Regulations and the Orders implement the Second Money Laundering Directive, which was adopted by the European Union in December 2001.

In Australia, money laundering is criminalized in accordance with Division 400 of the 1995 Criminal Code Act. Predicate crimes cover the laundering of money or property from all indictable offences (i.e. offences punishable with one year imprisonment or more) (FATF, 2005 Evaluation Report, p. 4). Punishments can range from six months to twenty-five years depending on the amount laundered and the level of knowledge of the offender (Busuioc 2007, p. 23).

The Netherlands, which explicitly criminalized money-laundering in 2002 through an amendment to the Penal Code (*i.e.* Bill 21 565) took the approach that the term predicate offences refers to 'serious crimes'. The category 'serious crimes' encompasses the offences mentioned in the Dutch Penal Code, Book 2 as well as the offences punishable under the Economic Offences Act (Graaf and Jurgens, 2003, p. 472). The maximum sentence for laundering is four years. Suriname, until its independence in 1975 a Dutch colony, largely copied the Dutch Money Laundering Law, but the Surinamese Wet Strafbaarstelling Money-laundering 2002 foresees much higher punishment for laundering, up to 20 years (see Unger and Siegel 2006).

Greece has a so-called 'exclusive and restrictive' approach to money-laundering in the sense that the relevant legal instrument (i.e. Law 231/95) provides a limited list of offences (16+ crimes) such as drugs, theft, several categories of fraud, illegal importation etc. Laundering of the proceeds of crimes not listed will not fall under the crime of money-laundering. (Busuioc 2007, p. 23)

German legislation also specifically pinpoints what constitutes a predicate offence to money laundering and the German Criminal Code § 261 (1) 2 lays out a restricted list of predicate offences. The maximum sentence for laundering is ten years. (Hufnagel 2003, p. 50)

Switzerland, not being a member of the European Union, had less pressure to implement the EU Directives on Money Laundering, but it also followed the FATF Recommendations in order to reach some minimum standards for money laundering in Europe and implemented an Anti-Money Laundering law on 1 April 1998, Artikel 305bis StGB. Switzerland does not have a list of predicate crime. Instead, money laundering refers to all serious crimes with sentences of more than one year in prison (crimes with 'Zuchthaus' sentences which can range from one year to twenty years as opposed to 'Gefaengnis' sentences) (Art.305bis Ziff.1 StGB) (Hufnagel 2003, p. 62f).[13] In Swiss Penal Law every type of fraud is classified as serious crime, as opposed to German Law, where simple fraud, theft, racketing, fencing and procuring is not part of the money-laundering definition (Hufnagel, 2003, p. 63). Contrary to this, simple narcotic offences and gainful or organized tax evasion are not part of the definition in Switzerland, while they are in Germany. The punishment for money laundering is between three days and three years (Art.305bis Ziff.1 StGB). In qualified cases of serious organized crime it can reach five years (Art.305bis Ziff.2 StGB). Money laundering is often up to the Kanton and not a federal jurisdiction, which can be quite different (Hufnagel 2003). Only if the crime has been committed in several Kantonen does federal law apply.

The United States legislation will be dealt with in Chapter 7. In the US, money laundering is, in principle, a state and not a federal state matter. However, some federal laws also apply. U.S.C. §§ 1956 and 1957 give a list of 130+ predicate crimes for money laundering and a cumulative sentence up to twenty years. Not only prison but money sentences as well are much higher than in Europe and can reach US$500,000 or the double value of the illegal proceeds.

One illustration of the incoherent approach to predicate crimes outlined above is, for example, the variety of national approaches to tax evasion as a predicate for money laundering. For example, in the US, tax evasion is a predicate for money laundering. Similarly, in Australia anti-money-laundering legislation covers the laundering of proceeds of all indictable offences and tax evasion (and even tax avoidance) is an indictable offence. In Germany however, tax evasion is not a predicate offence to money laundering. In Greece and Switzerland, tax evasion is not even a crime, and therefore the hiding or concealing of such proceeds does not amount to money laundering because the first requirement of the crime

---

[13] Both words, Zuchthaus and Gefaengnis, mean prison in the German language and seem to have different meanings only in Switzerland to distinguish serious crime from less serious crime.

of money laundering, the criminal origin of the proceeds, is not met (Busuioc 2007, p. 23f).[14]

Table 4.2 gives a tentative overview over the types of crime in money laundering definitions. The first five columns refer to types of predicate crime in the penal codes of the US, Germany, Austria, Switzerland and the Netherlands. Since the FATF typology of crime overlaps with the US definition, they were placed together in column 1. The last five columns refer to empirical studies of money laundering. As one can see, estimates of money laundering can differ quite a lot, because they include different types of crime.

MONEY LAUNDERING, THE SHADOW AND UNDERGROUND ECONOMY

If the illegally hired gardener can be a money launderer in some jurisdictions, what distinguishes money laundering from the shadow and underground economy? Figure 4.2 is an extended version of the typology of Schneider and Enste (2000). The formal sector consists of industry and households producing legal goods in a legal way, the latter in a do-it-yourself manner. In column 3 the formal sector produces legal goods such as watches, but in an illegal way (by faking the value added and falsely pretending that they were expensive watches), or by fraudulent book keeping. For money laundering this form of white-collar crime is particularly important when it happens across borders. The informal sector consists of a legal part, such as a neighbour's help, and an irregular and a criminal part. In the irregular sector a legal good or service (gardening) is being produced but in an illegal way (shadow work). In the criminal sector, the goods that are produced are illegal (drugs, for example) and are also produced and distributed in an illegal way. This illegal part is called underground economy.

Money laundering overlaps with these definitions. One part of it is white-collar cross-border crime, for example, fake invoicing and transfer pricing can be used for laundering.

Another part of it belongs to the informal irregular sector, such as proceeds from social fraud and tax evasion in some jurisdictions and also the

---

[14] Under Swiss law, tax evasion is a misdemeanour and not a crime (Visini and Haflinger, 2003, p. 584).

Table 4.2 Types of crime in money laundering definitions

Types of crime	FATF Recommendations (2002) and US Penal Code	German Penal Code	Austrian Penal Code	Swiss Penal Code	Dutch Penal Code	Walker (1995)	Van der Werf (1997)	CBS (2004)	Meloen et al (2003)	Unger et al (2006)
Drugs and narcotics	X	X	Only some heavy delicts and hard drugs	Only heavy delicts and hard drugs	Only serious crime and hard drugs	X	X	X	X	X
Prostitution	X				Only when illegal		X	X		X
Public order (against persons)										
Theft, burglary and fencing	X	Not including simple theft and fencing	Not including simple theft and fencing	X	Only serious crime	X	X	X	X	X
Robbery	X	X	X	X	X	X	X	X	X	X
Racketeering	X	X	X	X	X	X	X	X		X
Homicide	X	X	X	X	X	X			X	X
Assault and sexual assault	X					X			X	X

continued

119

Table 4.2 continued

Types of crime	FATF Recommendations (2002) and US Penal Code	German Penal Code	Austrian Penal Code	Swiss Penal Code	Dutch Penal Code	Walker (1995)	Van der Werf (1997)	CBS (2004)	Meloen et al (2003)*	Unger et al (2006)
Participating in criminal organisations	X	X	X	X	X				X	
Possession of arms	X	?	?	?	?				X	
Terrorism	X	X	X	X	X					
Environmental crime	X									
Kidnapping	X	X	X	X	X					
Extortion	X	X	X	X	X					
Smuggling										
Smuggling goods	X	Not simple smuggling	X	?	Only serious					
Trafficking in human beings	X	X	X	X	X			X	X	X
Financial economic crime										
Illegal activities in the labour market	Hiring illegal workers							X	X	X
Embezzlement	X	X	X	X	X					
Terrorist financing	X	X	X	X	X					

continued

120

Table 4.2 continued

Types of crime	FATF Recommendations (2002) and US Penal Code	German Penal Code	Austrian Penal Code	Swiss Penal Code	Dutch Penal Code	Walker (1995)	Van der Werf (1997)	CBS (2004)	Meloen et al (2003)*	Unger et al (2006)
Fraud and deception	X	only by businesses and criminal organizations	only by businesses and criminal organizations	X	X	X			X	X
Matching of people	X	only by businesses or criminal organizations	only by businesses or criminal organizations	X	X				X	
Terrorist financing	X	X	X	X	X					
Counterfeiting currency	X	X	X	X	X					
Insider trading and market manipulation	X	?	?	?	?					
Tax evasion	X	only by businesses and criminal organizations								
Illegal gambling	X						X	X		X
Illegal copying	X	?		?			X	X		X
Corruption (bribery)	X	X	X	X	X		X			

Source: Unger et al. (2005), Unger (2007), Hufnagel (2003) and own modifications

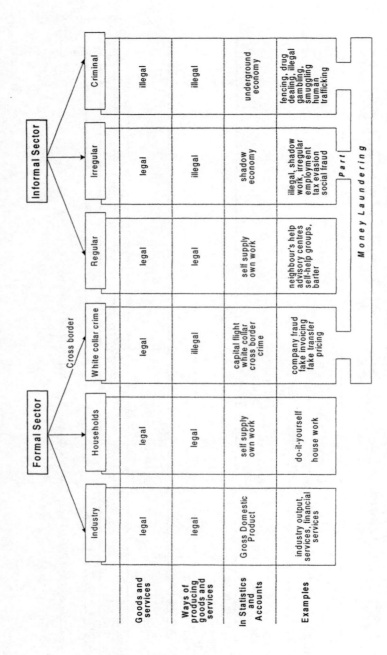

Figure 4.2 Money laundering and the shadow economy

illegal hiring of the illegal immigrant gardener, and another part deals with proceeds from the underground economy. These distinctions are especially important when measuring the sizes of these entities. The proceeds of crime, which are mostly used for measuring money laundering (see Walker 1995; IMF 1999; Unger 2007) are often not different from the value added or turnover estimates of those who estimated the shadow or the underground economy. Money laundering can, therefore, in empirical measures overlap or even be identical with some of these other definitions.

FOUR CASE STUDIES: IS IT LAUNDERING OR NOT?

The relevance of the differences in money-laundering definitions can be seen when analysing concrete cases suspect of money laundering. In this section four examples will be addressed. First, if a defence attorney gets paid by a criminal with contaminated money, does he launder by accepting this fee (Contaminated Attorneys' Fees from Defending Criminals)? Second, did the Dutch ABN AMRO Bank launder when dealing with Iran and Libya through its American branch, while this would have been legal had it done so through its Dutch headquarter (ABN AMRO Bank)? Third, can the Austrian BAWAG Bank that was involved in fraudulent activities in the Caribbean, be charged for laundering if the Austrian money-laundering law excludes self-laundering (The Austrian Bank BAWAG)? Fourth, can the Indonesian Bank Indover's bankruptcy in the early 1990s be linked to laundering (Indover Bank)?

Contaminated Attorneys' Fees from Defending Criminals

If an attorney defends a criminal who pays him with contaminated money, is the attorney then a money launderer? An attorney who defends a drug dealer cannot actually expect the money he receives to be obtained from honest business. Does he launder money? And can he be prosecuted for laundering?

According to our own definitions the attorney does not launder. The attorney does not accept a fee for defence in order to reduce special transaction costs, namely, concealing the illicit origin of the proceeds. He has no advantage if he gets paid from the proceeds of criminal money as opposed to getting paid from the legal activities of his defendant, except if the defendant pays him a higher price for accepting criminal money.

However, according to German and Austrian law, attorneys who subjectively have a reason to assume that the fee they get is from illegal origin are money launderers, no matter whether they receive the money in cash or via a bank transfer (Hufnagel 2003, p. 70). In Switzerland the attorney is not laundering. The disguise of assets is not explicitly mentioned in the Swiss Penal Code. Neither is the pure acceptance of dirty money a money-laundering offence (ibid., p. 72).

In the US, the attorneys' fees are explicitly exempted from the money-laundering definition. Section 1957 – 'Engaging in monetary transactions in property derived from specified unlawful activity' lists under f, 'but such term does not include any transaction necessary to preserve a person's right to representation as guaranteed by the sixth amendment to the Constitution'.

Given the precarious situation, the ideal answer for the attorney is to successfully defend the criminal. In this case there was no crime, hence no proceeds from crime and hence no money laundering possible.

Otherwise, there is a controversial trade-off between the right of a person to be defended and equal treatment of launderers. It is open to debate whether exemptions from laundering should only be valid for defending people with no income or also be valid for lawyers of choice, because then this could also give the impression that 'crime does not pay, except for attorneys' fees'.

ABN AMRO Bank

ABN AMRO is one of the world's largest banks. Incorporated in The Netherlands with its headquarters in Amsterdam, it has some 3000 branches and subsidiaries spread out over 60 countries. It is valued at some US$830 billion. In December 2005 the US Federal Reserve Board, the New York Banking Department and the Illinois Department of Financial and Professional Regulation fined ABN AMRO US$80 million for violating state and federal Anti-Money Laundering (AML) rules and regulations (US Federal Reserve Board 2005) (Unger 2007, Chapter 1).

If anything demonstrates more clearly the problems of defining money laundering and providing an accurate global base line for measuring the amounts and effects of laundered funds, it was ABN AMRO's dealings with Iran and Libya. Half of the US$80 million fine levied against the bank was authorized by the Office of Foreign Assets Control (OFAC), part of the Department of the Treasury. OFAC regulates and prohibits specified transactions between the US and Iran and Libya (US Federal

Reserve Board et. al. 2005). Economic measures against Libya are a response to its past involvement with international terrorism. All countries agreed to these sanctions and therefore any violation of them could give rise to allegations of money laundering that would be valid across borders. The Iranian Transactions Regulations, however, by which Washington imposes sanctions unilaterally on Iran, are specific to the US. Transactions with Iran would not be a predicate crime in the Netherlands or in any other major trading nation. Therefore, a US company dealing surreptitiously with Iran and without approval of the OFAC could be charged with money laundering. A non-US company could not be charged with money laundering.

ABN AMRO is defined as a foreign bank in the US, including its New York and Chicago branches. Despite this, OFAC regulations covering Iran and Libya apply to ABN AMRO regardless of whether or not transactions are routed through the US or a third country if they involve US individuals and/or corporate entities. These regulations effectively blur the boundaries between the US and third countries. If ABN AMRO had done the same deal via its other branches rather than via the US, it would not have laundered.

ABN AMRO's Chicago and New York branches were simultaneously dealing with a Libyan state chartered bank registered in the United Arab Emirates, the Arab Bank for Investment and Foreign Trade (ARBIFT). US authorities observed that 'Prior to August 1, 2004, the Chicago Branch of ABN AMRO cleared U.S. dollars checks for ARBIFT. The cleared checks were submitted by one of ABN AMRO's overseas branches, which had arranged for ARBIFT to not endorse or stamp the checks' (US Federal Reserve et. al. 2005: 6). These dealings with Iran and Libya were found to violate US regulations. If ABN AMRO had done the same activities in the Netherlands and cleared euro cheque for ARBIFT, this would not have been money laundering.

Finally, it seems interesting to mention that ABN AMRO was not found guilty of money laundering per se, but rather of engaging in 'unsafe and unsound practices' that increased the potential risk for criminal abuse (US Federal Reserve et. al. 2005: 6).

The Austrian Bank BAWAG

The 2005 collapse of the US securities trader Refco and the involvement of Austria's third largest bank, Bank für Arbeit und Wirtschaft – still owned at that time by the Peak Association of the Austrian Trade

Unions, the bank which administered the strike funds of Austrian work-
ers – reads like a series of money-laundering transactions. But was it
laundering?

Refco has been accused in the US courts of fraudulently concealing
US$430 million in losses and missing funds (Shapiro 2006). Prior to the
discovery of these financial irregularities, Refco borrowed US$21 mil-
lion from the trade-union-owned BAWAG bank. BAWAG had also par-
ticipated in New York-based Public Investment in Private Equity (PIPE)
trading schemes whereby companies short of liquidity raise equity by
selling stock at discount prices, often through hedge funds. BAWAG
used hedge funds based in Liechtenstein to facilitate its participation in
the highly speculative PIPE market. In the meantime, Refco incorporated
six companies on the Caribbean island of Anguilla, which were jointly
owned by a company called Liquid Opportunity and BAWAG. They in
turn held US$525 million in fake bonds in an entity incorporated in Ber-
muda (Shapiro 2006; Unger 2007, Chapter 1).

In October 2005, Refco's board learned that its CEO Bennett had
fraudulently hidden loans from Refco to his own companies, with which
he in turn borrowed money from BAWAG in an attempt to repay Refco.
However, the collateral for BAWAG's loan to Bennett consisted of
shares in the company itself. When this became public, there was a panic
run to the bank. In addition, Refco's creditors launched legal action
against BAWAG claiming US$1.3 billion, 'alleging that the bank ac-
tively helped Bennett to deceive the company' (Shapiro 2006). A crime
is committed (fraud) which has a financial gain, these gains are then
placed in a myriad of offshore and onshore corporate structures, they are
then layered to make them appear legitimate financing and reintegrated
as clean property or investments such as stocks and bonds.

Bennett got charged with securities fraud, not with money-laundering,
in the US. Since fraud is a predicate crime for laundering this would have
been possible. Could the Austrian BAWAG be charged for laundering?
According to Austrian law, self-laundering is not a money-laundering
crime. BAWAG could, therefore, not be charged for laundering its proceeds from fraud.

Indover Bank[15]

Indover is a Dutch bank with its headquarters in Amsterdam, specialized in Investment Banking, and in Trade and Corporate Finance. Its roots date back to 1828 (http://www.indoverbank.nl/index.php?pageID=1), to colonial times, where Indover was a branch of the Javanese Bank, the central bank that the Dutch colonial rulers had set up in the Dutch Indies. After Indonesia obtained its independence, the Javanese Bank got nationalized and was renamed as Bank Indonesia. Its Amsterdam branch was renamed as Indover, 'De Indonesische Overzeese Bank' or the Indonesian Overseas Bank, in 1965. Due to the historic circumstances, Indover was owned by a Central Bank, the Bank Indonesia. This unusual fact, that a Central Bank owns commercial affiliations, can bring about some conflicting interest. This is why Bank Indonesia was forced by the Central Bank Law of 1999 to sell off its commercial affiliation.

By that time, internal investigations led to the discovery that Indover was almost bankrupt. Indover was just one of many banks acting within Indonesia that had given out loans without proper risk analysis. Many loans were provided without checking the collateral, if there was any collateral at all. Political and personal considerations were sufficient to provide loans. According to Weissink (2004), Indover granted loans for US$90 million due to political and personal preferential treatment. In order to save Indover from bankruptcy, the Dutch Central Bank had to guarantee almost US$1 billion.

In 2000, the Indonesian public prosecutor Marzuki Darusman accused Indover of money-laundering practices. Also, Weissink (2004) found that Bank Indonesia and Indover could not blame the Asian monetary crises in 1998 for the deficiencies of Indover, but rather the bad loans.

Furthermore, Weissink (2004) discovered that Indover had dealings with former president Suharto, suspected of corruption on the scale of former Philippine leader Marcos. Suharto was, and probably still is, the chairman of many so-called charity foundations in Indonesia. These foundations extracted money through the state apparatus. For instance, at a certain time corporations were obliged to transfer 5% of their profits to one of those foundations. Government employees of Muslim faith had to relinquish a certain percentage of their salary to one of Suharto's found-

---

[15] I owe this story to Alexander Weissink, a journalist, who investigated in Indonesia and was kind enough to allow me to use it in this book. He has also written several articles in the Dutch newspaper *Het Financieele Dagblad* on this issue (see a.o. FD 12.6.2004).

dations. They had no choice since 'the donation' was simply deducted from their monthly wage. At least three of these charity funds in the 1990s had bank accounts at Indover Bank. These accounts were used for massive transfers (approx. US$450 million) in only a few days in 1990. On a weekly basis, up to a few million dollars were transferred to the account at Indover and within the same week, the money was transferred to accounts elsewhere.

Did Indover, which is under the supervision of the Dutch Central Bank, launder the criminal proceeds of former president Suharto? Did the dispersion of part of his ill-gotten wealth from corruption happen by a Dutch bank? Will we ever find out?

Between 1999 and 2004 the Dutch newspapers were eager to investigate (see http://www.antenna.nl/wvi/eng/indover/index.html for references to Dutch newspapers). Since then, media interest has stopped. The public prosecutor in Indonesia was replaced by a new prosecutor who stopped all investigations against president Suharto. The Dutch Central Bank and Indover claim that there were no relations between Indover and Suharto (Vasco de Boom 2004 in Unger et al. 2005). Also, the Dutch authorities did not investigate further. The relationship between Indonesia and the Netherlands has always been fragile. Maybe the transaction costs of damaging the fragile relationship between Indonesia and the Netherlands seem higher than the benefit from prosecuting Indover for money-laundering?

If the reproaches against Indover were justified, it did launder. But as the German proverb says 'wo kein Klaeger, kein Richter' (where there is no prosecutor, there is also no judge).

LATEST EUROPEAN EFFORTS TO HARMONIZE MONEY LAUNDERING DEFINITIONS

The Third Anti-Money Laundering Directive (2005/60/ EC) [16] is the most wide-ranging of the three and represents a significant step towards a more comprehensive approach. The directive incorporates FATF's 40 recommendations and thus brings about a certain degree of coherence between international and European measures for fighting money-laundering. The scope of the directive was extended to cover, in addition

---

[16] Directive 2005/60/EC of the European Parliament and of the Council of 26 October 2005 on the prevention of the use of the financial system for the purpose of money laundering and terrorist financing.

to the sectors and professionals identified by the Second EC Directive, trust or company service providers and all natural and legal persons who receive payments in cash of €15,000 or more as well.[17] Furthermore, for the purpose of the directive, predicate offences are serious crimes encompassing: terrorism related offences as laid out in Articles 1-4 of the Council Framework decision of 13 June 2002 on combating terrorism (2002/ 475/ JHA), drug-related offences as put forward in Article 3(1)a of the 1988 United Nations Convention against Illicit Traffic in Narcotic Drugs and Psychotropic Substances, the activities of criminal organizations as defined in Article 1 of the 1988 Council Joint Action (98/733/JHA), fraud, corruption and all offences punishable in the Member States by detention for a maximum of more than one year or for a minimum of more than six months (i.e. for states that have a minimum threshold for offences).[18]

The directive was formally adopted in October 2005 and will have to be implemented by the EU Member States before 15 December 2007. The adoption of the directive will smooth out many of the cross-country discrepancies relating to the issue of predicate offences. With regard to the implementation of the Second Anti-Money Laundering Directive (2001/97/EC) the Commission started infringement proceedings for failure to implement by issuing its 'reasoned opinion' against six Member States: France, Portugal, Greece, Sweden, Luxembourg and Italy (IP/04/180) (Busuioc 2007).

Another harmonization effort was made when the new Council of Europe Convention on Laundering, Search, Seizure and Confiscation of the Proceeds from Crime and the Financing of Terrorism was opened for signature in May 2005. The Convention was signed by 22 States including the Netherlands and Austria but so far there have been no ratifications[19]. Given that six ratifications are necessary for this, the 2005 Council of Europe Convention has not entered into force by the end of 2006.

The Convention leaves it to the latitude of each Signatory State to decide which approach to use (i.e. all crimes, penalty threshold or an enumerated list of offences) in determining predicate offences as long as the 20 crimes listed in the Appendix of the Convention are covered. For states having a threshold for offences, the threshold for money launder-

---

[17] See Art 2(1).

[18] Article 3 (5).

[19] For additional information concerning signatures and ratifications see <http://convetions.coe.int/Treaty/Commun/ChercheSig.asp?NT=198&CM=11& DF=7/10/2006&CL=ENG>

ing is offences punishable by detention for a maximum of more than one year or for a minimum of more than six months. However, relating to crimes other than those falling under the 20 categories explicitly identified in the Appendix of the Convention, states are likely to have different approaches to whether to regard them as predicate offences to money laundering or not. To this extent, transnational prosecution of money laundering will remain cumbersome with regard to certain offences, given the requirement of double criminality. Double criminality means that countries can only prosecute laundering if the predicate offence is a crime in both countries. If a Swiss tax evader launders in France or a French tax evader launders in Switzerland, he cannot be prosecuted in either of the two countries due to the lack of double criminality. Tax evasion is only a predicate offence in France, but not in Switzerland. For the same reason, the Netherlands cannot punish an Austrian drug dealer for money laundering if he self-launders, nor can Austria punish a self-laundering Dutch drug dealer for the laundering offence.

The harmonization efforts by the European Union, the EC Directives, the Council measures and Council of Europe Conventions show that money laundering is being taken seriously. However, there are still some loopholes left for launderers.

> Agreement has been reached on a list of crimes as well as a set of criteria for identifying additional predicate offences (e.g. the threshold criteria).[20] Nevertheless, variation remains with regards to offences falling outside the scope of the categories of predicate offences identified specifically in the Directive or the Annex to the Strasbourg Convention. To the extent that the threshold criteria is mentioned, this will not result in uniformity in the scope of predicate offences given that criminal penalties have not been harmonized so different countries have different penalties for the same crime. Consequently, although ground breaking and far reaching, the legal instruments discussed above still display weaknesses concerning the definition of money laundering given the fact that they fall short of imposing an 'all crimes' approach. (Busuioc 2007, p. 32)

---

[20] Ferwerda and Bosma (2005).

TECHNIQUES OF LAUNDERING[21]

After having investigated whether someone is laundering or not from a legal perspective, it seems interesting for empirical research to find out how money is being laundered. Which methods or techniques are used for laundering? The following section distinguishes money-laundering techniques by the three phases of laundering: the placement, the layering and the integration phase. Examples mainly refer to the Netherlands, where the original empirical study of techniques has been done (Unger et al. 2006).

Laundering Techniques in the Placement Phase

Smurfing and structuring
In the placement phase, smurfing and structuring (breaking up a large deposit into smaller deposits which helps avoid the currency transaction reporting requirements) is used for smaller amounts of illicit money. Since many countries now have reporting requirements for unusual transactions, launderers will try to stay slightly below the benchmark for reporting. The Dutch limit is equal €15,000. Launderers who do not want to risk reporting will smurf; that means putting amounts up to €14,990 on their accounts. By doing so, they stay slightly under the reporting mark. In order to launder €1.5 million, a launderer would have to present himself more than 100 times at a bank. This is why larger amounts are difficult to place by using smurfing techniques. The problem of over-reporting by banks was addressed recently in the Netherlands and the US (see Takáts 2006). Dutchmen's cash withdrawals for buying a new car costing €15,000 or more would have to be reported as an unusual transaction. Lately, the regulatory trend in the Netherlands is going in the direction of avoiding information dilution through too much reporting. According to this trend, banks should rely more on subjective, rather than objective criteria for identifying suspicious transactions.

Camouflage
One way of getting higher amounts into the banking circuit is by using false passports or other fake IDs. Passports and other items for changing one's ID can be bought on the Internet (see for example http://www.espionage-store.com/newidentityletter.html). Real passports

---

[21] This section closely follows Unger et al (2006 Chapters 3 and 4) and Unger (2007, Chapter 5 which has been co-authored by Madalina Busuioc).

from countries that do not exist anymore, such as British Honduras, are popular. The price for fake passports is around US$1000.

Currency smuggling

A launderer smuggles ill-gotten cash into a country with lax or non-existent money-laundering laws. He then places it in a bank there. Very often it is deposited in an offshore bank account and eventually wired back, say to the United States, at a later date.

Smuggling cash out of a country to another country with minimal Anti-Money Laundering standards and then sending it back via official bank transfers is a popular method. For example, the latest FATF evaluation report on Australia identifies cash smuggling as one of the more common typologies (FATF Third Mutual Evaluation Report, Australia, October 2005). However, there are two drawbacks inherent to this money-laundering method. First, cash is heavy and thus more difficult to transport inconspicuously and second, there is the danger of getting caught at the border.

If a drug trafficker sells heroin for one million dollars, he or she must transport 22 pounds of heroin, but then ends up with 250 pounds of currency (if there is an equal mix of 5, 10 and 20 dollar bills) (see Cuéllar 2003, p. 13). This means that there is great incentive to place money into the financial system or to use the cover of an existing cash-intensive business.

Smuggled cash has been found in cars, ships, bowling balls, coffins and the scuba diving oxygen tanks of supposed tourists. In 1998, Dutch customs caught 231 people who tried to smuggle cash over the border with a total value of €15 million. Often, it concerned more than €200,000 (Kleemans et al. 2002 p. 107-108). In a recent television report on money-laundering, the Dutch journalist Dirk Kageman (Witwassen, in Zembla, Nederland, 3 September 2006) interviewed a courier who transports €250,000 every week in his car from Amsterdam to Hungary. The courier proudly showed that the bills fit exactly under his seat. The fact that €500 bills exist means that cash smugglers can carry much less weight than if they had to carry the same amount in US dollars.

Travellers cheques

The purchase of travellers cheques with 'dirty money' is quite a lucrative laundering technique. The FATF has reported cases of the purchase of large quantities of cheques for cash in several of the FATF member states (FATF 2002b). The 'advantage' of the method is due to the fact that the cheques are easier to move across borders given the lack of reporting requirements. Moreover, given the fact that these types of cheques are issued by respectable companies, they are easily convertible into cash and will not give rise to suspicion that easily (ibid.)

Gambling, casinos

Casinos can be used for the first and third phase of money laundering. A launderer can clean cash by converting it into chips at a casino, then exchange it back into cash to deposit at a bank and obtain a cheque from the casino showing a legitimate transaction. In the third phase of laundering, the launderer can buy a casino. Casinos are a highly cash intensive business. The launderer can own a casino and claim that the large amounts of cash held are profits from the casino. This requires taxes to be paid but gives launderers a legal cover for their illegal activities. Unger and Siegel (2006) investigated laundering techniques in Suriname, a country suspected of being a trading port for cocaine from Columbia and ecstasy from the Netherlands, where casinos pop up like mushrooms. At the moment there are 27 casinos in its capital, Paramaribo, for a population of about 400,000 people. This adds up to one casino per 15,000 inhabitants. In comparison, there are 13 casinos in Australia for approximately 20 million people and 12 casinos in the Netherlands for 16 million people, which comes down to one casino per 1.3 million inhabitants. The difference doesn't seem to be due only to variances in gambling addiction.

In the Netherlands, gambling is a sizable enterprise with about 4500 employees. Recently, there has been much media speculation that Holland Casino, with its 12 casinos nationwide, was a major money-laundering institution. The casino in Amsterdam alone was said to whitewash several million euros per year. It was estimated that about 80% of the money gambled in casinos is criminal money. This was particularly juicy news, because Holland Casino is a quasi-public enterprise. It is a foundation with the Council of Commissioners[22] appointed by the Minister of Justice.

However, if one takes a closer look at how casinos operate, this does not seem realistic. Holland Casino falls under the Wet MOT and must, therefore, report suspicious transactions (above equal €10,000). This leads to the preference of customers to stay slightly underneath this limit

---

[22] In Dutch: Raad van Commissarissen.

(Paauw, 2005). In 2003, 1576 transactions were reported of which 509 were reported to the Ministry of Justice.

Large winnings are not paid out in cash but are transferred to a bank account. Holland Casino deposited €17.5 million directly to winners' bank accounts in 2003. From this, €7.5 million came from unregistered activities at gambling tables from 132 guests. This means that, on average, €27,000 are being deposited directly into clients' bank accounts. (The other €10 million was from gambling machines and jackpots won by 149 guests). The tax authorities are informed, customers are registered at the entrance, a photograph is taken, and more than 150 cameras record activities in the gambling hall. Paauw (2005) estimates that not more than €1.5 million can be whitewashed by means of bank transfers through Holland Casino per year.

The estimates for money laundering through casinos range between €1.5 million and €480 million (80% of turnover). Most experts interviewed think that money laundering through casinos is negligible and highly exaggerated in the Dutch media. However, in other countries, especially where casinos are owned by drug dealers, things might be different. Furthermore, a new loophole for money laundering is gambling via the internet. Legal enforcement in this regard is still very difficult (see Kaspersen, 2005).

Laundering Techniques in the Layering Phase

Correspondent banking

Correspondent banking involves one bank (the 'correspondent bank') carrying out financial services for another bank (the 'respondent bank'). By establishing networks of a multitude of correspondent relationships at the international level, banks are able to undertake international financial transactions in jurisdictions where they do not have offices. For example, there has been no Dutch bank in Holland's former colony, Suriname, since 2003. In order to send money from the Netherlands to Suriname, a sender in the Netherlands would go to a Dutch bank that works with one or more of the Surinamese banks. ABN AMRO, who was active in Suriname until 2003, has several respondent banks. One is RBTT, the Royal Bank of Trinidad and Tobago, which took over ABN AMRO in Suriname in 2004 (see Unger and Siegel 2006). The respondent bank can also be at some offshore centre, such as the Cayman Islands or Seychelles, which are historically known for lax anti-money-laundering regulations.

Correspondent banking frequently uses SWIFT, a Belgian industry cooperative that provides a standard format for transmitting payments, stock transactions, letters of credit and other financial messages to more than 7,500 member banks, broker-dealers and investment organizations around the world. Founded in 1973 as the Society for Worldwide Interbank Financial Telecommunication, millions of transactions worth several trillion dollars are sent each day with an average transit time of 20 seconds. Working in the same manner as a bank routing number, a SWIFT code is widely used to transfer funds between banks (see www.swift.com).

SWIFT got in the news in 2006 and into a heavy debate on privacy issues when the Dutch newspaper *Het Financieele Dagblad* on 11 April 2005 published the story that President Bush wanted a precise tracing of money in order to fight terrorism. In *Het Financieele Dagblad* of 28th June 2006, one could read that the Belgian SWIFT company had to give the Americans access to its entire database which constituted all money transfers.

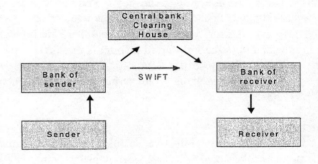

−Credit-transfer (wire transfer) via the bank (correspondent banking) SWIFT

Source: NVB (2006)

Figure 4.3 Correspondent banking

Correspondent banking could also make use of a Central Bank and use, for example, a US clearing house when US dollars are used for the transfer from the Netherlands to Suriname. Figure 4.3 shows the principles of correspondent banking graphically.

Correspondent banks can carry out a variety of services for the respondent bank ranging from cash management to payable-through accounts, international transfer of funds and exchange services. The correspondent bank must rely on the integrity of the respondent bank. Evidently, these relationships are vulnerable to misuse for money laundering. Correspondent banking can be a gateway for illegal funds into the regular banking system. Thus, 'shell banks, certain offshore financial institutions and banks from non-cooperative countries and territories (NCCTs) are of particular risk to legitimate correspondent banking relationships' (FATF 2002b). For example, Al Qaeda used the correspondent network of a Sudanese bank for cross-border dealings. These cross-border dealings included France's Credit Lyonnais, Germany's Commerzbank and the Saudi Bank in Jeddah in which ABN AMRO of the Netherlands has a 40% stake. (Nawaz et al. 2002). Once dirty money has leaked into the regular financial system, it is nearly impossible to detect (Unger and Busuioc 2007).

Bank cheques and bank drafts
According to the FATF, the use of bank cheques and one of its more specific forms, bank drafts, which allows for funds to be transferred between persons or jurisdictions, is usually not reportable and there are no identification requirements unless the transferred amount is in cash and it surpasses a certain threshold (e.g. €10,000 or €15,000). The use of these instruments as a technique for money laundering has been frequently identified (FATF 2002b).

Collective accounts
Dishonest professionals can use collective accounts as a way to launder money. Because the professional will have a reputable standing with the financial institution, they can pay in large amounts of cash and pay out to a variety of different people. These people will, of course, be associates of the launderer. This method is a more advanced form of smurfing.

Payable-through accounts
This process requires the launderer to have a bank account with a foreign bank that has a payable-through account system with a bank in a different country, such as the US. These accounts give the launderer the ability to conduct business in the second country as if he had a bank account in that country, without having to submit to those countries' banking regulations. For example, a launderer from Colombia can bank in the US if

the Colombian bank has a payable-through account with a US institution without having to notify the US financial authorities, which may require a greater degree of evidence of the origin of funds. These types of accounts are set up in the context of correspondent banking relationships (Unger and Busuioc 2007, p. 85).

Loan at low or no interest rates

A very easy method is to give interest-free loans. This allows the launderer to transfer large amounts of cash to other people and so avoid having to deposit the money into a bank or other institution. These loans will be paid back slowly, which avoids deposits hitting the reporting threshold. The receiver of the loan is likely to be aware of the dubious nature of the money, but will be put off from reporting it due to the benefits he receives from the preferential loan rates.

Sometimes these loans are given for special purposes. For example, in Suriname one can buy second hand cars without any savings and pay the lease rent back every month. In this case, the loan is given in the form of a car, which the money launderer pays for in cash with US dollars. The car market in Suriname is entirely in US currency and cash. The car dealer who is a launderer slowly gets clean money back from the lease then (Unger and Siegel 2006).

Back-to-back loans

Back-to-back loans are a construction used for currency hedging. They involve an arrangement in which two companies in different countries borrow each other's currency for a given period of time in order to reduce foreign exchange risk for both of them. For example, a US company loans 1000 US dollars to a British company in the US which in turn loans the equivalent amount in pounds sterling at the spot market exchange rate to the US company in the UK. This saves both from going to the foreign exchange market and running an exchange risk.

This hedging construction can also be used for laundering purposes. In the Netherlands, it is sometimes used when launderers want to buy real estate, which needs a Dutch bank guarantee. For example, a person takes cash to Paraguay and deposits it in a bank account there. This money is then transferred to Switzerland. The person then purchases real estate in the Netherlands using the bank deposit in Switzerland as a guarantee (see Unger et al. 2006).

Money exchange offices

Money exchange offices are a legal way of exchanging money into the currency of choice. But they can also be used for money laundering. In the first phase of laundering, this usually requires a corrupt exchange office as the levels of cash would raise suspicion. In the third phase of laundering, the launderer can operate an exchange bureau and thus incorporate the illegal cash as profits using money exchanging. Whilst the launderer would pay tax on these 'profits', it provides him with a simple explanation on the high levels of cash held. The paid taxes also give an added layer of legitimacy to the funds.

Money exchange offices[23] have been highly suspect of money-laundering in the Netherlands. They perform not only money exchange, but coupon cashing as well. Security coupons issued abroad (effectively, this includes bonds, shares and money certificates), mostly issued in Belgium and Luxembourg, are exchanged at the Dutch border. The money exchange offices cash these coupons. Later, the coupons are in turn cashed back in Luxembourg and Belgium. The total money flow here is €350 million. The EU's savings tax directive (ESD) should reduce this problem in the future. However, the ESD preserves bank secrecy arrangements for Luxembourg and Austria in the EU and Switzerland is outside this jurisdiction.

Money exchange offices can also be abused regarding unauthorized money transfers. Most of the Surinamese Cambios, for example, are only authorized to do money exchange but not international money transfers. However, many of them do (see Unger and Siegel 2006). The drug dealer gives money to the Dutch underground banker in cash. The underground banker calls the Cambio in Suriname, who pays out the money in cash in Suriname. Since the drug business is running both ways quite well (cocaine versus ecstasy pills), clearing is not needed very often. With this method, money does not have to leave the country anymore and avoids the risk of being confiscated at the border.

Money transfer offices

Money transfers via money transfer offices such as Western Union[24] and MoneyGram[25] seem to be important for money laundering. In the Nether-

---

[23] See the article about money exchange offices by Dirk van der Wal in DNB Report 2005.
[24] In the Netherlands there are three banks connected with Western Union: Postbank, Cash Express and Goffin Bank (Kleemans, 2002, p.110).

lands, the total amount of money transferred by the existing 30 Dutch money transfer offices is €325 million per year. According to Kleemans et al. (2002), these relatively expensive money transfers are mainly used for smuggling illegal immigrants and women. Though they are often expensive, they are fast. International money transfer agents are controlled to a different extent in different countries. In the Netherlands, for example, money transfer agents have to be licensed and are supervised by the Dutch National Bank. In Suriname, the same money transfer agents do not need a license and are not supervised (see Unger and Siegel 2006). It is, therefore, very likely that these agents also behave differently in different countries.

Insurance market

One way for the launderer to use the insurance market is to arrange insurance policies on assets, either real or fake, through a dishonest or ignorant broker. Regular claims on this insurance can then be made to return the cash to the launderer. To reduce the risk of detection, the launderer can ensure that the claims made are below the premiums paid so that the insurer makes a profit (Unger and Busuioc 2007, p. 87).

Fictitious sales and purchases

This method entails the use of false sales and purchase orders. These can be with legitimate organizations that will have no knowledge that these purchase orders exist. Fictitious sales documents are created to explain the extra income showing in the accounts, which has come from illegal activities.

Fake invoicing

Launderers can create fake invoices for high amounts and ship merchandise of low value or reverse this procedure as a way of concealing illgotten gains. This can be very difficult to detect. For example, if an exporter ships watches worth €1 million to a third country, but invoices the 'customer' (who may be a subsidiary of the supplier) only €100,000 for low-value watches, and the importer sells the expensive watches for €1 million in her/his country, then €900,000 are laundered by fake invoicing. The exporter, who has spent his illegal cash on watches in his own country, has thus 'frozen the money into watches' and has shipped it to

---

[25] In the Netherlands there are three banks connected with MoneyGram: Grens Wissel Kantoor (GWK), Thomas Cook and American Express (Kleemans et al. 2002, p. 110).

the other country with help from the importer. The importer makes honest earnings from selling expensive watches and puts the money on an account in his country for the exporter. In the exporting country (mostly also the one with high taxes) the exporter only declares low income from the export of cheap watches.

Unusual price movements and suspicion regarding under- or over-invoicing is one reason why the United States and some other countries have issued interquartile ranges for specific transaction prices. Every four months, price ranges are set and prices are not supposed to exceed these limits. In 1994, the US Internal Revenue Service issued 482 transfer pricing regulations. Prices that were not within the interquartile range were considered abnormal (Boyrie et al. 2005).

Zdanowicz et al. (1999) have analysed transfer pricing between Brazil and the US, and Boyrie et al. (2005) analysed transfer prices between Switzerland and the US. Every import and export transaction between Switzerland and the US for every month in the years 1995 to 2000 was analysed. Transactions that exceeded the transfer pricing range were considered abnormal. They found overvalued Swiss imports from the US and undervalued Swiss exports to the US. Between 1995 and 2000, the resulting capital outflows from Switzerland totalled some US$31 billion. They also found a significant increase in the amounts of capital outflows from Switzerland after the country passed anti-money-laundering legislation in 1998. One explanation is that stricter AML regulations encouraged launderers to switch from channelling the proceeds of crime through banks to invoicing.

The same method of transfer pricing was used to investigate discrepancies in Russian and US trade (Boyrie et al. 2005). The amount of capital flight from Russia to the US through abnormally priced trade between 1995 and 1999 was valued at US$8.92 billion, comprising US$7.24 billion in under-invoiced exports to the US and US$1.68 billion in over-invoiced imports into Russia (ibid., p. 259). Not all of it is due to laundering, but one can safely assume that quite a lot of it is.

Shell companies

Shell companies are 'businesses without substance or commercial purpose and incorporated to conceal the true beneficial ownership of business accounts and assets owned' (FATF Report on Money Laundering Typologies, 2002-2003). A number of shell companies are set up in countries known for strong bank secrecy laws or for lax enforcement of money-laundering statutes. They can also be in the form of Special Purpose Entities (SPEs) or International Business Companies (IBCs). The dirty money is then circulated within these shell companies.

Trust offices[26]
Trust offices in the Netherlands provide services in the field of tax and law for foreign companies. The foreign companies do not run businesses in the Netherlands, they are only placed in the Netherlands because of tax advantages on royalties or worldwide dividends. This is completely legal. They use a trust office in the Netherlands to manage their corporation. These trust offices have been in the news recently because of some international administration scandals at several multinationals (Gorkum and Carpentier 2004). Since 2003, there has been legislation to cover the supervision of trust offices[27]. This supervision is now in the first phase, with the DNB responsible for licensing trust offices. Actual research has not yet started; this is probably the reason that no unusual business has been found yet. There were cases of trust office closures, while some of them did not seek a licence. They might have disappeared underground. More might be found once the DNB starts actual research on the licences. The total amount of money flowing through trust offices is about €8 billion per year.

The amount of trust companies was reduced drastically after they came under the supervision of the Dutch National Bank in 2003. The number of licensed trust companies in 2006 was 119, whereas there were about three times as many before the law came into force (see Statistical Bulletin DNB different months and years).

The role of special purpose entities (vehicles)
Special Purpose Entities (SPEs), also known as Special Purpose Vehicles (SPVs), are companies settled in a country so that non-residents of this country are able to earn foreign income and can then redistribute it to third countries. From the Statistical Bulletin of the DNB (June 2003), one can see that in 2001-2002 there were, on average, €4000 billion per year flowing through these corporations in the Netherlands. Multinational companies frequently use SPEs for internal funds transfers between subsidiary companies. For example: Esso collects the receipts from all over the world in the Netherlands and then redistributes these to its branches or to financial institutions abroad. The reason why companies such as

---

[26] In Dutch: trustkantoren, which function differently from US trust companies.
[27] In Dutch: Wet op Toezicht Trustkantoren (Wtt), since 17 December 2003.

Esso are based in the Netherlands is very often to reduce global tax exposure. In 2002, there were 12,500 registered SPEs. Eighty percent of them were trust offices (as mentioned above). But these 80% only account for one quarter of all SPEs transactions. The very large companies are not represented through trust companies including large oil conglomerates, banks, telecommunication and automobile companies. Data released from the US Commerce Department in 2001 showed that US$107.8 billion in profits from US multinationals has been shifted to SPE/BFI subsidiaries located in 11 top offshore destinations (Sullivan 2004, p. 590). Of these, the Netherlands held the most with US$24.6 billion in company profits, followed by Ireland holding US$19.3 billion. In his analysis of these trends Martin Sullivan (2004, p. 589) stated that:

> Recently released data from the Commerce Department indicate that the IRS cannot prevent U.S. companies from artificially shifting profits to tax haven countries like the Netherlands, Ireland, Bermuda, and Luxembourg. In 2001 subsidiaries domiciled in those four countries were assigned 30 percent of all foreign profits of U.S. corporations, despite accounting for only five percent of the productive capacity and three percent of the employment of foreign subsidiaries of U.S. corporations.

Because the amount that SPEs transfer is so huge, about eight times the Dutch GDP, they are not included in the balance of payments calculations. In 2002, most transactions went to the UK (De Nederlandsche Bank 2003, p. 22).

Underground banking

In a broad definition, underground banking can be considered as any financial operation outside the conventional or regulated banking and financial sector. Due to their combination of informality, confidentiality, informal control and minimum request of information from customers, which can sometimes be, for example, illegal immigrants or legal immigrants with an unclear working status, these informal, naïve channels are extremely attractive and open to abuse. Thus, the said channels might satisfy the demand for illegal financial services and, more specifically, serve the purpose of money laundering and terrorism financing (Masciandaro, 2004; see also Nawaz et al. 2002).

Traditionally, it was thought that these informal channels could not sustain the flow of large sums of money, but there is evidence which suggests that these informal systems can indeed sustain large amounts of money (Passas, 2004). Dutch experts estimate that between 50 and 500 underground bankers are active in the Netherlands.

Black market of foreign currency

The launderer uses the foreign currency black market both to remove the risk of transporting large amounts of currency and to avoid depositing large amounts of foreign currency in domestic banks – for instance, a Mexican drug trafficker having large quantities of US dollars to deposit in a Mexican bank. These foreign exchange traders are used; they themselves are conducting an illegal enterprise and have no wish to attract attention to themselves by reporting the activities of the money launderer. Furthermore, the exchange traders charge high fees for their services. This costs the launderers money but removes some risk of having large amounts of cash on them (Unger and Busuioc 2007, p. 90).

The Integration Phase

In the third phase, money launderers want to park the laundered money safely without being detected and with profit.

Capital market investments

Capital market investments can happen in all phases of laundering. In the first phase, the launderer uses his ill-gotten cash for buying. The launderer can invest the money into financial assets so as to avoid having large amounts of cash. But he can also use capital market investments in the layering phase or for placing the money in its final spot. These assets, such as shares and bonds, are generally low risk and so the chances of losing money are small. Furthermore, the assets are highly liquid, which means they can be converted back into cash very easily. Laundered funds are co-mingled with lawful transactions.

Derivatives

These are financial assets and so can be purchased by the launderer in order to invest the cash in reputable enterprises. Again, a disreputable broker is probably needed. These assets are highly liquid and so can easily be resold in order to return the cash back to the launderer. However, derivatives are much more risky than traditional financial instruments.

Real estate acquisition
The launderer can invest the illegal cash into property, which is generally a non-depreciating asset. This would normally require a real estate agent who is willing to overlook the fact that the launderer wants to pay cash for an expensive asset. This asset can then be sold fairly easily to show a legitimate source of cash. The importance of this market for Dutch money laundering seems especially high.

The catering industry
The catering industry is often used by launderers because it is a highly cash-intensive business, just like casinos for example. The owner of a catering company can pay its employees – who often work illegally – in cash, and will often receive its payments in cash, which will serve as a justification for the large cash deposits. Usually, the company will have to use various fraudulent accounting practices in order to succeed in such an operation. The cash that is to be laundered is incorporated as profits. Similar exploitation of apparently legal cash intensive businesses can also be found with reference to hotels, cinemas and so forth.

The gold market
According to the FATF, gold offers the advantage of having a so-called 'high intrinsic value in a relatively compact form' and, consequently, represents one of the simplest and most effective typologies. Gold can be purchased easily in most jurisdictions regardless of whether it is in a rough or finished form (i.e. piece of jewellery). In situations where the gold is the actual vehicle for laundering, it is usually related to the laundering of funds from crimes such as narcotics trafficking, organized crime activities and illegal trade in goods and merchandise (FATF Report on Money Laundering Typologies, 2002-2003).

The diamond market
Hiding the illicit nature of funds is easier in this case as the identity of the person making the transaction may not be publicly revealed. Furthermore, diamonds and other precious gems offer some of the same advantages as those provided by gold such as the so-called 'high intrinsic value in a compact form'. Diamonds, in particular, can easily be concealed and transported and will be traded with little difficulty worldwide. 'The ease with which diamonds can be hidden and transported and the very high value per gram for some stones make diamonds particularly vulnerable to illegal diversion from the legitimate channels for the ex-

ploitation and profit of criminals' (FATF Report on Money Laundering Typologies, 2002-2003).

Buying jewels

Substantial revenues from wholesale and retail jewels sales laundered US$1.2 billion for Colombian drug kingpins in 18 months in Los Angeles in the operation La Mina, the gold mine (see Cuéllar 2003, p. 14).

Purchase of consumer goods for export

The launderer will invest in consumer goods (such as television sets, kitchen appliances and so on) because such purchases can be easily transported across borders without arousing suspicion. These goods can then be sold abroad and produce what appear to be legitimate commercial revenues.

Acquisition of luxury goods

The launderer follows a logic similar to the case of the purchase of consumer goods. These goods can be kept either for personal use or sold for export. One of the qualities of these products, which renders them extremely attractive, is the fact that large amounts of cash can be transformed into a less conspicuous form. Moreover, it is not unusual for purchasers of luxury goods to pay with cash and questions are unlikely to be asked as the shop is unwilling to upset the purchasers with personal questions.

Cash-intensive business

This laundering method is common in situations where the launderer uses a legitimate, cash-intensive business as a cover for laundering (such as an exchange business or a restaurant to help justify large currency deposits). It is the oldest form of laundering. The Chicago gangster Al Capone used launderettes for hiding illicit proceeds from alcohol during the American prohibition in the 1930s (see van Duyne et al. 2003, p. 73). The owner commingles the dirty money with the business's actual revenues, depositing them together into a single bank account.

Using currency to supplement an apparently legitimate transaction

The launderer could pay for a product worth €500,000 with a wire transfer of €300,000 and €200,000 in currency. The currency could be given to the seller under the table, who might be someone operating a currency-intensive business such as a restaurant.

Export import business
The export and import business can be used for the falsification of foreign trade prices. This is essentially a form of false invoicing and can be achieved either by overpricing imports or underpricing exports. In the first case, an importer who buys an item for an amount of US$1 million could request that the price be increased by 10% so that upon payment of US$1.1 million the extra US$100,000 is placed into his private bank account in the exporter's country. In the second situation (i.e. underpricing exports), an exporter will essentially sell an item to a foreign dealer for, say, 25% less than their negotiated value with the understanding that when the payment is made the extra 25% will be deposited into the exporter's foreign bank account in the dealer's country. Provided the willingness of the other party, this can be an easy means to move funds across borders and to detach it from the original crime.

Acquisition and smuggling of arms
The acquisition of arms with ill-gotten proceeds is particularly common amongst terrorist circles (see Unger et al. 2006). Moreover, arms smuggling is also a source of illegal proceeds in itself, which are subsequently subject to laundering. Combined with the proceeds of drug trafficking, organized crime and the funds derived from arms smuggling have been identified as one of the main sources of illegal proceeds for laundering especially in parts of Southern and Eastern Africa (FATF, Report on Money Laundering Typologies, 1996-1997).

New Money Laundering Risks

With the advent of the Internet, new forms of money transfers and possibilities for launderers have arisen.

On-line banking
On-line banking makes it easier for the launderers to conduct transactions as they can avoid having to go to banks and being seen or having to complete many forms. Furthermore, it is much more difficult to trace the operators of these accounts if they never go to banks.

E-cash
E-cash, or electronic cash, is even harder to trace than real cash as the ease with which it can flow around the world makes it twice as hard for the authorities to detect. Money becomes not a real commodity, but sim-

ply a line on a piece of paper or a computer screen. The launderer does not have to worry about depositing large amounts of cash then, as the money does not physically exist. All payments and receipts are made electronically.

E-gold

One can buy gold on the Internet, using addresses such as http://www.e-gold.com/examiner.html or http://goldmoney.com/. These sales and buys still need some identification, one has to register, but when used after having cleaned the money they still guarantee some anonymity.

Prepaid phone cards

Prepaid phone cards can be bought on the streets. One can pay with criminal cash for them and use the prepaid phone cards for shopping anonymously on the Internet. The possibilities and variety of products for sale increase steadily. The Dutch Banking Association calculated that payments over the Internet valued €2 billion (5-7 million transactions) in 2004. Payments via mobile phones amounted to about €1 billion in the Netherlands (NVB 2006).

Proprietary systems

Proprietary systems refer to a specific set of payment and funds transfer rights owned and patented, with intellectual property protections, by a financial services provider located anywhere in the world. Proprietary systems enable customers to access electronic banking or funds transfer routing systems located offshore and hence avoid local reporting requirements such as those specified in the FTR Act. This does not mean that customers are engaging in money laundering, but it does mean that customers can make undetectable financial transactions that may increase the risk of money laundering. These proprietary systems may include international funds transfers between offshore accounts/entities, cheque writing, trading facilities, letters of credit and securities trading. They also involve alternative payment systems with the conversion of funds into a virtual currency with e-credits, PayPal and e-gold. Funds can then be disbursed offshore without triggering the reporting requirements of the FTR Act (Hackett 2003, p. 3).

In 2002, the United States Internal Revenue Service (IRS) found that MasterCard alone processed 1.7 million offshore transactions for 230,000 US resident account holders with offshore debit/credit cards issued in 30 countries with strict bank secrecy laws and minimal FTR requirements (US Department of Justice, 25 March 2002).

New proprietary systems, electronic access and payment methods and interbank settlement protocols are all ways in which transactions can be concealed. The extent of their use for money laundering is unclear. However, it might be appropriate to consider these new technologies when determining which variables and values to use in the measurement of money laundering.

5. The Impact of Money Laundering

Brigitte Unger

INTRODUCTION

Money laundering can have diverse effects on the economy, society and politics. Its effects can be direct and indirect. Direct effects are the costs of the underlying crime itself to the victim and society, since without crime there would be no laundering. Estimates of costs of drugs for several countries amount to about 0.4% of GDP (UNDP 1996, p. 33). Costs from fraud are much higher, but given the huge differences in statistics, international comparison is still not possible. Costs from tax fraud alone are estimated to be about 2%-2.5% of GDP (see EU Memo 2006). If one takes into account the costs for society, for insurance, for the government, the legal system, the judges, the lawyers, the costs of prison, the social consequences such as dismantling the family or corruption, the costs of crime related to money laundering are certainly higher than the ones estimated.

Most of the effects of money laundering are, however, indirect. Unger (2007, Chapter 6 and 7) identified 25 different effects of money laundering in literature. Money laundering can affect business activities, relative prices, consumption, saving, output, employment and growth. It can also affect the financial sector – its liquidity, reputation, integrity and stability. Or it can affect the public sector through unpaid taxes. When criminals buy up public enterprises such as railways and electricity for laundering purposes, this can also mean a threat to privatization efforts. The monetary sector can be affected by means of higher capital inflows or volatile interest rates and exchange rates. There are also social effects such as increased crime, corruption, bribing, and contamination of legal activities through illegal activities. Political effects are the undermining of political institutions by criminals and an increase in terrorism.

This chapter focuses on the microeconomic, sector, and macroeconomic effects of money laundering. Laundering can have microeconomic effects such as changing the behaviour of people by giving wrong incentives to invest or consume. Criminals might behave differently from honest people, because 'not being caught' is an important factor when maximizing utility (see Chapter 1). Laundering can create extra demand for specific investment and consumption goods, which can have an impact on whole sectors, for example by an increase of prices. Laundering activities create extra flows of money, which can have macroeconomic effects such as a reduction of interest rate or inflation.

MICROECONOMIC IMPACT OF MONEY LAUNDERING

Different Spending Pattern of Criminals

Once the money is transferred from the victim to the offender, the latter will use the money in a different way than the former. The spending patterns of criminals might be different from those of ordinary citizens. Furthermore, the money-laundering activity itself involves the purchase of assets such as real estate, jewellery, art and other luxury products, since these assets offer launderers the possibility of concealing large amounts of illicit money without arousing suspicion (Barlett 2002, p. 19). These spending choices may differ from those of the victims who may have intended to use the money for their everyday expenses, old age or 'rainy days' (Walker 1995, p. 30).

Do criminals behave differently from normal people? From criminal case studies we can learn something about the behaviour of criminals and money launderers. Meloen et al. (2003) did a research on crime money, the amount, the characteristics and the spending of it in the Netherlands. They analysed 52 cases of criminals with unlawful advantages ('ontnemingszaken'), where the judge estimated the proceeds at more than 1 million guilders (€400,000) per case. I will refer to these as 'the 52 big criminal cases' in the following.

From the Dutch case studies one can learn about the individual behaviour of launderers. A small group of criminals makes a lot of money, while most criminals make small amounts of money. Eighty-three per cent of suspects in these case studies accounted for only 11.7%

of criminal proceeds, whereas 2.1% of suspects accounted for 57.9% of proceeds. This sounds pretty much the same as the income distribution of honest people.

Meloen et al. (2003) divided the spending behaviour of criminals into four categories: (1) hoarding the crime money (this happens mostly temporarily for later use); (2) consumptive lifestyle, spending the money on luxuries like jewels, art, expensive vehicles, boats or a plane; (3) conventional investment, temporarily putting it into a bank account or spending it on stocks, bonds or options or converting it into loans or other securities; (4) making irregular business investments or reinvesting in a business, legal or illegal, to influence it or use it for personal purposes. In Figure 5.1, one can see that 32% of the money spent in the 52 big criminal cases was for hoarding (9%) and irregular business investments (23%), 11% was for consumptive lifestyle, and 57% went into conventional investments. The 52 criminal cases referred to drug dealers and fraudsters mainly (plus four other cases) and all had to do with money laundering. Table 5.1 gives an overview of the behaviour of several thousand Dutch criminals, from small crime to big crime. The advantage of Table 5.1 is that the consumption and investment patterns are shown in detail. The disadvantage is that many of these cases might not refer to crime cases relevant to laundering, since part of the crime might not have been serious and hence not a predicate crime for money laundering. Table 5.1 demonstrates that small criminals hoard and consume more, whereas big criminals tend to invest more. This behaviour would also be expected from honest people. The big criminals tend to hoard 30%, to use 10% for consumptive lifestyle and luxury goods, and to invest 60%. If one compares the findings for criminals with the findings for launderers in Figure 5.1, one can see that consumptive lifestyle accounts for about 10% of all spending in both cases. This is much less than one would expect from the wasteful, opulent, squandering criminal that is sometimes described in the newspapers. If one adds irregular investment and hoarding as was done in Figure 5.1, then this amounts to 32% of launderers' spending as compared with 29% of criminals' hoarding in Table 5.1. Money is only hoarded temporarily; therefore hoarding can have the purpose of being available for further irregular business investments. Since Table 5.1 does not contain a section for irregular investment, it is likely that this falls under hoarding. Figure 5.1 shows that launderers spend 57% on investments and Table 5.1 that big criminals invest 59.3% of their money. One can, therefore, safely assume that criminals, including launderers, use about 60% of their money for investments.

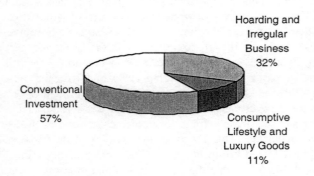

Source: Unger et al. (2006), calculations from Meloen et al. (2003, p. 246)

Figure 5.1 Spending behaviour in 52 big Dutch criminal cases

Table 5.2 shows, in more detail, what the money is spent on in the 52 big criminal cases. The most remarkable difference in spending behaviour is in the frequency of money being hoarded. For drug money, in 20 out of 26 cases, i.e. in 77% of cases, some of the money is hoarded in order to reinvest it in new drug sales. This happens much less often in fraud cases, where hoarding takes place in 23% of cases.

There can only be a distortion of consumption and savings if criminals behave differently from normal people with regard to consumption and savings. If one compares the case studies on criminal spending behaviour from Meloen et al. (2003) shown above, with household spending behaviour according to the Tilburg study done by Alessie et al. (2002, Chapter 9) one can see that criminals basically behave like normal people.

Table 5.1 Spending behaviour of Dutch criminals from large datasets

| Spending Pattern | Data Base Rapsody (the amount of crime money) | | | | | |
| | 1 to 100,000 | | 100,000 to 1 million | | 1 million and more | |
	guilders	%	guilders	%	guilders	%
Hoarding						
1. Cash Money NL	3,565,220	36.2	9,659,836	41.9	11,487,907	24.0
2. Cash Money Foreign	541,583	5.5	878,011	3.8	2,820,971	5.9
Consumption						
3. Consumptive Lifestyle	8,095	0.1	1,300	0.0	9,370	0.0
4. Consumption Goods	311,335	3.2	1,999,370	8.7	694,477	1.5
5. Jewellery, Musical Instruments, Art	667,787	6.8	948,484	4.1	1,012,104	2.1
6. Vehicles	1,672,090	17.0	2,874,646	12.5	3,179,762	6.7
7. Planes, Boats	172,805	1.8	829,598	3.6	227,435	0.5
Investment						
8. Bank Accounts	1,334,454	13.6	902,294	3.9	632,213	1.3
9. Immovable Property NL	718,850	7.3	4,527,500	19.6	13,476,500	28.2
10. Securities			69,157	0.3		
11. Fixed Interest Assets	854,516	8.7	375,963	1.6	14,246,988	29.8
Total	9,846,753	100.0	23,066,158	100.0	47,787,727	100.0
Total Hoarding	4,106,803	41.7	10,537,847	45.7	14,308,878	29.9
Total Consumption	2,832,112	28.8	6,653,398	28.8	5,123,148	10.7
Total Investment	2,907,821	29.5	5,874,913	25.5	28,355,702	59.3
Total	9,846,753	100.0	23,066,158	100.0	47,787,727	100.0
Total Number of Cases	2,399		2,786		1,666	

Source: Own calculations from Table 5.5 in Meloen et al. (2003, p. 116)

Table 5.2 Spending behaviour in 52 big Dutch criminal cases

Type of spending	Form of Spending	26 drug cases		22 fraud cases		4 other cases	All 52 cases	
		N°	%	N°	%	N°	N°	%
Hoarding	Cash Money NL	20	77	5	23	3	28	54
	Cash Money Foreign	13	50	2	9	1	16	31
Consumption	Luxurious Lifestyle	8	31	7	32	0	15	29
	Consumption Goods	11	42	5	23	0	16	31
	Jewellery, Music instruments, Art	10	38	7	32	2	19	37
	Vehicles	21	81	17	77	3	41	79
	Planes, Boats	11	42	6	27	0	17	33
Conventional Investment	Bank Accounts NL	17	65	13	59	1	31	60
	Bank Accounts Foreign	16	62	9	41	1	26	50
	Immovable Property NL	8	31	9	41	0	17	33
	Immovable Property Foreign	8	31	9	41	1	18	35
	Securities	9	35	12	55	2	23	44
	Fixed Interest Assets	18	69	15	68	2	35	67
Irregular Business Investment	Business Activities NL	20	77	15	68	1	36	69
	Business Activities Foreign	12	46	8	36	1	21	40
	Reinvestment	8	31	5	23	2	15	29

Notes: Percentages have to be read horizontally. For drug cases 100% equals 26 cases; for fraud cases 100% equals 22 cases; for the total of 52 cases 100% equals 52 cases; for the '4 other cases' no percentages have been attributed since there are too few cases.

Source: Unger et al (2006), own calculations from Table 14.2 in Meloen et al. (2003, p. 246)

Distortions of consumption and savings from money laundering are, given the relatively similar spending and saving pattern of Dutch households and of money launderers, not expected to be large in the Netherlands. From the Dutch findings, one can conclude that criminals behave like normal people. There are a few rich ones and many poor ones and those who are rich have a higher propensity to save. The difference between launderers and normal people does not seem to lie mainly in the saving and spending pattern, but more in the way they invest their money.

Different Investment Pattern

The negative impact of money laundering on investment stems mainly from the fact that in their investment choices, money launderers are primarily guided by the desire to escape control and detection rather than by investment return maximizing considerations. However, these investment choices can be detrimental to the economy because they lead to a redirection of funds to assets that generate very little economic activity or employment (Barlett 2002, p. 19).

Money launderers tend to opt for investments that afford them the largest degree of concealment even if this entails lower rates of return. This diverges income from good investments to risky and low-quality investments. Fullerton and Karayannis provide evidence that this is prevalent in the United States, where funds from tax evasion are directed to risky investments in the small business sector (Fullerton and Karayannis (1993) paraphrased in Quirk 1996).

Money laundering causes a misallocation of resources due to distortions in relative assets and commodity prices arising from money-laundering activities (McDonell 1998 and McDowell 2001). Money launderers are not looking for the highest rate of return on the money they launder, but for the investment that most easily allows the recycling of the illegally obtained money.

SECTOR IMPACT OF MONEY LAUNDERING

In which sectors do criminals invest? Criminals reinvest their criminal proceeds in companies and real estate with the purpose of making further profits, legal or illegal. Most of these investments are in sectors that are familiar to the criminal, such as bars, restaurants, prostitution, cars and transport (Kleemans et al. 2002, pp. 124-136). Criminals tend to invest in the country of their origin or the country where they perform their criminal activities. Dutchmen have a tendency to invest in the Netherlands, Turks in Turkey.

It also looks like as if each country has its own special attraction for money launderers. In Italy, Masciandaro (1999) found out that the bond market was particularly popular for criminal investors since it allowed one to disguise their true identity for quite some time. In the Netherlands, the real estate sector seems especially popular amongst criminals.

Artificial Increase in Prices

One specific effect in these sectors is an artificial price increase. Launderers have an incentive to invest their illegal proceeds in an attempt to disguise their illegal origin. Consequently, they are willing to pay for particular assets more than their actual worth as well as to purchase otherwise unappealing property or enterprises simply because it gives them the possibility to increase their share of a particular market and gain stronger foothold in a particular economy (Keh 1996a, p. 5).

This will lead to an artificial increase in prices. For example, in Colombia it appears that in the 1980s the Medellin group bought large tracts of land, which pushed prices up from $500 to $2,000 per hectare (ibid.). Investments in the capital market could work the same way, leading to an artificial increase in share prices. The danger that the real estate market is used for money laundering lies in the fact that buyers can pay far too high a price in order to disguise criminal money. This means that artificial price increases and unfair competition are connected with it.

Unfair Competition

Gresham's law that 'bad money drives out good money' seems to apply to money laundering as well. Holding on to illicitly obtained cash is incriminating for the offenders. Consequently, they will attempt to convert it into assets (i.e. real estate, business) which are less conspicuous and can give the appearance of legitimate wealth. To achieve this aim, money launderers engage in extensive purchases and due to their large availability of funds, they will be able to outbid potential honest buyers (Walker 1995, p. 33). Furthermore, since their interest in the respective asset does not stem from its actual value but rather from the benefits that accrue to it in terms of concealment, they are willing to pay far more than the true value of the asset. This will artificially drive purchase prices up and make them unaffordable to honest buyers (ibid.).

Moreover, if launderers acquire and operate a business and use additional criminal funds to subsidize it, this provides them with a competitive advantage over legitimate ventures to the point where they will drive them out of business (Keh 1996a, p. 5). This assertion can be substantiated by the study conducted by Arlacchi (1986) on the anti-competitive business behaviour of the mafia. It appears that 'the considerable capital sums acquired in the course of the mafia's illegal activity did in fact tend to be transfused into its legal entrepreneurial operations... The mafia had access to a reserve of its own finance capital that far exceeded the firm's own present dimensions – and far exceeded what was available to non-mafia firms, which often found themselves squeezed out by lack of credit and therefore subordinated to finance capital' (Arlacchi 1986, p. 102-103).

Illegal transactions can contaminate legal ones. According to Quirk (1997, p. 4), certain perfectly legal transactions involving foreign participants are reported to have become less appealing as a result of alleged association with money laundering. Quirk does not provide any evidence in support of his assertion, which was subsequently taken up as a given in the literature (FATF 2002a, p. 3 and Camdessus 1998). His contention seems, however, logical, given that association with money laundering or even just the possibility of such an association leads to erosion of other economic agents' confidence. On the other hand, it is also likely that such transactions and enterprises will become more appealing in launderer circles. By gaining a reputation of willingness to cooperate with launderers, they could potentially attract illegal capital (Alldridge 2002, p. 315, Unger et al. 2006).

Sectors Endangered of Getting Contaminated by Crime

The real estate sector

In the Netherlands, the real estate sector is particularly attractive for launderers. It is the largest sector for money laundering and is the most vulnerable to it. Real estate is important for money laundering because it is a non-transparent market, where the values of the objects are often difficult to estimate and where big value increases can happen. In the last few years, the real estate sector got a lot of attention due to the killing of real estate agent Willem Endstra. He was shot right out in the open on the street in Amsterdam in May 2004. He was suspected of fencing and of being connected to the mafia. The boss of the criminal organization under suspicion is Willem Holleeder, previously convicted for kidnapping beer-brewing magnate Heineken. Several people who wanted to testify against Holleeder were killed on an open street. Before his death, Endstra revealed the criminal circle and the money-laundering techniques in the real estate sector to the police. The protocols, which lasted 15 hours, were published without editing in the Dutch language in the so-called 'Endstra tapes' (Middelburg and Vugts 2006).

The real estate sector is very attractive for criminals and the Dutch real estate sector seems to be even more so. The Dutch real estate sector has relatively high investments. A comparison of the European Central Bank of investments with the housing sector within the EU shows that the Dutch are among the top four investors (after Ireland, Spain and Germany). Furthermore, prices increased more than with other assets. In the Netherlands, prices increased while they started to stagnate in other countries (CBS 2005a,b). There is speculation on land so that price movements in the real estate sector are less conspicuous (Nelen 2004).

Meloen et al. (2003) showed that criminals in 29 out of the 52 cases analysed invested in immovable property. In 19 of the cases the investments were in housing, ranging from apartments to villas. Second, investments in coffee shops, shops, brothels and hotels took place. Sometimes these are only financial investments, sometimes the goal is to earn on business. Also, investments in big construction projects are popular. The WODC (Kleemans et al. 2002, p. 132) also finds, from analysing 80 cases, that investing in real estate is an efficient method of placing large amounts of money. The price increase in real estate is profitable and the annual profits in the real estate business create a legal basis for income.

Nelen (2004) points out that investment in real estate has the following features, which make it attractive for criminal money:

- it is a safe investment
- the objective value is difficult to assess
- speculation is a tradition in this market
- it allows to distinguish between legal and economic ownership
- it allows to realize 'white' returns
- it can be used to perform criminal activities

Abuse of legal persons can happen because

- they can buy sleeping enterprise licenses
- there is no central registration of foreign corporations
- it is unknown what Dutchmen do with foreign legal persons abroad
- the European Court necessitates that foreign legal persons cannot be refused

Eichholtz (2004) points out that the real estate sector has the biggest value and exceeds the size of the bond market. Therefore, it attracts big wealth, both from legal and from illegal sources. Compared to the bond market, the real estate sector is less transparent and about three times as large. In 2005, the total value of the real estate sector in the Netherlands (this includes housing and business objects) was €1771 billion, as compared to an average total value of nominal bonds to €521 billion. The difference became even bigger when compared to the year before (Unger et al. 2006; CBS 2005).[1,2]

The bond market in Italy and the real estate market in the Netherlands are prone to laundering activities. It looks as if each country has its own specialties when it comes to how to reintegrate money. Investment distortion effects of money laundering on specific sectors such as the bond market, the real estate sector, and the gem sector are very likely.

Fijnault et al. (1998) classified the most vulnerable economic sectors as, on one hand, Dutch specific sectors and on the other hand sectors that are contaminated elsewhere. He identified the most sensitive sectors of the Dutch economy for the infiltration of crime to be transport, harbours, the automobile sector, slot machines, hotels, restaurants and nightclubs. The real estate sector has to be added due to its latest developments (see under Artificial Increase in Prices). The most vulnerable industries that are controlled by organized crime in other countries are the construction industry, the waste disposal industry, the garment industry, the insurance sector, the wildlife sector and the sector of nuclear material.

There are some infiltrations in the transport sector (for drug transport overseas, by air and by land). Criminal groups set up their own haulage

---

[1] Centraal Bureau voor de Statistiek (2005a). This is a provisional number. Taxations of real estate for real estate taxes (onroerend zaak belasting) were used as value per real estate object.
[2] Centraal Bureau voor de Statistiek (2005b). Nominal value of all outstanding bonds of Dutch companies and the Dutch public sector quoted at Euronext Amsterdam.

companies to import and export drugs. By trying to control the hotel, restaurant, nightclub and pub sector, criminal groups not only control this sector but also use its infrastructure for other illegal activities such as selling drugs, laundering money and installing illegal slot machines (Fijnault et al. 1998).

Legal professions

Crime can also contaminate legal professions. Money laundering needs lawyers. As Nelen and Lankhorst (2003, pp. 45-53) point out, for lawyers the specific interest of a client is more important than the general interest of society. They have to find a balance between this partiality and the code of conduct, which says that entanglements of interests due to financial or personal relationships should be avoided. Lawyers can assist money launderers in the following way:

- create complex legal arrangements such as trust companies
- buy or sell property
- perform financial transactions
- give financial and tax advice
- provide introductions to financial institutions
- receive cash and provide the client with cash
- pay money to third parties for transactions not connected with the lawyer's underlying retainer
- passing money through their own personal or business accounts
- assist criminals in laundering from prison

(see Nelen and Lankhorst 2003, pp. 47f).

The financial sector

Another profession that can get contaminated by crime is that of providers of financial services, since money laundering necessitates their cooperation, as is the case with lawyers and notary publics.

A great majority of authors are concerned with the effects of money laundering on the reputation of the financial sector. Organized crime can infiltrate financial institutions (FATF 2002a). Money laundering impairs the development of the financial sector for two reasons. First, it erodes financial institutions themselves, as there is a direct correlation between money laundering and fraudulent activities undertaken by employees. Second, customer trust is fundamental to the growth of sound financial institutions (Barlett 2002; Unger et al. 2006).

Once a financial institution becomes involved in money-laundering operations and this is detected, it will lose credibility and customer confidence (Barlett 2002). Due to the perceived risk of fraud and corruption associated with money laundering, economic agents will try to avoid such institutions and conduct their business elsewhere. This negative effect is not restricted solely to the particular institutions implicated. In smaller countries, the involvement in money-laundering operations of several of its financial institutions can result in the loss of reputation for the entire financial system (McDonell 1997, p. 9). Furthermore, money-laundering operations do not actually have to happen. Even the potential for such an involvement is sometimes sufficient to damage financial credibility.

MACROECONOMIC IMPACT OF MONEY LAUNDERING

Output, Income and Employment

Money laundering can, on one hand, increase output, income and employment, since extra means of money are brought into the financial circuit that are available for additional investment. On the other hand, money laundering can also dampen the economy if the victims from crime would have spent the money more productively than the perpetrators.

Money laundering reduces output and employment by diverting resources from sectors with high additional productivity (i.e. clothing, footwear) to sterile sectors (i.e. dwelling properties, jewellery, art). The multipliers for the latter are the lowest in terms of output, income and employment, thus resulting in a net loss to the total economy regardless of where the money would have otherwise been spent. Walker (1995, p. 32) tries to measure these effects by means of an input-output model and estimates that if $1 million of laundered money is invested in dwelling properties rather than in more productive sectors of the economy this would result, on average, in a net loss to the Australian economy of $1.126 million of output, $609,000 of lost income and 25 lost jobs (Walker 1995, p. 33). Once these figures are multiplied by the actual amount of money laundered, the effects become stark indeed.

Walker uses input-output data, from which he calculated multipliers per sector (see Table 5.3 for Australia). Read the first line the following way: 1 million of additional expenditures for agriculture spills over through the whole economy (farmers have to buy more fertilizers, stimulating the chemical industry, etc.), increases output by AUD$2.178 million and (net) income by AUD$0.38 million. Some part of this goes into imports (AUD$0.094 million) so that the domestic employment effect is 28 jobs.

He then calculates different scenarios, depending on the consumption pattern of victims and criminals. Suppose AUD$1 million is transferred from relatively poor victims, who reduce their consumption of clothing and footwear, and is laundered through real estate purchases. The loss of AUD$1 million regarding the demand for clothing and footwear will lead to a total loss of AUD$2.877 million in output, AUD$692,000 in lost wages and salaries and 34 jobs. Almost half of it would be from the clothing and footwear industry, the other half from the rest of the economy. On the other hand, the AUD$1 million increase in demand for real estate will increase output by AUD$2.611 million, generate AUD$786,000 extra wages and 29 new jobs. The net effect is a loss of AUD$266,000 in output, a gain of AUD$94,000 in wages and a decrease of five jobs.

Not knowing exactly how criminals spend their money, Walker states that if AUD$1 million of laundered money is invested in dwellings, this has the following effects:

- A net loss of output from AUD$578,000 to AUD$1,675,000.
- A net loss of income from AUD$199,000 to AUD$1,019,000.
- Net imports will fall by AUD$46,000 to AUD$250,000.
- Net employment will fall by 7 to 42 jobs.

Walker's (1995) idea behind the multiplier model was that criminals and victims have different spending behaviour. In particular, he assumed that criminals spend and invest the money less productively. If our findings about Dutch criminals and Dutch households are right, then such a difference in spending behaviour is not as marked.

Criminals and households have similar spending behaviour, differences might only occur with regard to less productive investments by the former. Similar input-output tables could be used for all countries in order to measure the effects of money laundering on output, income and employment.

Table 5.3 Input-output multipliers, by sector of industry for Australia

Industry	Output	Income	Imports	Employment
AUD\$1 million increase in demand for industry in Column 1 produces the indicated total changes in output, income, imports and jobs:	AUD\$ million	AUD\$ million	AUD\$ million	# jobs
1. Agriculture	2.178	0.38	0.094	28
2. Forestry. fishing, hunting	2.485	0.646	0.128	26
3. Mining	2.136	0.428	0.114	15
4. Meat and milk products	3.008	0.511	0.097	29
5. Food products nec	2.926	0.588	0.137	27
6. Beverages, tobacco prod.	2.629	0.495	0.132	22
7. Textiles	2.778	0.582	0.239	26
8. Clothing and footwear	2.749	0.692	0.282	34
9. Wood, wood products nec	2.877	0.704	0.202	34
10. Paper. printing etc	2.595	0.646	0.226	27
11. Chemicals	2.597	0.512	0.243	21
12. Petroleum and coal products	2.438	0.339	0.239	12

continued

Table 5.3 continued

Industry	Output	Income	Imports	Employment
AUD$1 million increase in demand for industry in Column 1 produces the indicated total changes in output, income, imports and jobs:	AUD$ million	AUD$ million	AUD$ million	# jobs
13. Non-metallic mineral prod.	2.630	0.564	0.145	22
14. Basic metals and products	2.642	0.463	0.154	16
15. Fabricated metal products	2.911	0.639	0.189	27
16. Transport equipment	2.554	0.552	0.265	22
17. Machinery etc nec	2.649	0.631	0.252	26
18. Miscell. manufacturing	2.641	0.601	0.239	26
19. Electricity, gas and water	2.386	0.459	0.078	17
20. Construction	2.694	0.632	0.158	27
21. Wholesale and retail	2.656	0.772	0.105	35
22. Repairs	2.549	0.759	0.165	33
23. Transport, communication	2.463	0.638	0.128	27
24. Finance, property, etc	2.611	0.786	0.094	30

continued

Table 5.3 continued

Industry	Output	Income	Imports	Employment
AUD$1 million increase in demand for industry in Column 1 produces the indicated total changes in output, income, imports and jobs:	**AUD$ million**	**AUD$ million**	**AUD$ million**	**# jobs**
25. Ownership of dwelling	1.558	0.14	0.032	5
26. Public admin., Defence	3.233	0.951	0.194	36
27. Community services	2.983	1.159	0.124	42
28. Recreational etc services	2.762	0.747	0.131	36

Source of data: Australian Bureau of Statistics, 1994, Australian National Accounts, Input-Output Multipliers 1989-90 (Cat. #5237.0)

However, this model is designed for a closed and not for a small and open economy. Walker (1995) himself does not see a problem there. He claims that laundered money flowing into the open economy should be treated the same way as laundered money produced within this open economy. They would have the same output effect, whereas laundered money that leaves this open economy would produce its effects in the country where it is received. Even if one accepted this, one would still have to know in detail what the victim and the offender do with the money.

Walker discusses the effects of money laundering for Australia by using a model that assumes one big closed economy. However, money laundering mainly refers to transferring illegal and laundered money all over the world. The big problem in the Netherlands, to give an example, is not the illegal money generated and laundered in the Netherlands, but the money coming in from illegal activities abroad, which flows partly through the Netherlands, and is partly invested in the Netherlands.

Furthermore, the input-output multipliers do not replace a model for economic effects. They only concentrate on the amounts of demand in other sectors that are generated by an original stimulus of demand in one sector. These amounts are 'technically' determined through the technical relations of the production function, which shows how much output can be maximally produced if one increases the input by one, but the effects of changed behaviour are missing.

In order to measure macro-economic output and employment effects one would need to know about the effects of large amounts of extra money flowing into an open economy through laundering. Such a model is no longer available for countries within the euro zone.

For the Netherlands, Unger et al. 2006 found that

> most likely, the Dutch profit from money laundering. The large amount of money flowing through the country stimulates financial services, employs lawyers and financial experts. These are among the highest paid and, hence, highest productive jobs. If the money is reintegrated into the Dutch real estate or diamond sector, this again creates jobs. However, a lot of the money-laundering just flows through the Netherlands, referring hence to the layering phase of money laundering which creates less real effects than at the reintegration phase.

Changes in Imports and Exports

Money-laundering activities can also bring about a distortion of a country's imports and exports if launderers tend to engage in (often imported) luxury consumption. As a consequence, there will be balance of payment problems. Such imports do not generate domestic economic activity or employment and can depress domestic prices, thus reducing the profitability of domestic enterprises. This appears to be the case in developing countries in particular (Barlett 2002, p. 20).

Furthermore, money laundering affects imports and exports in terms of prices. One of the most common tactics used for laundering money and generating illegal flight capital is to overprice imports and to underprice exports (Baker 1999, p. 33). For example, an importer of particular foreign machinery could make an agreement with the seller that the purchase price be increased by a considerable margin (e.g. 30%). The purchaser can pay the seller the whole sum in cash on the understanding that the addition in price (i.e. the 30%) be placed on his account in the foreign country. Clearly, if these activities are conducted recurrently and on a large scale this can artificially affect import and export prices.

Boyrie et al. (2005) use transfer prices and show that overpricing and underpricing imports is very common between Russia and the US. They measure capital flight by analysing transactions with abnormal transfer prices. They estimate the average volume of capital flight from Russia to the United States from 1995 to 1999 to be between $1.86 billion and $8.92 billion. They suggest that this could be attributed to either money laundering and/or tax evasion.

Losses of Income of the Public Sector

Money laundering can have a detrimental effect on government revenues by decreasing government income from tax. Money laundered also represents income that evades taxes (Quirk 1996, p. 19 and Alldridge 2002, p. 315). Misreporting or underreporting income is one of the most common methods of conducting money laundering. Consequently, money laundering negatively affects tax collection efforts.

At the same time, an increase in predicate offences and money laundering demands public enforcement expenditure, which draws further on public revenues (McDonell 1998, p. 10). This will indirectly impact honest taxpayers by bringing about an increase in tax rates.

Table 5.4 shows the revenue losses of the public sector through tax fraud and tax evasion. In the Netherlands, losses from tax fraud and tax evasion are estimated to lie between 6% and 15% of GDP. EU wide, the losses from tax fraud alone are estimated to be about 2.5% of GDP.

A point not mentioned in the literature is that money laundering can also increase the revenue of the public sector. Criminals want their money to be 'legal'. A way of doing this is to pay taxes on income. Non-existent high turnovers from restaurants with no clients are sometimes voluntarily declared to the tax authorities. This way, the illegal money is turned into taxed legal money. A country is particularly attractive for this kind of 'official' laundering if it has low tax rates. Yaniv (1999) developed a model demonstrating how money launderers respond to tax policies. He shows that the incentive to launder increases with lower tax rates and lax money-laundering regimes. The Netherlands is one of the most popular countries for multinationals because of low taxes. As shown in Chapter 3, the Dutch are classified by the American tax authorities IRS as one of the biggest tax havens in Europe. 'Internal Revenue Service cannot

prevent companies from artificially shifting their profits to tax haven
countries like the Netherlands, Ireland, Bermuda and Luxembourg.
Subsidiaries in these four countries were assigned 30% of the profit from
US corporations' (Sullivan 2004, p. 589). Also, other organizations such
as the OECD on Harmful Tax Practices or the Primarolo Rapport by the
European Union classify the Netherlands as an intense tax competitor.

Table 5.4 Fiscal fraud and tax evasion

Type of Fraud	Country and Year	Amount of Estimate	Source of Estimate
Fiscal fraud and social fraud	The Netherlands 2004	7-15 billion euros if 5%-10% of total fraud is discovered	Unger et al. (2006)
Tax fraud and financial fraud discovered	The Netherlands 2003	698 million euros	FIOD-ECD 2003
Fiscal fraud, tax evasion	The Netherlands 2003	20-70 billion euros or 6%-15% of GDP	CBS, de Kam 2004
Value added tax fraud	EU wide	10-15% of VAT tax revenues	EU Memo 2006
Tax fraud	EU wide	2-2.5% of GDP 200-250 billion euros	EU Memo 2006

The Dutch government announced in 2004 that it would cut the
country's corporate tax rate from 34.5% to 31.5% in 2006, with a further
cut to 30% slated to take place by 2007. The Netherlands has 100 tax
treaties in place (Belgium has 66, Denmark has 78 and the UK has 110).
The greater a country's network of double taxation treaties, the greater its
leverage to reduce withholding taxes on incoming dividends. An
elaborate network of double taxation treaties is, thus, a key factor in the
ability of a territory to develop as an attractive holding company
jurisdiction (see Unger et al. 2006).

When a Dutch holding company falls within the 'participation
exemption rules', all income received by the holding company from the
subsidiary, whether by way of dividends or otherwise, is tax free. The

criteria that have to be fulfilled in order to qualify for the participation exemption rule are, for example, the 5% rule: the Dutch holding company must hold at least 5% of the subsidiary's shares. This share is much lower than in many other countries and makes the Netherlands very attractive for holding companies and other investors (see http://www.lowtax.net/lowtax//offon/netherlands/).

Though tax rates might be low, and many holding companies are tax free, the large volume of transactions will, nevertheless, create extra tax income, if only from employing additional Dutchmen in the financial sector.

The suspicion is that a lot of money laundering takes place through these big entities. The public sector does not lose income because the Netherlands is a transit country for money laundering and does not suffer from the negative effects of it. According to de Kam (2004) the Netherlands received €500 million in taxes as a result of being a tax haven.

Changes in the Demand for Money, Exchange Rates and Interest Rates

Money laundering also affects the money demand. The IMF found that a 10% increase in crime results in a 6% reduction in overall money demand (Quirk 1997, p. 3). A 10% increase in crime, will, furthermore, discourage the demand for this country's currency equally. Money laundering can, therefore, have a negative impact on the demand for money, on the exchange rate and on interest rates.

Quirk (1997) gets these results by running the following regression: $M_i = M_i (y, ep, id, L_j)$. The demand for money M_i depends positively on income (y), negatively on the expected inflation (ep), the deposit interest rate (id) and on money laundering (L_i). Proxies for *ML* are crime, fraud and drug offences. Separate proxy variables can be included for money-laundering associated with crime ($L1$), with tax evasion ($L2$) and with unemployment and labour participation ($L3$).

In another study done by Tanzi (1997), the IMF estimated that US$5 billion per year was being taken out of the US in cash through the illegal drugs trade in 1984. This creates a potential instability for the world financial system because of the possibility that these dollars could be unloaded in exchange for foreign currency. In order to estimate these US$5 billion, Tanzi calculated the difference between the money printed and the money circulating in the US.

Money laundering leads to volatility in exchange rates and interest rates due to unanticipated inflows and outflows of capital (Tanzi 1996, p. 8; McDonell 1998, p. 10; Camdessus 1998, p. 2; FATF 2002, p. 3 and Boorman and Ingves 2001, p. 9). As Tanzi points out, a large inflow of laundered money can result in the depreciation of the exchange rate and/or an expansion of the country's monetary base (Tanzi 1996, p. 8). An increase in exchange rates is associated with a reduction in exports and a heavier reliance on imports whereas an expansion of the monetary base would bring about an increase in prices (ibid.). Additionally, as mentioned above, interest rates are also affected because launderers invest funds where their schemes are less likely to be detected rather than where lending rates are lower or rates of return are higher. Moreover, due to the unpredictable character of such choices impacting economic fundamentals, the soundness of economic policy is also affected (McDowell 2001).

Negative or Positive Effect on Growth Rates

Money laundering has a significant negative impact on growth rates. Since, in the context of this activity, funds are redirected from sound to risky ventures, from productive to sterile investments and crime and corruption are facilitated, economic growth can suffer (Barlett 2002, p. 1). When a particular venture or industry is no longer appealing to launderers, they simply tend to abandon it, causing the potential collapse of these sectors and serious damage to the respective economies (McDowell 2001). Moreover, through its damaging effect on financial institutions, which is crucial for economic growth, as well as through its distorting effect on the allocation of resources, laundering further dampens economic growth (Tanzi 1997, p. 96).

However, money laundering can also have positive effects on growth. For example, if a country is a transfer country for criminal money flows, additional value added is created for financial services without the countries having to bear the costs of crime. Money is simply flowing through.

If money is transferred from the country with criminal activities to the laundering country, then the latter does not bear the negative effects of predicate crimes associated with money laundering. It benefits from crime abroad; it is a free rider on criminal activities. This is the case, in particular, for countries with less strict anti-money-laundering regulations than neighbouring countries because less strict regulation can have a positive effect on the capacity to attract illegal capital. The reverse is true as well. The more strict the anti-money-laundering regulations, the more the country will suffer from a negative externality effect, the inability to attract illegal capital (Bagella et al. 2003).

Ferwerda and Bosma (2005) did an empirical research regarding the effect of money-laundering on economic growth. They based their estimations on the work of Quirk (1996 and 1997) who extended a model by Barro (1991) and replaced human capital with a proxy for money laundering, the level of crime. In their model, growth depends on private domestic capital, government consumption, education measured as student enrolment at the tertiary level, and on crime.

Quirk did his study for 18 industrial countries for the period 1983-1990, and found that reductions in annual growth rates were associated with increases in money-laundering activities (Quirk 1997, p. 6). He found that the most significant difference in the regressions he ran emerged when he excluded government consumption. Instead of being positive and significant, the sign became negative. According to Quirk (1996), this implied that money laundering was closely and positively related to the level of government consumption. The more the government consumed, i.e. the higher the number of civil servants, the more money was laundered. Knowing this, Quirk (1996) estimated the effect of money laundering on economic growth by using the following equation:

$$DGDP = C + \beta1(PI) + \beta2(TER) + \beta3(CRIM) + \varepsilon$$
$$DGDP = -1.94 + 1.06(PI) + 0.068(TER) - 0.015(CRIM) + \varepsilon$$

where

$DGDP$ = Growth of GDP, 1983-1990
PI = Private gross domestic capital formation in constant prices
TER = Student enrolment at the tertiary level (in millions)
$CRIM$ = Total number of offences contained in national statistics

From this equation, Quirk (1996) concluded: 'The elasticity at the means in the equation is an estimated 0.1 percentage point reduction in industrial country annual GDP growth rates for each 10 percent rise in money-laundering associated with crime' (Quirk 1996, p. 20).

The problem with Quirk's results is that they are outdated and because of his elasticity approach cannot be applied to other countries. Money laundering has increased substantially since the 1980s. Furthermore, some improvements can still be made such as relating crime to the size of the population or per 1000 of population, in order to account for the country size.

Ferwerda and Bosma (2005) did an update of the Quirk study. Because money laundering worldwide is 'heavily concentrated in Europe and North America' (Walker 1999), they estimated the growth effect of money-laundering for Europe (EU-15[3]) and North America (US and Canada). The countries in these areas display the same economic structure and forms of development and have the best international comparable crime statistics. Taking these countries into account results in a similar number of countries as in the Quirk study (1996).[4] Several proxy variables have been selected for money laundering, and a pooled regression has been done. The pooled data set contained the 17 countries mentioned above for a 6-year period, from 1995 to 2000. This gave a total of 102 observations (see Unger 2007, Chapter 7 for more details).

Bosma and Ferwerda (2005) found that if money laundering increases from its initial level with US$1 billion, the economic growth will decrease by 0.03 to 0.06 percent points in the 17 countries explored. This confirms the results of Quirk (1996). They showed that this overall effect of money laundering on growth can be separated into two effects. First, money laundering increases growth between 0.06% and 0.14%, but it also increases crime. Money laundering has a very small but positive effect on growth, but crime dampens growth. The overall effect of, on one hand, a positive effect of money laundering on growth and, on the other hand, a negative effect of crime on growth is negative, since the crime effect outweighs the money-laundering effect.

The danger of money laundering for the economy is not that it directly affects macro-economic variables such as output, employment or growth. The danger lies in the fact that money laundering increases crime. And it is crime that has negative effects on the economy. Crime reduces growth by 0.12% to 0.45%.

It is, therefore, very important to study the relationship between money laundering and crime. If crime increases so will money laundering and this dampens growth.

---

[3] EU-15 is Austria, Belgium, Denmark, Finland, France, Germany, Greece, Ireland, Italy, the Netherlands, Norway, Portugal, Spain, Sweden and the United Kingdom.

[4] In this chapter the number of countries is 17, while Quirk (1996) used a dataset of 19 countries.

Crime Increase

In Chapter 1 we assumed that money laundering triggers financial flows, which lead to more investment in illegal activities in the country. There is, therefore, a spillover mechanism from criminal money to crime. Because of the possibility of money laundering in the financial sector, reinvestment of the money in illegal activities in the real sector will be the consequence (see also Masciandaro 1999).

A fixed proportion y of this illegal money has to be laundered, since even criminal activities need some legal money. A part c of the criminal money gets lost in the verge of the money-laundering process. These costs c include both legal regulations (which increase c for the launderer) and costs for the individual criminal who tries to bribe somebody, has to buy a false passport, has to find somebody to bring the money across the border and loses some money while whitewashing it in the casino etc. The laundered money can be reinvested in either legal or illegal activities. A fixed share (q) of it goes back into the illegal sector and bears an interest of r_i, $(1 - q)$ gets reinvested in the legal sector and has an interest rate r_l. If the decision of how much money is put into the illegal sector (q) depends on the difference in the interest rate between the illegal and the legal sector $r = r_i - r_l$, then this interest difference must stay constant over time.

The original multiplier of Masciandaro (1999) was:

$$AFI = y/[1 - yq(1 - c)(1 + r_i)]ACI$$

Here we assume r_l to be almost zero compared to the high illegal interest rate, hence $r = r_i$

Assumptions:

y = fixed proportion of crime money that needs to be laundered
c = fixed proportion of transaction costs of laundering
q = fixed share of laundered money reinvested in illegal activities (depends on difference between r_l and r_i)
r_l = return in legal economy
r_i = return in illegal economy

Note that $1 > y$, q, $c > 0$ since they are shares by definition. But the interest rate r_i has basically no 'natural' restriction.

Barone (2006) interpreted the model slightly differently. She claimed that the numerator in Masciandaro's (1999) and Unger and Rawlings' (2005) model should be $y(1 - c)$. So the multiplier should be:

$$AFI = y(1 - c)/[1 - yq(1 - c)(1 + r_i)]ACI$$

Masciandaro (1999) looked at $yACI$ the criminal proceeds which are planned to be put into the laundering process. He chose an input oriented approach. Barone opts for an output oriented approach. She looks at the money which has been already laundered $(1 - c)\ y\ ACI$ and is then reinvested. With this assumption her multiplier is always slightly smaller than the first one we have presented.

Possible operationalization of the variables
The fixed proportion of crime money (y) that needs to be laundered is 70% (from Smekens et al. 2004) and 80% (from Walker 1995). The actual percentage will depend on the type of crime: a large percentage of crime money from drugs and fraud is being laundered, whereas other types of crime like theft, burglary, robbery etc. lead to proceeds of which only about 10% are being laundered. However, since drugs and fraud are the largest components of crime that are relevant for money laundering, we will assume y in the range of 0.70-0.80. The way in which we will present the multiplier allows us, nevertheless, to look at other possible proportions to be laundered also:

c (transaction costs of laundering): What percentage of money is lost through the laundering process? It depends, amongst other things, on anti-money-laundering policy. If money is laundered through the casino, the expected return is 46% (except if you play red and black only, then it is definitely higher, almost 100%, except for the zero, but this might be too conspicuous). If you only have to declare the gains, which are then whitewashed, and forget about the losses, playing in the casino seems to be the best strategy. But this strategy is not good for very large amounts. You get videotaped; the casino does not hand out larger amounts in cash and reports suspicious transactions to the authorities etc. But laundering in the casino means that the expected return, c, is 46%. Another argument we found is that money laundering means that the criminal does want to pay taxes. There should, therefore, be at least the loss of the corporate tax of 34% (in the Netherlands) plus some fees for the bank or the (Dutch) income tax rate of maximum 52%. This is why Unger (2007) found it quite reasonable to assume that $c = 0.5$. Half of the criminal money is lost when it is laundered, either through casino losses or through taxes.

'However, when one takes the criminal money over the border and then places it into a bank account, the transaction costs c might be substantially lower and the share of money successfully laundered $(1 - c)$ might be much higher $(1 - c = 0.9)$' (Unger 2007, Chapter 7). Truman and Reuter (2004) have estimated low laundering costs of between 5% and 15% (see also Chapter 7 of this book). This means that $c = 0.05 - 0.15$ and $1 - c = 0.95 - 0.9$. The way in which we present the multiplier below, allows us to see the value of the multiplier for different values of c.

q (laundered money reinvested in the illegal economy): This variable is difficult to evaluate. Experts of the DNB think that there is a high incentive to make money dirty again because of the high profits in the criminal sector. There will be less of an incentive, though, to reinvest clean money into dirty business than the other way around, except for terrorism financing or if return differences are very high. But even with high returns on criminal activities, it still seems more likely that some of the illegal money will be hoarded for further illegal business purposes rather than running through the risky laundering process and then reinvesting the clean money illegally again. Following Masciandaro, however, one always needs some clean money to do illegal business. In the following we assumed that 20-50% of the laundered money is made dirty again, $q = 0.2$, $q = 0.5$.

r_i (the average return of illegal business) is also difficult to estimate. For drugs, the sales value of 1 kg of heroine can exceed the costs of production by 600%. However, for cocaine the difference between wholesale and retail price or the value added is about 100%. For example, one gram of 100% pure cocaine retailed for $4.30 in Colombia is ultimately sold for between $59 and $297 in the United States. The gross profit margin, or value added, is therefore between 93% and 98.5% of the retail value (see UNDCP 1996, p. 3). For other sorts of crime much lower rates of return might apply. We assume r_i to be between 50% and 100%.

The following graphs display the multiplier for different assumptions regarding the variables mentioned above. Read the graph (Figures 5.2 and 5.3) as follows: along one line (for example changes in q, top dark line in Figure 5.2) one can read how big the multiplier is if q changes, as long as the other three variables stay at their level (in the first graph $y = 0.7$, $c = 0.5$ and $r_i = 0.5$). If $q = 0.2$, the multiplier is about 0.78. If – given that the three other variables do not change – q increases to 0.95, the multiplier is 1.39. If $q = 0.75$, the multiplier is 1.15 and if $q = 0.5$ the multiplier is 0.95. Along the upwards sloping, top line the change of the multiplier can be seen for all values of q. In the same way one can look at the downwards sloping, light grey line for c, the share of money lost with laundering. If the other three variables stay at $y = 0.7$, $r_i = 0.5$ and $q = 0.2$ the multiplier is 0.87 if only 5% of money is lost through laundering, it is 0.78 if 50% is lost and it is 0.70 if 95% of money is lost through laundering. In the same way variations in y and r_i can be analysed.

In Figure 5.3, illegal returns $r_i = 100\%$, i.e. are double those in Figure 5.2. One can see that the multiplier slightly increases in that case. The stability condition for the multiplier model is that the lower part of the fraction, the denominator, cannot become zero. If the interest rates get high, say 600%, and $y = 0.7$ and $c = 0.5$, then the model will explode if q = 0.85 or more. This problem applies in particular to the interest rate, which is not necessarily smaller than 1, whereas all the other variables are between 0 and 1 by definition.

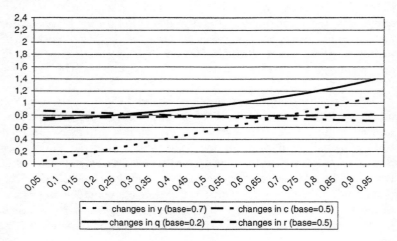

Figure 5.2 The crime multiplier with an illegal interest rate of 50%

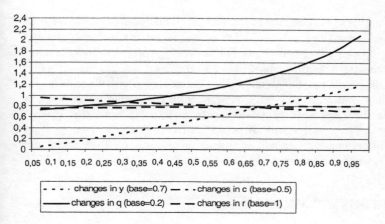

Figure 5.3 The crime multiplier with an illegal interest rate of 100%

If the costs of laundering are lower, say only 5% instead of the 50% assumed in the graphs above, then the multiplier would lie between 1.04 and 1.16 if q was between 0.25 and 0.30 respectively. It would also be 1.04 if y was 0.75 instead (if all the other base values stayed the same). Barone's multiplier would lie between 0.90 and 1.10 in these cases.

Our multiplier lies between 0.9 and 2 in most cases and under more likely assumptions it is about 1.06-1.1. This means that proceeds from crime will increase through money laundering by about 6% to 10% (see also Unger 2007) of the original amount. Money laundering triggers an additional 6%-10% of more laundering through an increase in illegal activities.

This means that criminal money will attract more crime because the financial returns from it will partly be reinvested in additional criminal activities. The Masciandaro (1999) and Chapter 1 model is a closed economy model. Money that is being laundered will be reinvested in the closed economy. In an open economy, as long as the reinvestment in illegal activities happens abroad, the country that accepts money-laundering will not suffer. But it seems more likely that opportunities to launder will eventually also attract criminals.

Countries that have hardly any regulations against money laundering are, in principle, free riding on those countries that suffer from high crime. They accept the returns from crime as investments, but this goes either at the cost of other countries or − and this seems more likely − will backfire eventually.

Once crime is settled, the economic, social and political consequences can reach from the control of entire economic sectors to corruption and bribery up to the undermining of politics through criminal organizations. As Kleemans (2006) pointed out for the Netherlands, the criminal consequences of money laundering are not necessarily the establishment of a hierarchic criminal organization, such as the Italian mafia, but can also be the emergence of flexible network organizations that emerge through a 'snowball effect' between relatives of ethnic groups. Both forms of organized crime will eventually undermine and erode social and political values and norms.

TERRORISM INCREASE

Money laundering can contribute to an increase in terrorism in two ways. First, laundered money can be used to fund terrorist activities. A typical example is the financing of terrorism with the proceeds from the production and marketing of narcotics (Masciandaro 2001). Most experts agree that the sale and trade of drugs seem to be a sizable financial contributor to terrorist organizations. According to Schneider (2004), the origin of terrorist wealth can be broken into the following sources of financing: drug business (mainly transporting) 30-35%, donations or tribute payments of governments 20-30%, classic criminal activities (blackmail and in particular kidnapping) 10-15%, unknown 30-35%. The Taliban, for example, profited from the trafficking of opium and taxing the drug trade in areas under its control and these funds were subsequently used to support terrorist organizations like al-Qaeda. Also, profits generated from the sale of opium and heroin have been used to buy weapons and to finance the training and support of terrorists around the world (Hedges 2001). Usually, the drug money used for financing terrorism will first be 'laundered'. This serves two purposes: concealing the illegal origin of the money as well as the illegal destination of the funds. In other words, 'in those specific situations, at least on the logical level, the importance of transaction costs is at least doubled, since the need to lower the probability of incrimination concerns both the crimes that generated the financial flows and the crimes for which they are intended' (Masciandaro 2004b, p. 131).

However, it should be made clear that very often terrorism is financed not only with illegally derived funds but also with clean money, which was never connected to a criminal activity. Supporters, friendly governments and also unsuspecting benefactors provide these clean funds. It is often the case that well-off individuals make donations to organizations that they believe to be real Islamic charities but which later on turn out to be a cover for supporting terrorism. The financing of terrorism with clean money involves a process completely different from money laundering: money dirtying (i.e. reverse money laundering). In that case, the funds are not derived from criminal activity and need to be laundered in order to 'separate' them from the original crime, but on the contrary, the money is clean and needs to be separated from its original source because it will be used for a criminal purpose (i.e. terrorism). This brings us to the second connection between money laundering and terrorism. Even if terrorism is financed with clean funds and one would be tempted to dismiss any connection between the two, such a conclusion would be erroneous. In this situation there is, just as in the case of money laundering, an incentive for concealment, a need to separate financial flows from their source and destination in order to avoid the crime of terrorism being discovered (Masciandaro 2004b, p. 131). 'Money dirtying can also perform an illegal monetary function, responding to the demand for covertness expressed by individuals or groups proposing to commit crimes of terrorism' (ibid.).

Thus, in their efforts to avoid detection, terrorists will exploit the same weaknesses in the international financial system as launderers and will tend to use the same channels.

The empirical study of Blomberg et al. (2004) uses panel data for 177 countries from 1968 to 2000. These data are taken from the Penn World Table, the ITERATE data set for terrorist events and data sets of external and internal conflict. By means of a cross-sectional and panel growth regression analysis and using a structural VAR model, they estimate the following equations:

$$\Delta y_i = \beta 0 + \beta 1 \, D1 + \beta 2 \, D2_i + \beta 3 \ln y0 + \\ \beta 4 \, I/Y_i + \beta 5 \, T + \beta 6 \, I + \beta 7 \, E_i + \varepsilon_i$$

Country i's average per capita growth Δy_i depends on the log of initial GDP $y0$, Investment ratio I/Y_i, Terrorism T, Internal Conflict I, External Conflict E plus two dummies D1 and D2 for non-oil-exporting countries and for Africa. In the US, there were 20.4 terrorist events per year on average, the second highest number after Lebanon, followed by Germany in third place with 19.3 events and by France with 17.9. Terrorism mainly takes place in the US and Europe (this might have changed with regard to the situation in Iraq, Israel and so on, though).

They find a strong positive correlation between terrorism and internal conflict ($\rho = 0.15$) and between terrorism and income ($\rho = 0.20$). The more internal conflict a country has and the richer the country, the more terrorist attacks it has to expect.

Terrorism leads to a slight decline in per capita growth. If there were one terrorist event every year, this would lead to a 1.5% reduction of per capita income growth over the whole period (1968-2000). One would have to divide this by 33 to get the effect estimated for a year. The effect is, hence, quite small, much smaller than from external conflicts. But terrorism has a strong negative impact on business investment. The Investment/GDP ratio falls by 0.5% points, while government expenditures increase by 0.4% points. Investment reacts more negatively to terrorism than other spending components and government expenditures get crowded in.

References

Alessie, R., S. Hochguertel and A. van Soest (2002), 'Household Portfolios in the Netherlands', in L. Guiso, M. Haliassos and T. Jappelli (eds), *Household Portfolios*, Cambridge, MA: MIT Press, 340-388.

Alldridge, P. (2002), 'The Moral Limits of the Crime of Money Laundering', *Buffalo Criminal Law Review*, 5.

Arlacchi, P. (1986), *Mafia Business, the Mafia Ethic and the Spirit of Capitalism*, London.

Bagella, M., L. Becchetti and M. Lo Cicero (2003), 'Regional Externalities and Direct Effects of Legislation Against Money Laundering: A Test on Excess Money Balances in the Five Andean Countries', *Journal of Money Laundering Control*, 7 (4), 347-366.

Baker, R.W. (1999), 'The Biggest Loophole in the Free-Market System', *Washington Quarterly*, 22 (4), 29-46.

Barlett, B.L. (2002), 'The Negative Effects of Money Laundering on Economic Development', *Platypus Magazine*, (77).

Barone, R. (2006), Comments on 'Competing for Criminal Money' by Unger B. and G. Rawlings, Discussion prepared for the Lawless Finance-Workshop in Economics & Law, Bocconi University, Milan.

Barro, R.J. (1991), 'Economic Growth in a Cross Section of Countries', *The Quarterly Journal of Economics*, 106, 407-443

Blomberg, S.B., G.D. Hess and A. Orphanides (2004), 'The Macroeconomic Consequences of Terrorism', *Journal of Monetary Economics*, 51 (5), 1007-1032.

Boorman, J. and S. Ingves (2001), 'Financial System Abuse, Financial Crime and Money Laundering', IMF Background Paper, International Monetary Fund.

Boyrie, M.E. de, S.J. Pak and J.S. Zdanowicz (2005), 'Estimating the Magnitude of Capital Flight due to Abnormal Pricing in International Trade: The Russia-USA Case', *Working Paper Series* (1), Center for International Business Education and Research, Florida International University.

Burgstaller, M. (2001), Geldwäscherei durch Annahme eines Rechtsanwaltshonorars? AnwBl (Österreich), Seiten 574-587.

Busuioc, M. (2007), 'Defining Money Laundering. Predicate Offences – The Achilles' Heel of Anti-Money Laundering Legislation', in Unger B. (2007), *The Scale and Impacts of Money Laundering*, Edward Elgar: UK, 15-27.

Camdessus, M. (1998), 'Money Laundering: the Importance of International Countermeasures'. Plenary meeting of the FATF, Paris, February 10.

Centraal Bureau voor de Statistiek (2004), 'Statistical Yearbook of the Netherlands 2004'. Voorburg/Heerlen: Statistics Netherlands

Centraal Bureau voor de Statistiek (2005a), 'Nominale waarde obligaties op Euronext Amsterdam'. Statline Database: www.cbs.nl

Centraal Bureau voor de Statistiek (2005b), 'Waarde onroerende zaken'. Statline Database: www.cbs.nl

Cuéllar, M.F. (2003), 'The Tenuous Relationship Between the Fight Against Money Laundering and the Disruption of Criminal Finance', *The Journal of Criminal Law & Criminology*, 93 (2-3), 324.

De Nederlandsche Bank (2003), 'De Nederlandsche Bank, Statistics Bulletin Juni 2003, DNB Juni.

Duyne, P.C. van, K. von Lampe and J.L.Newell (eds) (2003), *Criminal Finances and Organising Crime in Europe*, Nijmegen: Wolf Legal Publishers.

Eichholtz, P. (2004), 'De Vastgoedwereld: Spelers, Activiteiten en Geldstromen'. Presentation held at the seminar 'Zicht op misdaad en onroerend goed', 15 December, Centre for Information and Research on Organised Crime, Amsterdam, Vrije Universiteit.

European Union (2006), 'EU coherent strategy against fiscal fraud'. MEMO/06/221, Brussels, 31 May.

FATF (1996), Financial Action Task Force on Money Laundering, 'The Forty Recommendations', (Revised on June 2003) www.oecd.org/fatf/

FATF (2002a), 'Basic Facts about Money Laundering', FATF website (www1.oecd.org/fatf)

FATF (2002b), 'Report on Money Laundering Typologies 2001-2002', Paris.

Ferwerda, J. and S. Bosma (2005), 'The Effect of Money Laundering on Economic Growth', paper for Onderzoekskeuzevak Economie van de Publieke Sector, Utrecht School of Economics.

Fijnaut, C.J.C.F., G. Bruinsma and H. van der Bunt (1998), *Organized Crime in the Netherlands*, The Hague: Kluwer Law International.

Fullerton, D. and M. Karayannis (1993), 'Tax Evasion and the Allocation of Capital', NBER *Working Paper* (4581), National Bureau of Economic Research, Cambridge.

Gorkum, W.M.E. van, Carpentier, J.R. de (2004), 'Toezicht op Trustkantoren', Bank Juridische Reeks 50, NIBE-SVV.

Graaf, F. and M. Jurgens (2003), The Netherlands, in Graham, T. (ed.) (2003), *Butterworths International Guide to Money Laundering Law and Practice*, Second Edition, Butterworths.

Graham, T. (2003), *Butterworths International Guide to Money Laundering Law and Practice*, Butterworths second edition.

Graycar, A. and P. Grabosky (1996), 'Money Laundering in the 21st Century: Risks and Countermeasures', Australian Institute of Criminology Research and Public Policy Series. Seminar held on 7 February 1996 Canberra, Australia.

Hackett, A. (2003), 'AUSTRAC Submission No. 2, Inquiry into Cybercrime', Parliamentary Joint Committee on Australian Crime Commission, Sydney: AUSTRAC.

Hedges, M. (2001), 'Afghan Opium Benefits Taliban/Al-Gaeda Protects Heroin Smuglers, Collects Drug Tax', *Houston Chronicle* (online), Houston.

Hufnagel, S. (2003), 'Der Strafverteidiger unter dem Generalverdacht der Geldwäsche gemäß § 261 StGB – *eine rechtsvergleichende Darstellung (Deutschland, Österreich, Schweiz und USA)*', Juristische Reihe TENEA/www.jurawelt.com; Bd. 74, PhD of the Johann-Wolfgang-Goethe Universität Frankfurt am Main
http://download.jurawelt.com/download/dissertationen/tenea_jurawelt bd74_hufnagel.pdf#search=%22Definition%20Geldwaschen%20im%20Strafrecht%22

IFAC (2001), International Federation of Accountants, 'Money Laundering and Frauds – Changing Expectations From Accountants', Accounting Profession Issues and Trends, by M.A. Baree, FCA, President, Institute of Chartered Accountants of Bangladesh, SAFA Conference at Goa, India, October/December 2001 http://www.ifac.org/library.

IMF (2004), International Monetary Fund, 'The IMF and the Fight against Money Laundering and the Financing of Terrorism, a Fact Sheet', September http://www.imf.org//np/exr/facts/aml.htm

Indover Reports in Dutch Media:
- Nederland steunt de Soeharto's fiscaal NRC Handelsblad, 22 Juli 1999

- Indover Bank in opspraak vanwege gelden Suhartoclan Indisch Nieuws, november/december 2000
- Kamervragen over Soeharto-miljarden Ingezonden 8 november 2000
- Onderzoek Indover in Nederland Trouw, 4 Jan 2001
- Indover versluisde miljarden Trouw, 31 Jan 2001
- De jacht op de Soeharto-schatten XminY, 2001
- Bank wil boek Baarspul uit schappen Mediafacts, 2.4.2002
- Rechtbank 's-Gravenhage Vonnis in kort geding van 16 april 2002
- Roman Baarspul mag van rechter in handel blijven Volkskrant, 19 april 2002
- Fraude bij Indover Het Parool, 06-12-2004
- Getover van Indover Kleintje Muurkrant actueel, 6 december 2004
- Indover Bank al jarenlang corrupt zibb.nl, 6 december 2004 http://www.antenna.nl/wvi/eng/indover/index.html

Interpol General Secretariat Assembly in 1995, http://www.interpol.int/Public/FinancialCrime/MoneyLaundering/defa ult.asp).

IOSCO (1992), International Organization of Securities Commissions, 'Technical committee, Report on Money Laundering', October, (25).

Kam, F. de (2004), 'Belastingparadijs Nederland, Judasloon voor de Schatkist', NRC Handelsblad, March 6.

Kaspersen, H.W.K. (2005), 'De Wet op Kansspelen en Handhaving in Cyber Space', presentation held at the seminar 'Gokken en Georganiseerde Criminaliteit', April 2005, Centre for Information and Research on Organised Crime, Amsterdam, Vrije Universiteit.

Keh, D.I. (1996a), 'Drug Money in a Changing World: Economic Reform and Criminal Finance', UNODC.

Keh, D.I. (1996b), 'Economic Reform and Criminal Finance'. *Transnational Organized Crime*, 2 (1), 66-80.

Kleemans, E.R. (2006), 'Organised crime, transit crime, and racketeering', in Tonry M. and C.J.C. Bijleveld (eds.), *Crime and Justice in the Netherlands*, Crime and Justice. A Review of Research, 35.

Kleemans, E.R., M.E.I.Brienen and H.G. van de Bunt, (eds) (2002), 'Georganiseerde criminaliteit in Nederland, tweede rapportage op basis van de WODC – monitor', Ministerie van Justitie, Wetenschappelijk Onderzoek- en Documentatiecentrum.

Masciandaro, D. (1995), 'Money Laundering, Banks and Regulators, an Economic Analysis', Working Paper (73), Innocenzo Gasparini Institute for Economic Research.

Masciandaro, D. (1998), 'Money Laundering Regulation: The Micro Economics', *Journal of Money Laundering Control*, 2 (2).

Masciandaro, D. (1999), 'Money Laundering: the Economics of Regulation', *European Journal of Law and Economics*, (7), 225-240.

Masciandaro, D. (2004a), 'Combating Black Money: Money Laundering and Terrorism Finance, International Cooperation and the G8 Role', Economics Working Paper (56/26), University of Lecce.

Masciandaro, D. (2004b), 'Global Financial Crime: Terrorism, Money Laundering, and Off-Shore Centres', *Global Finance Series*, Aldershot: Ashgate.

Masciandaro, D. and A. Portolano (2002), 'Terrorism and Organised Crime, Financial Regulation and Non Cooperative Countries: Inside the Black (List) Box', Economics Working Paper (32/14), University of Lecce.

Masciandaro, D. and U. Filotto (2001), 'Money Laundering Regulation and Bank Compliance Costs. What Do Your Customers Know? Economics and Italian Experience', *Journal of Money Laundering Control*, 5 (2), 133-145.

McDonell, R. (1997), 'An Overview of the Global Money Laundering Problem, International Anti-Money Laundering Standards and the World of the Financial Action Task Force'. Paper delivered at the International Conference on Global Drugs Law, New Delhi, 28 February.

McDonell, R. (1998), 'Money Laundering Methodologies and International and Regional Counter-Measures'. Presented at 'Gambling, Technology and Society: Regulatory Challenges for the 21st Century', Rex Hotel, Sydney, 7-8 May.

McDowell, J. (2001), 'The Consequences of Money Laundering and Financial Crime, Economic Perspectives', *Electronical Journal of the US Department of State*, 6 (2).

Meldpunt Ongebruikelijke Transacties (2004), '*Jaarverslag 2003, vooruitblik 2004*', MOT, Ministerie van Justitie, Breda: Koninklijke Drukkerij Broese & Peereboom.

Meloen, J., R Landman, Miranda, H. de, J. van Eekelen and S. van Soest (2003). 'Buit en Besteding, Een empirisch onderzoek naar de omvang, de kenmerken en de besteding van misdaadgeld'. Den Haag: Reed Business Information.

Middelburg, B. and P. Vugts (2006), 'De Endstra-Tapes', Nieuw Amsterdam.

Mills, J. W. and I. Robert (2004), 'Responding to terrorism and achieving stability in the global financial system: Rational policy or crisis reaction?', Journal of Financial Crime, 11(4), 380-396.

Ministry of Justice, Ministry of Finance (2004), 'Meer aandacht voor vervolging en opsporing van witwassen'. Letter to parliament. 11th May. www.minjus.nl

Mitchell I. (2002), 'Money Laundering and the Proceeds of Crime Act 2002', International Centre for Commercial Law ™ in association with The Legal 500, http://www.legal500.com/devs/uk/cc/ukcc_002.htm

Morais, H.V. (2002), 'The War Against Money Laundering, Terrorism, and the Financing of Terrorism', Lawasia Journal, 1-32.

Morris-Cotterill, N. (2001), 'Think Again: Money Laundering', Money Laundery Special, Sanders Research Associates.

Napoleoni, L. (2003), Modern Jihad: Tracing the Dollars Behind the Terror Networks', London: Penguin Books.

Napoleoni, L. (2004), Terror Inc: Tracing the Money Behind Global Terrorism', London: Penguin Books.

NATO Parliamentary Assembly (1998), Transnational Organised Crime - an Escalating Threat to the Global Market.

Nawaz, S., R. McKinnon and R. Webb (2002), 'Informal and Formal Money Transfer Networks: Financial Service or Financial Crime?', Journal of Money Laundering Control, 5 (4), 330-337.

Naylor, R.T. (1999), 'Follow-the-Money methods in Crime Control Policy'. Nathanson Centre for the Study of Organized Crime and Corruption, Toronto, University of Toronto Press.

Nederlands Wetboek van Strafrecht (2004), 'XXXA: Witwassen'. Artikel 420bis, 420quarter and 420ter 18 Oktober.

Nelen, H. (2004), 'Criminaliteit en onroerend goed'. Presentation held at the seminar Zicht op misdaad en onroerend goed. 15th of December, Centre for Information and Research on Organised Crime, Amsterdam, Vrije Universiteit.

Nelen, H. and F. Lankhorst (2003), 'Legal professions', 45-53 in: Bunt, H.G. van de, Schroot and van der C.R.A. (2003), Prevention of Organised Crime, WODC 215. Meppel, BOOM Juridische Uitgevers.

NRC (2006), Interview with Brigitte Unger by Roel Janssen, NRC Handelsblad, February 2006.

NVB (2006), 'De Nederlandse Vereniging van Banken', The Dutch Banking Association, sheets Simon Lelieveldt.

Paauw, K. (2005),'Witwassen in een Nederlands casino'. Presentation held at the seminar 'Gokken en georganiseerde criminaliteit'. 6th of April, Centre for Information and Research on Organised Crime, Amsterdam, Vrije Universiteit.

Passas, N. (2004), 'Informal Value Transfer Systems and their Mechanics', paper presented at a 2004 APEC Conference in Tokyo.

Quirk, P. J. (1997), 'Money Laundering: Muddying the Macroeconomy', Finance & Development.

Quirk, P.J. (1996), 'Macroeconomic Implications of Money Laundering', Working Paper, International Monetary Fund, (96/66).

Savona, E. U. (1997), 'Responding to Money Laundering', ISPAC, 3.

Schneider, F. and D.H. Enste (2000), 'Shadow Economies: Size, Causes, and Consequences', Journal of Economic Literature, 38, 77-114.

Schneider, F. and D.H. Enste (2002), 'The Shadow Economy, An International Survey'. Cambridge: University Press.

Schneider, F. (2004), ´Shadow Economies around the World: What Do We Know?´. Institute for the Study of Labour (IZA) Bonn, Discussion Paper (1043), March.

Shapiro, G. (2006), 'Austrian bank hit by Refco scandal', in Law and tax news.com, 2 May, http://www.lawandtax-news.com/asp/story.asp?storyname=23481

Silberbauer, K. and R. Krilyszyn (2003), 'Austria', in Graham, T. (eds) (2003), *Butterworths International Guide to Money Laundering Law and Practice*, Second Edition, Butterworths.

Smekens, M. and M. Verbruggen (2004), 'De Illegale Economie in Nederland.' Centraal Bureau voor de Statistiek, 20 September.

Sullivan, M.A. (2004), 'US Multinationals Move More Profits to Tax Havens', Tax Notes International 27(4), 589-593.

Tanzi, V. (1996), 'Money Laundering and the International Financial System', Working Paper, International Monetary Fund, (96/55).

Tanzi, V. (1997), 'Macroeconomic Implications of Money Laundering', 91-104 in Savona, E.U. (1997), Responding to Money Laundering, International Perspective, Amsterdam: Harwood Academic Publihers.

Takáts, E. (2006), 'A Theory of "Crying Wolf": The Economics of Money Laundering Enforcement', paper presented at a workshop organized by Donato Masciandaro at Bocconi University, Milan March.

Takáts, E. (2006), 'A Theory of "Crying Wolf": The Economics of Money Laundering Enforcement', paper presented at a workshop organized by Donato Masciandaro at Bocconi University, Milan March.

Truman, E.M. and P. Reuter (2004), 'Chasing Dirty Money: Progress on Anti-Money Laundering', Institute for International Economics, November.

The Money Laundering Regulations (2003), 'Statutory Instrument 2003'. (3075), United Kingdom.
http://www.opsi.gov.uk/si/si2003/20033075.htm#1

Unger, B. and G. Rawlings (2005), 'Competing for Criminal Money' paper prepared for the Conference of the Society for the Advancement of Socio-Economics (SASE). Budapest 1.7.2005.

Unger, B. and M. Siegel (2006), 'World Bank Report on Suriname Remittances', mimeograph.

Unger, B., J. Ferwerda. W. de Kruijf, G. Rawlings, M. Siegel and K. Wokke (2006), 'The Amounts and the Effects of Money Laundering'. Report. for the Dutch Ministry of Finance, February 2006.
http://www.minfin.nl/binaries/minfin/assets/pdf/old/06_011a.pdf

Unger, B. (2007), *The Scale and Impacts of Money Laundering*. Edward Elgar: UK.

Unger, B. and M. Busuioc (2007). 'How Money is Being Laundered', in Unger B. (2007), *The Scale and Impacts of Money Laundering*, Edward Elgar: UK, 89-109.

UNDP (1996), United Nations Development Programme, 'Human Development Report 1996', Oxford University Press: New York, Oxford.

United States Department of Justice (2002), 'Department of Justice Seeks Offshore Credit Card Records', press release, Washington DC: Department of Justice, March 2002.

United States Federal Reserve et al (2005). 'In the matter of ABN AMRO N.V. Amsterdam, The Netherlands, ABN AMRO BANK N.V. New York Branch, New York, New York, ABN AMRO BANK N.V. CHICAGO BRANCH, Chicago Illinois. Order of Assessment of a Civil Monetary Penalty, Monetary Payment and Order to File Reports Issued Upon Consent'. FRB Dkt. No. 05-035-CMP-FB. US Federal Reserve. Washington DC.

Visini, S. and R. Haflinger (2003), 'Switzerland', in Graham, T. (eds) (2003), *Butterworths International Guide to Money Laundering Law and Practice*, Second Edition, Butterworths.

Walker, J. (1995), 'Estimates of the Extent of Money Laundering in and through Australia'. Paper Prepared for the Australian Transaction Reports and Analysis Centre. Queanbeyan: Jonh Walker Consulting Services.http://www.austrac.gov.au/text/publications/moneylaundesti mates/index.html.

Walker, J. (1999), 'How Big is Global Money Laundering?', *Journal of Money Laundering Control*, 3 (1).

Walker, J. (1999), 'Measuring the Extent of International Crime and Money Laundering'. Prepared for KriminálExpo, Budapest, June 9th.

Weissink, A. and J.M. Slagter (2001), 'Soeharto had geen rekening bij Indover', *Het Financieele Dagblad*, 2001.02.13.

Weissink, A. (2004), 'Indover Bank speeltuin voor corruptie' and 'Jarenlange corruptie bij Indover Bank', *Het Financieele Dagblad*, 2004.12.06.

Werf, R. van der (1997), 'Registration of Illegal Production in the National Accounts of the Netherlands', submitted by Statistics Netherlands and presented at the Conference of European Staticians.

Yaniv, G. (1999), 'Tax Evasion, Risky Laundering, and Optimal Deterrence Policy', *International Tax and Public Finance*, 6 (1), 27-38.

Zdanowicz, J., Pak S. and M. Sullivan (1999), 'Brazil-United States trade: capital flight through abnormal pricing', *The International Trade Journal*, XIII (4), 423-443.

PART THREE

Anti-Money Laundering

6. Domestic Money Laundering Enforcement

Előd Takáts

INTRODUCTION

This chapter reviews how money laundering is fought and explains the specific features of enforcement.[1] Throughout the chapter the United States' anti-money-laundering (AML) regime is discussed as a leading example. There are two main reasons to do so. First, the basic principles are roughly the same across different industrialized countries. Hence, understanding the principles in one country makes it very easy to explore their workings in others. Second, money laundering is a problem highly relevant in the United States. According to some lawmakers (FBI 2001) half of all monies laundered globally are laundered through the United States and its banking system.[2] Hence, the US AML regime is relevant to study on its own right. In addition, Chapter 3 has discussed the legal problems of European AML enforcement.

The chapter is organized as follows. First, money laundering is defined as the objective of enforcement efforts. Second, the AML regime's set-up and short history are introduced. Third, the AML regime's goals and available tools are discussed.

---

[1] The chapter uses the findings of Takáts (2006) on reporting as a starting point to explore the general problems relevant for domestic money laundering enforcement. Hence, the chapter is completely different from the paper. Those readers who are interested in the formal treatment of the 'Crying Wolf' problem are advised to read Takáts. Those who are interested in money laundering law enforcement problems in general will find this chapter more useful.

[2] These estimates are also consistent with various other calculations, presented in detail in Chapter 3.

The fourth part investigates how these tools are used to deter and prosecute money launderers. Fifth, the economics of how the financial system's integrity preserved is analyzed. The need to apply AML measures widely in the transfer sector and the need for properly set marginal deterrence is then investigated. Finally, the lessons learned from the exposition are summarized for the reader.

MONEY LAUNDERING: ILLICIT FUND TRANSFER

Money laundering is defined as an illicit money transfer, in other words a transfer that ideally should not take place. Obviously, defining money laundering as an illicit fund transfer is a simplification to ease discussion. Money launderers use a variety of methods which sometimes puzzles even the experts. The Financial Action Task Force on Money Laundering (FATF) typologies provide a good overview of these methods, the most important of which are summarized in Table 6.1.[3]

However, most (if not all) of the above mentioned money-laundering methods can be interpreted as fund transfers. The main idea behind all these transactions is to transfer funds from their present form or place to somewhere else; either to use it there or to conceal the origins of them. Hence, the different money-laundering methods share the illicit fund transfer, which will be in the focus of the subsequent discussion.

What is the problem with this illicit fund transfer? Obviously, it is not the cash deposit or the electronic fund transfer itself which warrants so much attention. Money-laundering transfers are socially harmful, because they are linked to and facilitate the so-called predicate crime. Money laundering is harmful, because it *necessarily* coexists with crime.

There are three main kinds of predicate crimes which are facilitated by money laundering. First, drug dealers are traditionally the most infamous money launderers. They are not only laundering large sums, but their predicate crime is also extraordinarily harmful. Drug dealers cannot use directly the huge amount of cash (usually in small denomination notes) which results from their trade. Hence, they need to transfer funds through the financial system until the illegal origins are concealed and they can use these monies freely. Second, tax evasion also requires money laundering in order to hide the monies from tax authorities. Monies need to be transferred until their origin (from tax evasion) is hidden.

---

[3] For an exhaustive list of money-laundering methods please refer to Chapter 4.

Table 6.1 Money-laundering methods

Wire transfers	The primary tool of money launderers to move funds around in the banking system. These moves can conceal the illicit origins of the funds or just place the monies where the launderers need them. Often the funds go through several banks and even different jurisdictions.
Cash deposits	Money launderers need to deposit cash advances to bank accounts prior to wire transfers. Due to anti-money-laundering regulations they often 'structure' the payments, i.e. break down large to smaller amounts. (This is also called '*smurfing*'.)
Informal value transfer systems (IVTS)	Money launderers need not rely on the banking sector, other transfer providers, such as the *hawala* or *hindi* are readily available to undertake fund transfers. These systems consist of shops (mainly selling groceries, phone cards or other similar items), which are also involved in transfer services. IVTSs enable international fund transfers, as these shops are present in several jurisdictions.[4]
Cash smuggling	Money launderers might mail, Fedex or simply carry cash with them from one region to another, or even to different jurisdictions.
Gambling	Casinos, horse-races and lotteries are ways of legalizing funds. The money launderer can buy (for 'dirty' cash) winning tickets – or in the case of casinos chips – and redeem the tickets or the chips in a 'clean' bank check. Afterwards, the check can be easily deposited in the banking sector.

continued

---

[4] The basic idea can be understood through a simple example. There is an immigrant worker in the United States, who would like to transfer monies to the Emirates to his family. He knows in the US a hawala dealer (*hawalador*) and tells him his family's address. The US *hawalador* contacts another *hawalador* in the Emirates who gives the money (usually in cash) to the designated family members. The *hawaladors* will clear their balance after some period of time, usually through invoicing adjustments related to goods trade.

Table 6.1 continued

Insurance policies	Money launderers purchase single premium insurance (with dirty cash), redeem early (and pay some penalty) in order to receive clean checks to deposit. Longer term premium payments might make laundering even harder to detect.
Securities	Usually used to facilitate fund transfers, where underlying security deals provide cover (and legitimate looking reason) for transfers.
Business ownership	Monies might be laundered through legitimate businesses, where laundering funds can be added to legitimate revenues. Cash-intensive operations, such as restaurants, are especially well suited for laundering.
Shell corporations	Money launderers might create companies exclusively to provide cover for fund moves without legitimate business activities.
Purchases	Real estate or any durable good purchases can be used to launder monies. Typically, the item is bought for cash and resold for clean monies, like bank checks.[5]
Credit card advance payment	Money launderers pay monies in advance with dirty money, and receive clean checks on the balance from the bank.
ATM operations[6]	Banks might allow other firms to operate their ATMs, i.e. to maintain and fill them with cash. Money launderers fill ATMs with dirty cash, and receive clean checks (for the cash withdrawn) from the bank.

Tax evasion is an important predicate crime, because it involves huge amounts of money laundering, which in fact far exceeds money laundering for other purposes. Third, terrorism financing also requires money laundering. There the problem is not to clean the monies (which might well be clean enough), but how to transfer them for illegal

---

[5] In order to combat the money laundering high-value purchases are usually regulated. For instance, purchasing real estate with cash is illegal in the United States.

[6] This piece is based on the author's interview with Federal Reserve officials.

purposes, i.e. to finance terrorist attacks. Though the sums are small, terrorism is harmful enough as a predicate crime to warrant additional attention. Finally, the other predicate crimes involving money laundering are summarized on Table 6.2.

Table 6.2 Predicate crimes linked to money laundering

Drug dealing	Drug dealers almost always engage in money laundering, because their trade results in vast sums of cash in low denomination.
Tax evasion	Tax evaders usually need to transfer funds to different jurisdictions (or tax havens) so as not to raise tax authorities' suspicion.
Terrorism financing	Terrorists need to transfer funds from their base to different jurisdictions in order to finance terrorist attacks.
Fraud Smuggling (non-drug) Racketeering Embezzlement	Proceedings from criminal activities cannot be used directly without raising suspicion. Hence, the need to launder and thereby clean the funds, so that they would appear to be of legal origin.[7]

From an enforcement perspective, there are two main kinds of illicit money transfers. First, traditional money laundering entails transferring illegally obtained funds to conceal their origins and make them appear legal. For example, drug dealers deposit cash revenues in banks and later transfer them until the funds appear to originate from legitimate sources. Tax evaders are also interested in such traditional money laundering.[8] Second, terrorism financing entails transferring mostly legal funds for illegal purposes. For instance, legal charity donations are transferred to fund terrorist attacks. For all the differences it is worth noting, that both

---

[7] Estimates vary on the size of laundering related to fraud, but the sums are substantial; please refer to Chapter 3 for further details.

[8] The GAO (1996) defined money laundering accordingly: 'Money laundering is the act of converting money gained from illegal activity, such as drug smuggling, into money that appears legitimate and in which the source can not be traced to the illegal activity.' The definition also highlights why some authors discuss money laundering *and* terrorism financing. For the sake of simplicity, this chapter defines money laundering so as to include terrorism financing as well. This definition is in line with FATF policies: the original 40 recommendations were amended by 9 recommendations so as to include terrorist financing.

forms of money laundering are characterized by illicit fund transfers. Figure 6.1 illustrates the differences.

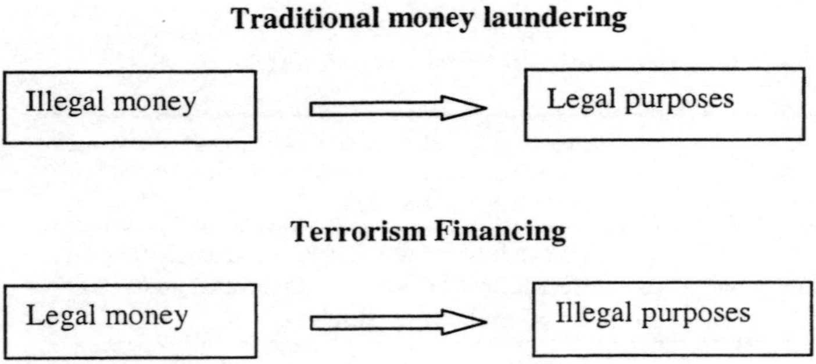

Traditional money laundering

| Illegal money | ⟹ | Legal purposes |

Terrorism Financing

| Legal money | ⟹ | Illegal purposes |

Figure 6.1 Two kinds of money laundering

There is an obvious danger evident from Figure 6.1. If terrorism financing and traditional money laundering is combined, then the need to launder funds dramatically decreases. For instance, terrorists engaging in drug dealing need not launder the monies, only transport it to the place where it is planned to be used. Hence, it is understandable that law enforcement and security officials are especially worried about such co-operations.[9]

Money laundering, the illicit fund transfer can happen through various intermediaries. Bank transfers, both wire transfers and checks, are the most common channel for illicit money transfers simply due to the size of the banking sector. Hence, the discussion of money-laundering enforcement focuses on banks in this chapter.

However, there are other kinds of transfer providers (as was shown in Table 6.1). Money transmitting businesses such as Western Union are also used by money launderers as detailed in the *Wall Street Journal* (2004b).[10] In the grayer area of finance, informal value transfer systems (IVTSs) provide money transmitting services usually without a proper paper trail. These transfer providers use an informal network of dealers

---

[9] For instance, the topic arose on the 2004 October 17-19 Quito meeting of the Western Hemisphere defense ministers.

[10] Furthermore, these businesses are typically franchised or owned by individuals, who might have stronger incentives to turn a blind eye to money laundering than bank branch-managers.

to transfer monies from one country to another as described in El-Qorchi (2002). Unfortunately, most such systems, for instance the hawala or hindi used and operated by certain ethnic communities, do not maintain reliable paper trails for transactions. This has prompted negative attitudes, for instance, *Time* (2001) magazine called hawala 'a banking system built for terrorism'. Precisely because of this it is very important to note, that there are many rational and legal economic reasons to use these systems. Most importantly, hawala transfers can be both cheaper and faster than official bank transfers.

Summarizing, there are different methods through different providers to undertake money laundering. Yet all of them share the core of money laundering: the illicit fund transfer. In the following, where abstraction is needed, the chapter focuses on the illicit fund transfer aspect of money laundering.

Finally, a few words on how significant money laundering is. There are three useful metrics to measure the importance of money laundering. First, one can estimate the amount of monies laundered.[11] According to Camdessus (1998) the consensus range of money-laundering volume is between 2 and 5% of the global GDP. The United Nations (2005) estimates the volume of global laundered funds to fall between $500 billion and $1 trillion.

Second, one might want to estimate the size of social harm caused by the predicate crimes attached to money laundering. Money laundering might cause harms potentially even larger than the size of the funds transferred. This is definitely the case for terrorism financing. According to *The 9/11 Commission Report* (2004) the tragic attack needed less than half a million dollars of funding. These monies are dwarfed by the enormous losses inflicted.[12] Obviously, in the case of tax evasion the social harms are likely to be much smaller than the amount of the funds laundered.

---

[11] There are two main kinds of estimation techniques. Microeconomic estimates work bottom-up: first money laundering linked to certain crimes is estimated and second the number of criminal acts is estimated (including latency). Chapter 3 estimates are examples of such microeconomic or bottom-up estimates. Macroeconomic estimates work top-down: they are trying to estimate how much more currency circulates in the economy (linked to money laundering) than what is needed for legal transactions.

[12] The direct losses alone are estimated to be around $135 billion (Thachuk, 2002).

Finally, one might think about money laundering as an industry, which provides transferring services for criminals in exchange for some fees. The laundering fee, that is what money launderers charge to their criminal clients, is estimated between 5 to 15% of the laundered amount according to Lal (2003) and Reuter and Truman (2004). Thus, money laundering, including self-laundering, is estimated to be a $25 to $150 billion global 'industry'. There are in fact professional money launderers who are transferring their clients' monies. The most infamous of these professional launderers is Stephen Sacoccia, who laundered up to $750 million and received a 10% commission for that (Reuter and Truman 2004).[13]

ANTI-MONEY LAUNDERING (AML)

Fighting money laundering requires government action, because it involves externalities. The reason is that money laundering (the transferring of funds) is not harmful per se. It is only harmful because it facilitates some other illicit activity, the predicate crime. Hence, economic agents interested in the fund transfers do not internalize the social harms caused by the predicate crime. For example, a bank might want to accept funds from drug dealing, as the social costs of drug trade are external to the bank. This externality warrants government intervention and setting AML regimes.

Yet, fighting money laundering is no free lunch, it involves trade-offs. Anti-money-laundering measures limit even legal citizens' privacy to some extent. They might be required to provide data, or their private data could be stored and used by several government agencies. Furthermore, enforcement systems are costly both for the private and public sector. This creates the following trade-off: stronger enforcement yields increased costs and reduces the privacy of citizens.

Not surprisingly, the evolution of the AML regime depended on the relative weight policy makers put on the harms stemming from money-laundering, and their preferences for maintaining privacy (and avoiding costs). Consequently, anti-money-laundering legislation developed mainly as a response to the drug epidemic of the 1970 and the 9/11

---

[13]Although, being known in this industry (as the joke goes on even in banking supervision) is usually a bad sign. Most well-known money launderers are either in jail or dead.

terrorist attacks in the United States. Both of these developments dramatically changed the trade-off between enforcement efficiency and privacy needs.

The AML regime started in the 1970s as a response to the growing drug problem in the United States. Before the 1970 the US government focused on fighting predicate crimes directly. However, with little or no anti-money-laundering effort criminals are effectively encouraged to commit crimes, because the criminal gains are readily accessible. The criminals might buy property, vehicles or invest these proceeds as they wish. In other words, if a criminal can get away with the crime, he or she does not have to worry about enjoying the resulting criminal gains. The anti-money-laundering regime reinforces deterrence by making the criminal worry not only about the predicate crime, but also about how to use the proceeds, or in other words about how to launder the monies.[14] Following the 1970 enactment of the Banking Secrecy Act, which in fact curbed bank secrecy in order to fight money laundering, the AML regime started to evolve as displayed in Table 6.3. The legislation was gradually amended and made stronger throughout the 1980s and 1990s.

The shock of 9/11 radically changed the anti-money laundering trade-off. Policy makers had to realize that that not only drug dealers or tax-evaders rely on money-laundering, but also highly dangerous terrorists. It resulted in a significant toughening of the AML regime by the Patriot Act in 2001.

The anti-money-laundering regime focuses on banks and other financial institutions – as it is clear from Table 6.3.[15] The reason is that financial institutions are in a position to gather information on certain transactions (or clients) and report them to law enforcement agencies. These agencies use the information to focus their attention on the most likely signs of money laundering.

---

[14] Furthermore, anti-money-laundering measures might provide additional deterrence by allowing civil law proofs into the fight against crime. For instance, law enforcement officials might not be able to show 'beyond reasonable doubt' – the criminal law bar – that a person dealt with drugs. However, they might be able to show that the person was likely engaging in money laundering. In such a case, the person will not be convicted for drug dealing (the criminal law part), but his gains might be confiscated for money laundering offences. Some similarities might be seen with the much-publicized O.J. Simpson case. The criminal proceedings found him not guilty – at least not beyond reasonable doubt, but the civil court awarded damages to the family.

[15] Of course, other institutions such as casinos or car dealers are also expected to participate in AML activities both in the United States and abroad.

Table 6.3 United States anti-money-laundering legislation

Year	Legislation
1970	Bank Secrecy Act (BSA) Racketeer Influenced and Corrupt Organization Act (RICO)
1977	Foreign Corrupt Practices Act (FCPA)
1986	Money Laundering Control Act (MLCA)
1988	Anti-Drug Abuse Act Money Laundering Prosecutions Improvements Act
1990	Crime Control Act
1992	Annunzio-Wylie Money Laundering Act
1994	Money Laundering Suppression Act
1995	Regulation of fund transfers Revision of currency transaction report (CTR)
1996	Simplified suspicious activity report (SAR)
1998	Money Laundering and Financial Crimes Strategy Act
1999	Foreign Narcotics Kingpin Designation Act
2001	Patriot Act (Money Laundering Abatement and Anti-Terrorist Financing Act which formed Title III of the USA Patriot Act)

AML GOALS AND TOOLS

The ultimate goal of the AML regime is to deter criminals from laundering monies, and thereby deter them from committing predicate crimes in the first place. This goal is achieved through two intermediate objectives.

First, the AML regime is supposed to directly deter and prosecute criminals.[16] The AML regime deters criminals through three main channels:

---

[16] Reuter and Truman (2004) call these two goals prevention and enforcement respectively. However, this chapter disagrees with their definition, because prevention and enforcement cannot be separated. Enforcement actions, such as investigation, prosecution and eventual sanctions do contribute to prevention. Hence, they are treated similarly here, and the deterrence role of prosecution is emphasized.

1. Financial institutions use customer due diligence (CDD) procedures to establish the legal nature of their clients' businesses. The CDD procedure forces potential money launderers to camouflage their operations so that they would appear to be legal businesses. This might be infeasible or just costly, in either case providing disincentives to commit the crime.
2. Financial institutions report transactions and clients as prescribed by the law. The two most important kinds of reports are the currency transaction reports (CTR) and the suspicious activity report (SAR). Through reporting banks can provide additional information to law enforcement, which improves on investigation efficiency – and thereby deters criminals.
3. Finally, banks can use the huge amount of financial information to provide additional help to law enforcement investigations. In the United States, all banks provide client contact information to law enforcement agencies through the 314(a) form. This makes it more difficult for criminals to hide their transactions and monies in the financial sector.

Second, the anti-money-laundering regime is designed to protect the integrity of the financial system. The AML regime wants banks to operate legally and not facilitate money laundering willfully. In other words, the AML regime enforces that banks are not the criminals themselves.[17] Furthermore, preserving integrity also entails that banks do not fail to be reasonably informed about their clientele, i.e. when the integrity of the financial system is preserved banks do not turn a blind eye to money-laundering or its suspicion. Note, however, that preserving integrity is less demanding than deterrence. Integrity is a necessary precondition for efficient deterrence, but by no means sufficient.

In the following the economics of the AML regime will be analyzed. First, the above three deterrence and prosecution tools are analyzed. Second, the economics of preserving integrity is investigated.

---

[17] A good example is the money laundering depicted in the 'Scarface' movie, where corrupt bankers let drug dealers deposit cash directly into the bank's vault. A real life example is that of the Broadway National Bank or that of the Bank of Credit and Commerce International (BCCI).

DETERRENCE AND PROSECUTION

This section discusses the economics of different deterrence and prosecution tools in subsections. The sixth subsection summarizes the findings. The final subsection concludes by contrasting the economic problem of anti-money laundering enforcement with similar, well-known economic problems.

Customer Due Diligence

Banks and other financial institutions are expected (and legally obliged) to validate their clients' background and identity. This procedure is called customer due diligence (CDD).

The aim of the procedure is twofold. First, it provides a mechanical background check that makes illegal banking more difficult. Potential money launderers need to use proper paperwork (or very high quality fake ones) in order to be able to establish bank accounts. Thus, anonymity of financial transactions, a major money-laundering tool, is limited.

Second, the CDD provides a solid ground for the financial institution what to expect from a certain client. For instance, an undergraduate student is not supposed to deposit large sums of cash at branches situated in drug-affected areas of the city. In other words, the financial institution builds a client profile, which determines the institution's expectation about client activity. Based on this profile the institution is able to flag those transactions which seem to contradict the profile.

The economics of background checks is straightforward. Banks and financial institutions must check certain identification forms and usually retain a photocopy of the documents. Hence, banking supervision needs only to audit banks with some (potentially very low) likelihood and verify that the copies indeed exist and the institution did not open accounts without proper CDD. If the bank fails on this audit, supervision might fine the bank. The problem is a combination of deterrence models in the style of Becker (1968) and costly state verification models.[18]

The CDD procedure also has other uses besides eliminating anonymity. Spotting 'out of profile' transactions is useful for two reasons. First, the financial institution can further refine its profile based

---

[18] For a more detailed description of these models, please refer to the section on rule-based reporting.

on the new information. Referring to the student example, the institution might realize that the student has supportive relatives in the drug-ridden part of the city, and the deposits are simply gifts to support his or her education. Secondly and most importantly, the financial institution might find the transactions indeed suspicious and report them to law enforcement.[19] In the example, the bank might not find any reasonable explanation for the student's deposits, and thus informs law enforcement officials about the suspicious deposits.

Reporting

Banks – and some other financial institutions – are supposed to provide information to law enforcement agencies by reporting certain transactions. There are two main kinds of reports; rule-based and discretionary reports. Rule-based reports are used where the government prescribes exactly what kind of transactions should be reported to them. For instance, banks must file a currency transactions report (CTR) for any cash transactions exceeding $10,000.

Soon, an ex post obvious problem surfaced with rule-based reports. No matter what the reporting requirements are, money launderers are able to circumvent them, because they are known before they start laundering. For instance, money launderers might want to break up cash transactions to smaller sums below the $10,000 threshold. This is known to be very frequent and called smurfing.

The solution to the problem was provided by introducing discretionary reporting. An example is the suspicious activity report (SAR). Here, banks are not given prescribed rules, but rather told to report transaction which they judge to be suspicious. In theory, money launderers are unable to foresee the working of such reporting. Hence, discretionary reporting is able to provide very high quality information. Table 6.2 below summarizes the different kinds of reports, according to whether they are rule-based or discretionary and it also lists the agency to whom they are filed.

In the following first the economics of rule-based, and then the economics of discretionary reporting is investigated.

---

[19] Note that CDD and client profile building is a necessary prerequisite of discretionary reporting. Because of this, the economics of profile building will be discussed together with the economics of discretionary reporting in the following subsection on reporting.

Table 6.4 Reports

Report	Filing	Receiving agency
Currency Transaction Report (CTR)	Rule-based	Internal Revenue Service (IRS)
Currency and Other Monetary Instruments Report (CMIR)	Rule-based	Customs service
Suspicious Activity Report (SAR)	Discretionary	Financial Crime Enforcement Network (FinCEN)[20]

Rule-based reporting

Rule-based reporting relies on the following structure. The government prescribes some reporting rules. For instance, in the case of currency transaction reports (CTRs) each and every cash transaction exceeding $10,000 needs to be reported to the Internal Revenue Service (IRS). Banking supervision forces banks to comply with these rules. Banks are audited, and if reporting omissions are found, then they are fined.

The following simple economic model outline can help the further discussion of rule-based reporting: there is a single transaction, which either requires reporting or not. For the sake of clarity, the transaction which needs to be reported is called the high volume one, and the one not needing reporting is the low volume one. The bank observes the transaction (high or low volume) and decides whether or not to report it.

The bank needs incentives to report, as it is a costly action. (There are both administrative costs and the implicit cost of losing some clients.) The government provides these incentives by auditing and fining the bank. First, the government chooses the likelihood with which to audit the bank in case of not receiving the report.[21] Auditing reveals – either

---

[20] FinCEN is an agency of the US Treasury Department.

[21] As the bank is perfectly informed, it has no incentive to report transactions which are not supposed to be reported. The reason is the existence of reporting costs. Hence, without the loss of generality one can assume away reporting if the

with certainty or with some likelihood – the volume of the transaction. Obviously, a higher auditing likelihood leads to higher costs, so the government prefers to save on auditing costs. Second, the government decides how much to fine the bank, should it observe an unreported high volume transaction.

The economic problem is a mix of the Becker's (1968) deterrence model and a costly state verification model. Furthermore, the costly state verification part can be understood as a specific investigation action in the Becker model. Hence, the result is the same as Becker's seminal result: there is a need for maximum deterrence, and minimal investigation (auditing). Banking supervision should apply very high, cheap fines for compliance failures, but should save on costly investigations and auditing.

The intuition is the following: the government prefers to save on costs and minimize the likelihood of investigation. However, banks are deterred from shirking in reporting by the strength of deterrence, which is a function of auditing likelihood and nominal fines. In a risk neutral environment it can be expressed as follows:

Deterrence = Likelihood of auditing * Nominal fine

Thus, maximizing costless fines and minimizing costly auditing is the optimal solution for the government. The government prefers to set up as high fines as possible, and as low (but always strictly positive) auditing likelihood as possible to still provide sufficiently strong deterrence. This solution is called maximum deterrence.[22] Furthermore, the bank always files rule-based reports optimally, if the fines are sufficiently high.[23]

---

transaction ought not to be reported. This also implies that in any equilibrium the government would not audit reported transactions.

[22] The original 1968 paper was used in policy debates to argue for harsher sentences, if the cost of punishment is low enough. In the case of banks, the punishment is not only costless, but it in fact brings in revenues.

[23] Note for the sake of completeness that there is a need for some kind of commitment device on the side of the government. The reason is that with perfect deterrence and without commitment the government does not have any incentive to audit the bank. However, without auditing, the bank would not report any transactions. In practice, governments have strong commitment power through, for instance, their internal organization structure. Government commitment is especially not an issue in the United States' case – though it might be interesting for some other weaker countries.

Finally, in practice one can see maximum punishment working. Fines are high, and banks are seldom audited for rule-based reports. Still, banks are reporting CTRs correctly, and there is no mention of reporting problems in the United States concerning rule-based reports,[24] aside, of course, from the standard criticism of rule-based reports, i.e. even if banks report transactions as prescribed the information value of the reports might be low. In case of CTRs too many innocent customers might need enough cash to be reported – and too many money launderers might be able to smurf their transactions below the reporting threshold.

Given that the result is intuitive and the system seems to work well, one might ask what is the need to review the economics of rule-based reporting. Many readers would not have needed even as much formalism as was given to understand the mechanism. However, the reason is that one needs to understand the economics of the simple, rule-based reporting to understand how the much more complicated discretionary reporting works. In particular, it will be shown that the intuitive maximum deterrence result will not hold in the discretionary reporting case.

Discretionary reporting[25]

Rule-based reporting can make money laundering more difficult. Yet, money launderers can always devise ways to circumvent fixed rules as the example of smurfing shows. Discretionary reports were introduced because of these considerations. The government trusts the bank to recognize transactions which look suspicious and report them – without the need to rely on formal rules.

Discretionary reporting involves two tasks on the part of the bank. First, banks and financial institutions use the customer due diligence (CDD) procedure to establish a client profile. Furthermore, based on incoming information, such as new transactions and client activities, they continuously update this profile.

Second, the bank reports those transactions which are suspicious and 'out-of-profile' based on the client profile. In practice, banks flag those transactions which do not fit into the client profile, and investigate them

---

[24] In some less developed countries there might be problems even with rule-based reporting. For instance, the Caribbean FATF's (2005) AML report in Suriname criticizes similar problems.

[25] Discretionary reporting is modeled formally in Takáts (2006), where the interested reader is referred. Here, only the intuition behind the results is outlined.

further. If the flagged transaction or activity proves to be truly suspicious, then the bank files a Suspicious Activity Report (SAR) to the Financial Crime Enforcement Network (FinCEN). [26]

The main idea is that banks are able to spot activities that do not necessarily fall into the prescribed, rule-based reporting categories, yet are highly suspicious. Ideally, the vague notion of 'suspicious' is changing with money-laundering practices. [27] Obviously, if a client deposits cash only slightly below the CTR reporting threshold several times, then the transactions can be suspicious ('smurfing'). However, what can be considered as suspicious depends on a number of factors such as geographic location, kind of business etc. In the previous example, for instance, it is not obvious what should be the reporting for suspicious activities. (What is slightly below the threshold?) However, banks know their clientele and should be able to distinguish legal activities from illegal copy-cat cover activities. Hence, the need for banks' well-established CDD procedures to establish client profiles.

Suspicious activity reporting is a fairly recent tool in the fight against money laundering. Reporting suspicious activities was started – at least de facto – as early as the mid 1980 in the United States. De jure suspicious activity reporting was started by the Annunzio-Wylie Money Laundering Act in 1992, yet SAR filing took up only from 1996. Since then reporting has expanded very quickly, and SAR filing entered the focus of money-laundering enforcement.

Regulatory sanctions are used to incentivize banks to exert substantial monitoring effort (CDD) and incur reporting (SAR filing) costs. Regulatory sanctions fall into three main categories. First, regulators might make banks pay civil money penalties (basically fines). Second, banks under publicly announced investigation face significant reputation costs and loss of legitimate business. [28] This second effect is partially a

---

[26] Furthermore, banks are able to recognize high volume but innocent transactions, and not flag them as suspicious.

[27] Suspicious activity reporting provides yet another example of constructive ambiguity. In this case, creating ambiguity forces banks to work on identifying truly suspicious activities – and thereby keep money launderers uncertain. Constructive ambiguity is generally used to keep market participants uncertain about central banks' market moves.

[28] It is an interesting question though, whether banks could profit from such negative publicity by attracting significant money laundering transfers and funds. The question is obviously very tough to measure empirically – as are most money laundering issues. At first sight, it seems that stock markets value such potential new funds less than the cost of increased regulatory attention.

market-disciplining device, yet the trigger is pulled by the regulators when they disclose money-laundering compliance problems. Third, regulators can impose so-called law enforcement actions on banks. Law enforcement actions prescribe specific policies and procedures for banks to improve their compliance. Private law enforcement actions are called 'memoranda of understanding' and are not disclosed to the general public. (Yet, compliance is usually costly.) Public law enforcement actions, which are called either 'cease or desist orders' or 'written agreements' also trigger market reaction. In the following, these sanctions will be simply referred to as fines in order to ease discussion and acknowledging that regulators pull the trigger for any sanctions.

Fines are levied based on deficiencies in reporting and flagging suspicious activities. More precisely, banks are essentially fined for false negatives, i.e. for not reporting transactions which the regulators find ex-post suspicious. In other words, banks might face sanctions for too few suspicious activity reports, but not for too many. The regulators do not second guess the validity of good faith suspicious activity reporting, thereby punishment is meted out only for false negatives.

Recently, there were several examples of regulatory sanctions and fines for reporting non-compliance. AmSouth Bank was fined with $50 million for failing to file SARs in a highly publicized case (FinCEN, 2004b). Riggs Bank – besides paying $25 million – was forced to close down in 2004 (FinCEN 2004a). Arab Bank was fined $24 million for failing to file SARs and complying with the Banking Secrecy Act (FinCEN 2005g). In line with the description of fines only for false negatives, there were no fines for too many reporting.

Economic building blocks The economic problem of discretionary reporting can be described by four main economic building blocks:

1. Coarse communication
2. Coarse incentive (fines only for false negatives)
3. Uncertainty
4. Dual tasks: monitoring and reporting

Communication is coarse because banks cannot tell the law enforcement agencies all they know about the transaction. They can only identify a certain transaction as suspicious by reporting it.[29] The reason for this coarseness is due to the fact that bankers are in a much better position to judge what is suspicious, and it is simply impossible to communicate several years of banking experience in a short report.

Coarse incentives, the use of fines for false negatives, have already been discussed. It might be worth adding, however, that fines for false negatives are not as illogical or unique as they might seem to be. First, banks are supposed to report suspicious activities. Hence, it would be strange to fine them for doing (maybe in a rather overzealous manner) what they are supposed to do. Second, fines only for false negatives are general in legal situations related to information provision. For instance, in product information and liability cases, companies are also effectively fined for false negatives. If they do not disclose a feature which is harmful, they can be rightfully sued. If they claim too many features to be dangerous, including some harmless ones, they cannot be sued.

Uncertainty is crucial as banks do not know which transactions are money laundering and legal with certainty.[30] Big cash deposits in drug ridden areas of the city can be perfectly legal, whereas small wire transfers between respectable looking clients might conceal terrorism financing. Hence, banks need to use their judgment in selecting which transactions or activities to report.

Finally, dual tasking comes from the fact that banks need first to monitor their clients (through CDD profiling) in order to recognize and be able to report the suspicious activities (by filing a SAR). Hence, banks need to undertake two costly actions: one to monitor their clients, and a second to report the suspicious activities.

It is crucial to notice that the bank's information at the time of reporting is not ex-post verifiable. Hence, it cannot be modeled with some costly state verification model. The government must rely on observable actions of the bank (such as whether or not it reported the transaction) and on what it learned about the transaction (whether it was prosecuted as money laundering).

Two policy implications The four main economic building blocks allow us to discuss the two most important policy implications:

---

[29] This coarseness is similar to the Stein (2002) soft information concept in banking.
[30] This is a major difference from rule-based reporting, where banks always know what they are supposed to do.

1. Optimal, not maximal fines are needed
2. Under certain conditions reporting fees are needed

The optimal fine conclusion rests on the first three building blocks. Coarse communication implies that both too little and too much reporting is harmful. No reporting is obviously uninformative: without reports the government does not know which transactions to focus on. Excessive reporting,[31] on the other hand, is also suboptimal. Taking the extreme point, if the bank identifies all transactions as suspicious, it is exactly as uninformative as identifying none of them. Hence, an optimal number of reports is needed.

An optimal number of reports requires optimal fines. Obviously if fines are too low, banks will not undertake costly monitoring and reporting activities. However, if fines are excessively high, uncertain banks will prefer to err on the safe side and report even fewer suspicious transactions. This excessive reporting is harmful, because of coarse communication as described before. Consequently, optimal – neither to strong nor too weak – fines are needed.

Of course, the question is whether optimal fines do exist. On one hand, optimal monitoring requires strong fines, so as to force the bank to undertake this costly action. On the other hand, optimal reporting requires sufficiently low fines. Unfortunately, nothing guarantees that such optimal fines do exist.

The basic problem is that if reporting costs are too low, then fines sufficiently high to elicit monitoring will also elicit harmful excessive reporting. Hence, the model's second policy implication on reporting fees. If reporting costs are so low that optimal reporting cannot be implemented with fines, then the government can introduce simple reporting fees to increase reporting costs. Such an increase in reporting costs can create a wedge for optimal fine setting. Figure 6.2 illustrates the case.

Economic model Based on the above discussion a simple model of discretionary reporting can be drawn.[32] There is a single transaction, which is either money laundering or legal. There is a private profit maximizing bank and a social welfare maximizing government the latter of which embodies law enforcement, banking supervision, FinCEN and other government agencies.

---

[31] Excessive reporting is called 'crying wolf' in Takáts (2006).
[32] For a formal modeling exercise please refer to Takáts (2006).

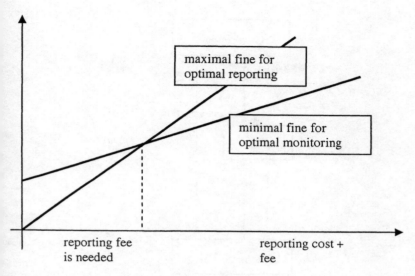

Figure 6.2 Reporting fee and optimal reporting

The bank needs to monitor the transaction so as to receive more precise information in the form of a signal. Based on the signal, the bank decides whether or not to report the transaction as suspicious.[33] The government decides on the intensity of the investigation decision based on whether it has received a report from the bank. Finally, if the government's investigation is successful and prosecutes the money launderer, and if the bank did not report the transaction as suspicious, then the government fines the bank.[34] Figure 6.3 summarizes the model.

Predictions and empirical evidence The model's main prediction is that optimal fines are needed. Too weak fines result in suboptimal reporting, whereas excessively strong fines increase the number of reports but decrease their information value. In other words, increasing fines show an Information Laffer curve: increasing fines first increase the number of successful investigations and prosecutions but later on decrease it. (However, the number of reports monotonically increases in fines.)

---

[33] Note that if the bank did not monitor the transaction it cannot report it.
[34] Successful investigation can mean the successful prosecution of the money launderer.

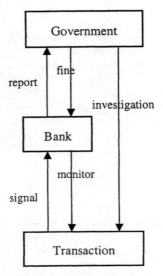

Figure 6.3 Modeling discretionary reporting

The Information Laffer curve result is illustrated in Figure 6.4.

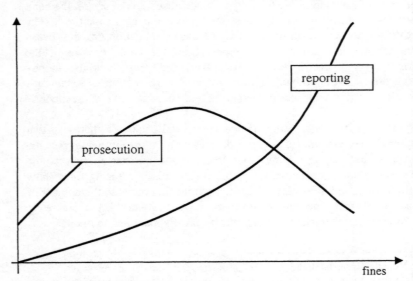

Figure 6.4 Information Laffer curve

The interesting question is how these results compare with what we observe in the data. First, before investigating the Information Laffer curve directly, one needs to look at an implicit assumption behind the model. The economic model and the Laffer curve implicitly assumes that money-laundering volumes are unchanged, and hence only (or at least mostly) fines are affecting reporting and prosecution numbers. First, this implicit assumption is checked through money-laundering volume estimates.

Independent studies estimate the volume of money laundering in the United States to be constant during the period of interest. Microeconomic estimates[35] show money-laundering volumes around 8% of the US GDP according to Reuter and Truman (2004). Though criminal earnings (without tax evasion) declined from 2.8% of the GDP in 1995 to 2.3% in 2000, increases in estimated tax evasion (from 5.2% to 5.6%) compensated the decline. Besides these microeconomic estimates, macroeconomic estimates[36] also show negligible variance and confirm that the underground economy is roughly 8.8% of the US GDP (Schneider, 2002). Of course, money laundering is a clandestine activity and it cannot be estimated precisely. Nevertheless, available evidence is consistent with the assumption that the volume of money laundering is essentially unchanged in the period examined in the United States.

In the next step the model's prediction on fines, reporting and prosecution numbers are investigated. First, fines show a steep increase during the period under consideration. There are many possible measures of fines in the United States, and all of them show a marked increase. All fines and restitutions, including fines on non-depository institutions as well as individuals, increased six-fold between 1996 and 2001 on the basis of US Sentencing Commission information (Reuter and Truman, 2004). GAO (2004) also confirms steep increases in civil money penalties, though without providing exact figures. FinCEN provides detailed statistics of its fines for neglecting SAR filing duties.[37] FinCEN started to levy fines in 2002, and the volume grew quickly from $0.1

---

[35] Microeconomic estimates work bottom-up: first money laundering linked to certain crimes is estimated and second the amount of crimes is estimated (including latency).

[36] Macroeconomic estimates work top-down: they are trying to estimate how much more currency circulates in the economy, than what is needed for legal transactions. This extra cash is then linked to money laundering.

[37] http://www.fincen.gov/

million in 2002 to \$24.5 million in 2003 and finally to \$35 million in 2004.

Second, reporting has also increased steeply. Reporting data are published in FinCEN (2005e), and the data are depicted in Figure 6.5. In order to correct for the widening range of reporting institutions, SARs filed by depository institutions are primarily discussed. As is evident from Figure 6.5 depository SARs grew exponentially, and the growth does not seem to saturate.

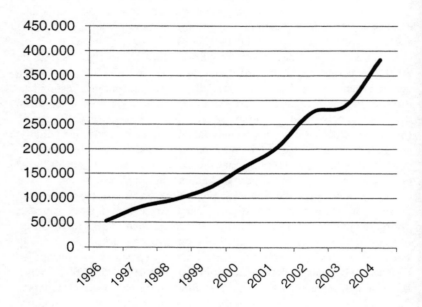

Figure 6.5 Suspicious activity reporting by depository institutions

Third, the number of prosecutions depicts a hump-shaped curve – exactly what one would expect based on the Information Laffer curve. Money-laundering prosecution peaked in 1999 and declined thereafter. Both measures of money-laundering prosecutions, filed and terminated cases, show the same qualitative picture as depicted in Figure 6.6. According to both measures prosecutions rose until 1999 and declined thereafter. Summarizing, the empirical evidence is consistent with what one would expect based on the Information Laffer curve.

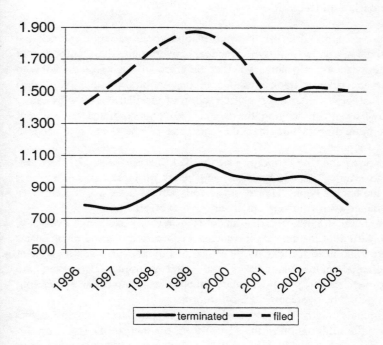

Figure 6.6 Money laundering prosecution

Furthermore, a congressional testimony from FinCEN (2005b, p. 3) provides further evidence that the observed excessive reporting is harmful:

> We estimate that if current filing trends continue, the total number of Suspicious Activity Reports filed this year will far surpass those filed in the previous years. ...it fuels our concern that financial institutions are becoming increasingly convinced that the key to avoiding regulatory and criminal scrutiny under the Banking Secrecy Act is to file more reports, regardless of whether the conduct or transaction identified is suspicious. ... If this trend continues, consumers of the data – law enforcement, regulatory agencies, and intelligence agencies – will suffer.

Information on Request

Banks are supposed to provide information about certain clients, if the government requests it. In practice, government law enforcement agencies can ask all banks whether they are in business contact with certain individuals. Banks respond to that inquiry through the 314(a) form – so called after the specific section of the Patriot Act – by either acknowledging or denying the contact. Of course, if the government needs more information than the existence of the contact it needs a proper subpoena.

On one hand, the economics of the 314(a) forms is straightforward. The government is able to check and verify business contacts ex post from the bank's books. Hence, sufficiently strong fines will force proper compliance even with very small verification effort.

On the other hand, the government faces a tricky problem. Obviously, it can learn a lot from the 314(a) forms. Prosecution is made much easier if there is no need for lengthy investigations to discover banking contact of potential money launderers and other criminals. However, the government might give involuntary hints to criminals about impending investigation by overusing the 314(a) form.

Criminals might get information about investigation, because banks can use the information in the 314(a) form for their CDD procedure. In particular, they might reasonably conclude that the client is more suspicious than what he or she was before learning that law enforcement officials are interested in his/her dealings. If banks conclude that it is not worth conducting business with the client in the light of the 314(a) information, they might involuntarily tip off the criminal by closing the account.

Summarizing, the government needs to balance how much information to ask for. Too many requests might just tip off criminals and eventually hinder law enforcement.

Summary: Information and Fines

As a summary, it is worth reviewing how fines affect the value of information provided by different kinds of reports. Table 6.5 below collects the different reports and shows what the optimal incentives and potential safe rules are.

Safe rules denote the kind of actions that uncertain decision-makers should rely on. For instance, under rule-based reporting uncertain decision-makers should rely on larger fines (punishment), because larger fines – if anything – will improve the value of information provided. Table 6.5 highlights the special feature of discretionary reporting, namely that there are no safe rules. Setting fines too low or too high can be equally harmful to the information value of reports. Hence, setting SAR policies based on experience gained in other reporting policies is clearly dangerous.

Table 6.5 Information and fines

Information form	Optimal incentive	Safe rule
CDD (paperwork)	Maximum deterrence	Maximum punishment
Rule-based reporting (CTR, CMIR)	Maximum deterrence	Maximum punishment
Discretionary reporting (SAR)	*Optimal deterrence*	*No safe rule*
Information on request: 314(a)	Maximum deterrence	Maximum punishment

Discussing Excessive Information Provision

As a conclusion to the reporting subsection it might worth considering what is new in the harmful effects of excessive reporting not known from earlier works in economics. There are two similar problems: defensive medicine and information overload. Yet, both are distinct at their core.

Defensive medicine is superficially similar to excessive reporting as it is also triggered by excessive fines, i.e. threat of lawsuits. Furthermore, defensive medicine does not only reduce social welfare, but it might also hinder general medical goals. For instance, unnecessary X-rays might harm patients' health. Yet the crucial difference is that in excessive reporting social welfare is decreased through information dilution. Excessive reporting destroys the information available for law enforcement. However, defensive medical practices do not destroy information in any ways.

Second, excessive reporting is different from information overload as described for instance in Posner (2004) and Garicano and Posner (2005). Information overload arises as a result of inefficient information processing. For example, in information overload intelligence data cannot be processed on time to start counter-terrorist measures. In excessive reporting the problem is not with processing information, but rather with the coarseness of communication. Law enforcement agencies can see all the reports, they just cannot figure out which reports are relevant.

Finally, it is worth investigating the dual role of reporting. The reporting subsection focused on the identification role of reports. This is a correct approach, because reports are essentially supposed to identify suspicious activities. However, these reports have an additional role: one can use the data to form a database. This reporting database can be used for searches and data mining – and for this purpose excessive reporting is not harmful. In fact more reporting provides more information for database use.

The distinction between data provision and identification explains why agencies interested in fighting money laundering (such as FinCEN) try to curb excessive reporting, while agencies with broader law enforcement goals (such as the FBI) prefer even more reports. Thus, database building is consistent with the FBI position that SAR filings are not harmful (*American Banker*, 2005a). However, the decreasing number of prosecutions supports FinCEN's point of view: the increasing number of reports is not useful for specifically fighting money-laundering.

PRESERVING INTEGRITY

The second major role of the anti-money-laundering regime is to preserve the integrity of the financial system. Preserving the integrity of the financial sector means that banks should not 'willfully and systematically' ignore AML compliance. For instance, they should not actively seek money-laundering funds – and later try to hide them from the authorities.

This integrity is the necessary condition that financial institutions and banks behave as honest intermediaries. The section on reporting assumed, for instance, that banks are not criminals themselves, i.e. they do not take part actively in, nor solicit, money laundering. This needs to be enforced, as banks might have financial incentives to solicit money laundering. Most importantly, even if only a single bank allows or seeks money laundering, that can compromise the integrity of the whole financial system. Transfers from such banks can reach all institutions. Moreover, after these transfers the illicit origins of the funds can be hard or impossible to detect. In other words, a single bank can potentially contaminate large parts of the financial sector.

Active solicitation of money laundering is rare, yet there are some US examples. For instance, Broadway National Bank (a small New York-based financial institution) engaged in helping money laundering in 2002. The bank's management authorized wire transfers following huge one-time or structured deposits, – without filing suspicious activity reports. The security guards were even advising certain clients when law enforcement investigators were around. According to some convicted money launderers' (admittedly unreliable) testimony, the bank was well-known for its lax approach in laundering circles.[38] Broadway National Bank was not closed, but it was fined $4 million, a huge amount for an institution with $89 million in total deposits.

An even more interesting example is that of Riggs Bank in 2004. Riggs Bank, which served the Washington diplomacy as well as several eminent politicians, 'willfully' violated its reporting duty. The bank failed to report large cash transactions by Saudi Arabian accounts. Furthermore, the bank was also suspected for hiding Augusto Pinochet's money. The authorities' response was harsh: the bank was forced to pay fines of $25 million. In addition, the public scrutiny made the institution unviable as a standalone bank, and amid the nudging of banking supervision it was sold to PNC Financial Services Group.

As the examples show, fines and even potential closure follow if a bank compromises the integrity of the financial system. These fines are larger than those levied for simple negligence so as to deter banks from criminal behavior.

The crucial point in preserving the financial system's integrity is to distinguish between negligence and willful deficiencies.[39] Hence, investigators need to clarify the intent of the bank as an institution.

The intent problem is slightly more complicated, however, in the case of banks than in the case of individual criminals, because banks are complex institutions. Some employees might solicit money laundering without approval or knowledge from management. This was the case at the Bank of New York, where low-level management was involved in laundering, without the higher level management knowing about it. In such cases it necessary is to judge the existing checks and controls within the bank in order to evaluate whether management intentionally turned a blind eye to the illicit activities.

---

[38] Joseph Vershish's testimony.
[39] Identifying intent is a standard problem in criminal law and the economics of criminal law. For instance, intent differentiates manslaughter from murder.

In spite of the institutional difficulties major bank in the United States do not seem to have problems with willful money laundering. Banks understand the serious consequences of engaging in money laundering (and if not that, then the serious consequences of actively soliciting it). Unfortunately, this is not necessarily the case globally, which will be discussed in the next chapter.

BANKING SYSTEM CLOSURE

Money-laundering enforcement is an increasingly important consideration for banks. Certain clients might prove to be unprofitable, because they need so much costly attention (monitoring, reporting) – and having business contact with them might eventually result in fines. Naturally, banks might want to cease contact with such unprofitable clients, which they are able to do legally. Hence, AML decisions should also be scrutinized on how they affect banks' service provision.[40]

The problem with closing banking services to certain groups of clients is that these clients are forced to find even less transparent transfer providers. They might even turn to informal transfer providers, who cannot be trusted to provide the same quality information as banks. Hence, the decision, that makes sense for a private profit-maximizing bank might be outright harmful for social welfare maximizing regulators.

Such harmful closures can happen in practice. For instance, in early 2005 US banks started to refuse providing services to money service businesses on such a scale that the closure threatened the money service industry (FinCEN, 2005a). In order to solve the problem, FinCEN (2005d) published amended guidelines which effectively decreased the likelihood that banks are fined for dealing with money service businesses.[41]

Concluding, the anti-money-laundering regime must also be cautious of the banking sector participation constraint. Tougher enforcement might backfire, if clients are forced underground.

---

[40] The closure problem is presented in a separate subsection so as not to blur the clarity of the reporting problem's exposition. As adding this additional point to the earlier discussions is straightforward, the structure will hopefully be easily accessible for the readers.

[41] In addition, there are worries that AML concerns will turn to ethnic profiling – especially in the case of terrorism financing.

EQUATING MARGINAL DETERRENCE

There are several transfer providers available for money launderers to execute the illicit fund transfer. Hence, money-laundering enforcement must pay attention to proper marginal deterrence of money launderers.

The term marginal deterrence is usually applied in the economics of crime literature. For instance, murder is widely accepted to be a more harmful crime than theft. Marginal deterrence means that murderers should expect stronger punishment than thieves. Thus, uncertain criminals, who cannot be deterred from committing crime, would rather engage in stealing than in killing. In sum, the optimal punishment of one crime should also consider punishments meted out for other crimes.

In money-laundering enforcement marginal deterrence should be equated between different transfer forms, i.e. enforcement should be roughly equally strong for different legal transfer providers. For instance, if enforcement is very efficient in banking, then money launderers will transfer funds through alternative transfer providers. In the extreme, only the most weakly enforced laundering channel is used, and efforts in other channels are wasted. In other words, the minimum of enforcement efficiency determines the system's efficiency, and the weakest chain describes the strength of the system.

Hence, there is a danger that excessively efficient AML regulation in banking – without similarly efficient measures in other transfer channels – simply directs money launderers to other transfer providers. Hence, excessively strong but insufficiently broad enforcement might miss its target.

CONCLUDING REMARKS

The chapter shows that domestic money-laundering enforcement poses challenges even in the United States which has one of the toughest anti-money-laundering (AML) regimes and political will to support it. Besides the obvious threats stemming from weak enforcement, the chapter has shown two main channels through which excessively strong enforcement can backfire and weaken AML efforts.

First, excessively strong fines can dilute the information value of discretionary reporting. Excessively strong fines distort banks' incentive to report only the truly relevant activities as suspicious. Excessive reporting produces a large number of false leads, which in turn decreases the efficiency of law enforcement investigations.

Second, excessively strong AML enforcement can make banks close services to certain client groups. This latter effect might increase the market share of informal transfer providers resulting in even less useful information – and potential more or easier money laundering.

In sum, the chapter's lesson is that optimal, neither too weak nor excessively strong, incentives are needed in anti-money-laundering enforcement. In the chapter the negative effects of excessively strong measures are emphasized more, for the reason that this point, the backfiring of excessively strong measures, is often missing from the public policy perspective on money laundering.

7.   International Enforcement Issues

Előd Takáts

INTRODUCTION

International enforcement is different in many respects from domestic enforcement, although the broad goals of the international and domestic AML regimes are similar:

1. Prosecute and deter money launderers through information acquisition
2. Preserve the integrity of the financial system

However, the tools for and problems in reaching these goals are substantially different. These differences are discussed in three main steps. First, the specificities of international money laundering are discussed. Second, international enforcement and its differences from domestic enforcement are discussed. Third, the potential problem of reversing financial globalization is introduced. The chapter concludes by contrasting the lessons learned for domestic and international money-laundering enforcement.

INTERNATIONAL MONEY LAUNDERING

The chapter on domestic enforcement started with defining what money laundering is: the illicit transfer of funds. As it was shown there, the fund transfers are not harmful *per se*, money-laundering transfers cause harms to society through their link to the predicate crime. The need for government intervention – i.e. anti-money laundering enforcement – arises precisely because of this externality in the domestic setting: those involved in the fund transfers do not internalize the harms of the predicate crime.

This externality is much worse in the international settings. The predicate crime and the subsequent money laundering can happen in different jurisdictions. Thus, there might not be a single agent (such as the government in a single country case) to internalize all the externalities.

Furthermore, the basic unit of money laundering, the illicit fund transfer, is also somewhat different in an international setting. It can be hard to follow the money across jurisdictions, even if a proper paper trail exists. Law enforcement officials need cooperation from their foreign partners which might be hard to get. The basic problem is that unlike in a domestic case there is no single authority to sort out disagreements between sovereign states and their law enforcement agencies.

The section is structured as follows. First, it introduces the laundering externality problem, which shows why countries have an economic incentive not to cooperate in fighting money laundering. Second, the section shows how this externality can result in different predicate crime definitions in an international setting. Finally, it is discussed how transfers crossing jurisdictions are different from domestic transfers.

The Laundering Externality

Undertaking money laundering and the predicate crime in different jurisdictions involves an externality, called the laundering externality. The predicate crime is harmful, but the harms are concentrated in the jurisdiction where it is committed. However, money laundering in itself is not harmful; on the contrary it brings revenues to the laundering jurisdiction. Hence, countries do face an externality: it is worth turning a blind eye to money laundering linked to predicate crimes committed elsewhere.

The situation is similar to the well-known Prisoner's dilemma. Countries do have an incentive, *ceteris paribus*, to allow laundering monies linked to predicate crimes committed elsewhere. However, if all countries act on such narrow self interest, then this behavior tremendously eases money laundering. In the language of game theory, the competitive Nash equilibrium of the Prisoner's dilemma is ultimately worse for all players than cooperation. Thus, countries might fail to take common action against money-laundering – to the eventual detriment of all countries.

It is worth illustrating the Prisoner's dilemma in the specific case of the laundering externality.[1] In the rows of Figure 7.1 there are the choices available for country A: being tough on foreign money laundering (Tough) or lax (Lax) on it. In the columns of Figure 7.1 country B's similar choices are depicted. In the matrix the payoffs are depicted given country A and B's choice of action. The first number denotes the payoff of country A, and the second that of country B. For instance, if country A is tough and country B is lax, then country A's payoff is −1 and country B's is 6.

	B Tough	B Lax
A Tough	5,5	−1,6
A Lax	6, −1	0,0

Figure 7.1 Prisoner's dilemma and the laundering externality

The explanation of the payoffs is as follows: If both countries are tough on foreign money laundering, then money laundering (and committing predicate crimes) is harder. The resulting lower crime yields higher utilities, in the example above 5 units, for both countries. If, for instance, country A is tough and country B is lax, then money laundering is easier in country A − as launderers can also use country B's facilities with few obstacles. Naturally, country A suffers from higher money-laundering and predicate crime levels, hence it has a −1 payoff. In addition, country B receives laundering revenues from laundering the criminal monies linked to predicate crimes committed in country A. This income results in higher revenues than tough enforcement, numerically 6 unit payoffs. Finally, if both countries are lax on foreign money laundering, then money laundering is easy and predicate crime levels are high in both countries. Note, however, the 0 unit payoffs are not as low when predicate crime is concentrated only in a single country (−1). The reason is that even though both countries suffer from high levels of predicate crime, they also enjoy laundering revenues from predicate crimes committed in the other country.

The economic problem is that what is collectively good for both states is not the best strategy for any one of them individually. The countries

---

[1] Readers familiar with game theory and the Prisoner's dilemma are asked to skip the following few paragraphs.

can maximize their joint payoffs (the sum of their payoffs) by running tough AML enforcement regimes on foreign laundering. This strategy yields profits of 5 units for each one of them. Thus, collaboration yields joint payoffs of 10.

However, individually each country is better off by deviating from this strategy. No matter what country B's strategy is, country A prefers to have lax regulation. If country B is tough, country A can increase its payoff from 5 to 6. If country B is lax, country A can still increase its payoff from −1 to 0. Hence, no matter what the other country is doing each country is better of following a lax strategy on enforcing other countries' predicate crimes.[2] Following this individually optimal strategy the resulting Nash equilibrium yields only 0 joint payoffs. The individually optimal strategy brings substantially lower payoffs (0) than common action and cooperation (5 for each country).

The laundering externality can be best exemplified through the case of offshore financial centers (OFCs). Transactions in OFCs do not affect and are not linked to the OFCs' economy – besides realizing some revenues from them. Hence, for OFCs money laundering is someone else's problem – and for them it is only a revenue base. [3] Thus, as explained in the Prisoner's dilemma, OFCs have very weak if any incentives to fight money laundering. Why undertake costly AML actions when the country does not suffer from the consequences of money laundering and its predicate crime? It is a confirmation of the theory and no surprise that many of these centers were initially reluctant to enact strong AML regulations.[4]

Obviously, the really interesting policy question is how to establish the cooperative equilibrium which yields higher payoffs for all. How to convince countries not to follow their narrowly defined self interest in order to reach better joint outcomes? The case of OFCs shows that the answer lies in international cooperation – even including some international pressure. The precise methods of international cooperation will be discussed later.

---

[2] In the language of game theory, the tough strategy is strictly dominated by the lax strategy for both players.

[3] By definition, money laundering in an OFC is related to foreign predicate crimes.

[4] International pressure can, however, change these incentives substantially. According to the IMF (2003) offshore financial centers have improved their AML regimes and enforcement since the international community (and the IMF) started to review them.

Defining International Predicate Crimes

The laundering externality, as was shown above, pushes countries to accept some levels of money laundering linked to predicate crimes committed elsewhere. The way such decisions are implemented is often through the definition of the predicate crime. Countries might exclude crimes committed abroad, or those not truly relevant for them, from the definition of domestic predicate crimes.[5] Hence, domestic law enforcement agencies would not prosecute money-laundering related to these "foreign" predicate crimes. Thus, international cooperation might break down if there are serious differences in establishing what a predicate crime is.

However, harmonizing predicate crime definitions is not always easy. Even absent economic arguments presented, for instance, in the laundering externality, countries might want to keep their own predicate crime definitions. Enforcing costly and privacy reducing regulations needs domestic justification. If there is no consensus that the predicate crime is harmful (or even that it is a crime), then it is hard to prosecute money-laundering related to that specific predicate crime. Furthermore, differing legal standards of predicate crimes can also stem from different value systems. What is crime in one country can be virtue in another, and this is particularly true when totalitarian dictatorships and democracies interact.[6] As a result, national law enforcement agencies might react differently to the very same offense.

Such differences in predicate crime definition often arise in international settings – as one would expect from the economic forces of the laundering externality. First, let us consider the handling of tax evasion and drug dealing in the United States and Latin America. On one hand, tax evasion and channeling capital to the United States is a major problem for Latin America. However, it is surely not a major problem to the United States, which maintains that every country should enforce its

---

[5] There is an interesting technical point here. The United States (and Japan) defines money laundering as a crime related to a specific list of predicate crimes. Most other countries do not have an explicit predicate crime list, and define laundering as to be related to a serious crime. However, the crucial point is what is considered to be a predicate crime, i.e. what is on the US list or what is viewed as a serious crime elsewhere.

[6] The often used example is of helping persecuted people transfer some of their monies out of Nazi Germany. Technically, this is an act of money laundering – though one would not expect democracies to support such transfer restrictions.

own tax system. On the other hand, drug dealing is a crucial crime for the United States. Before terrorism drug dealing was the number one predicate crime behind money laundering. The drug problem is, however, much less important for Latin America – especially compared to the tax evasion problem.

Second, a similar problem exists between the United States and Europe. European personal taxes are, by and large, higher than American ones. Hence, European money flies to the United States and evades taxes back home. European governments would prefer the US taking strong actions to stop this predicate crime – and enforce AML regulations on the related money laundering. The US government held the view for quite a while that it is unreasonable to expect countries with lower tax rates to enforce higher tax rate countries' tax codes. These costs seemed to be unjustified. Interestingly enough, after 9/11 the tables turned.[7] The United States was ready to share information to gather information on terrorists, whereas the European Union voiced concerns over data protection (or rather about the lack of it) in the United States.[8]

Third, unofficial exchange of currency is a crime in several countries with regulated foreign exchange markets, for instance in India. Currency regulation usually provides revenues for the government by forcing transfers through official exchange rates. However, *hawala* or *hindi* systems circumvent currency regulation and deprive the state of exchange income. Not surprisingly, these operations are illegal in India – and in many other countries with regulated foreign exchange markets. However, operating these informal value transfer systems is not criminal in the United States, where it is regarded only as yet another kind of business.

Interestingly enough, even agreement on what to exclude from the list of predicate crimes can be harmful. A prime example is the traditional 'money-laundering consensus' between corrupt dictators and financial centers. In case of dictators' monies no official party is interested in prosecuting the money laundering. On one hand, corrupt dictators such as Mobutu of Zaire, Abacha of Nigeria, Marcos of the Philippines or Suharto of Indonesia, who have laundered billions of dollars abroad,

---

[7] Not least, because by a simple analogy: 'it is unreasonable to expect countries with lower risk of terrorist attacks to enforce the expensive laws of countries with much higher terrorism risk'.

[8] For the sake of fairness though, it has to be acknowledged that the European position was rather stable and the turnaround was due to changing US policies motivated by new terrorism concerns.

have certainly no interest in prosecuting their own crimes. On the other hand, and most unfortunately, developed countries' financial centers felt they had a similar position, as they only enjoyed the benefits of the fund transfers.[9] A related point is that most countries did not regard bribery abroad a criminal offense, some viewed it is a 'way of doing business'. The United States, although officially foreign bribery was outlawed in the 1970, only started to enforce anti-bribery laws after the passage of the Patriot Act in 2001.[10]

The preceding discussion has established that countries have an economic incentive to turn a blind eye to laundering monies linked to foreign crime – and also that one way to do so is to establish different predicate crime categories. With different predicate crime definitions countries can fail to enforce other countries' money laundering rules, in a very implicit manner.[11]

It is evident from the above discussion that some harmonization of predicate crime definitions is necessary. Fortunately, the above examples are rather exceptions than the norm: most countries, especially the developed, democratic ones, have a strong common ground to define predicate crimes. Yet the existing differences can still foster money laundering, if money launderers can shop around for the best legal environment for their specific laundering needs.

International Fund Transfers

International fund transfers are different from domestic ones. Funds crossing jurisdictions are harder to evaluate and check – both for banks and government law enforcement agencies. Furthermore, crossing jurisdictions can very quickly conceal the true origins of the funds involved.[12]

---

[9] As the Laundering externality would predict.

[10] The past tense is justified, because the 'consensus' seems to fade away as financial centers realize the externalities caused by facilitating money laundering. In fact, the international community has focused significant attention on stopping laundering by politically exposed persons (PEPs).

[11] In the language of the laundering externality, countries can pursue 'lax' policies related to laundering of the proceed of foreign predicate crimes by intentionally having different predicate crime definitions.

[12] Of course, differences in predicate crime definitions can pose further problems as it was discussed in the previous subsection.

International bank payments are conducted mainly through correspondent banking relationships. Banks needing foreign currency transactions usually have several correspondent banking relationships. In effect, they have an account in foreign banks from which they can execute payments for their clients.

The problem with correspondent banking is the following: the host bank only sees the foreign bank, but does not have much further information about the clients behind the transfers initiated by the foreign bank. This way, the foreign bank can effectively tap into the financial system of the home country through the correspondent bank. Hence, if the foreign bank is lax in its monitoring and reporting duties money launderers can gain access to the financial system of the home country – even if the home country's regulation is sufficiently tough.

International transfers outside of the banking sphere are even more obscure. For instance, transfers conducted through informal value transfer systems (IVTSs) usually lack a proper trail and are very hard to verify. Cash transmitting services (such as Western Union) usually have much less sophisticated monitoring regimes than banks have. Other transfers, such as cash smuggling, are even less transparent.

Not surprisingly, money launderers often transfer funds through jurisdictions. Several international transfers can fully conceal the illicit origins of the funds. The structural differences, along with potential differences in enforcement strength or predicate crime definitions, make international laundering very attractive.

INTERNATIONAL ANTI-MONEY LAUNDERING

The major difference between domestic and international AML efforts is how to harmonize national AML regimes. The steps taken to fight money laundering a unified way is analyzed first. Next, international prosecution and deterrence is discussed. Finally, the specific problems related to preserving the integrity of the international financial system are discussed.

Harmonizing National AML Regimes

National AML regimes have a strong economic rationale to diverge due to the laundering externality even though cooperation would be preferable to maximize joint payoffs. As it was hinted at earlier, international cooperation can fix the situation. This section reviews the main channels for international cooperation and for establishing the cooperative equilibrium.

Harmonization can be undertaken through three main channels: unilateral, bilateral or multilateral negotiations. All approaches have different advantages and disadvantages.

The idea behind the unilateral solution, mainly used by the United States, is to provide a model anti-money-laundering regime that other countries can imitate. Ideally, countries could adopt AML practices without further negotiations. The unilateral approach can be useful if the AML priorities of the two countries converge and differences in the size of the economy render negotiations wasteful.[13] Unilateralism is especially useful if the leading country can provide know-how from its model AML system. In this case, both countries clearly benefit from harmonization. Unfortunately, if AML priorities are sufficiently different showing a model AML system as an example will not suffice.

Bilateral negotiations are used to harmonize two countries' AML regimes. In theory, bilateral talks have the advantage of faster conduct than multilateral negotiations. Bilateral talks are especially useful if the two countries have very strong economic ties. Then, it might be worth skipping wider harmonization for faster harmonization. The price, however, is that international money laundering outside of the two harmonized systems is not mitigated. In fact, bilateral harmonization might encourage money laundering, if the two converging systems diverge together from the rest of the world, from the global standards.

Multilateral negotiations are used to harmonize AML practices across several countries (like the group of developed countries or certain geographic areas). Multilateral talks involve the following trade-off: as the number of countries increases so does the potential gain from harmonization. However, as the number of involved countries grows it gets more difficult to reach common ground and the negotiations grew lengthier. Realizing these trade-offs most multilateral talks involve an optimal number of similar countries.

Multilateral negotiations are naturally facilitated by international organizations. The most important such organization in the fight against money laundering is the Financial Action Task Force (FATF) on Money

---

[13] For instance, it might not be worth changing the existing AML practices of a large country to conform to a small country's AML practices. It is easier to conform the small country's system – with, of course, due compensation.

Laundering. It was established in 1989 as a temporary body under the OECD. As the need for anti-money-laundering coordination remained stable, the original five year mandate was extended several times, last in 2004 for additional five years. The FATF has only 33 member nations and operates by consensus; both potentially constraining its activities' scope.

The FATF issued the Forty Recommendations on how to deal with money laundering which – with its modifications[14] – is the cornerstone of international AML cooperation. The recommendations focus on technical issues such as, for instance, the need for cash transaction reporting. The implementation of these technical guidelines provides a major step towards a unified global AML framework. Moreover, the FATF Forty Recommendations represent fairly high standards. Even the United States, with its tough AML regime, failed to fully comply with all the recommendations by 2003. (Though the implementation of the Patriot Act is likely to change that.)

The FATF also proved to be able to exert influence outside its member states. It uses a 'name and shame' policy to identify countries with lax regulation. The first such warning concerned the Seychelles in 1996.[15] Starting from 2000 the FATF lists 'non-cooperative countries'. Most of these non-cooperative countries were small, but the list included some bigger ones such as Nigeria, Egypt or Russia.[16]

The Egmont Group of Financial Intelligence Units coordinates anti-money-laundering effort on a more daily level. It was established in 1995 to coordinate the work of financial intelligence units (FIUs). The organization is more comprehensive than the FATF as more than 80 countries' FIUs participate in its work.

The International Monetary Fund (IMF) and the World Bank also participate in assessing – though on a voluntary basis – AML regulations and the level of compliance. Furthermore, the Organization for Economic Cooperation and Development (OECD) ratified the Convention on Combating Bribery of Foreign Public Officials in International Business

---

[14] Most importantly, the original recommendations have been amended to include nine additional recommendations covering terrorism financing.

[15] Condemning the 'Seychelles strategy' of welcoming money laundering worked out effectively.

[16] It might worth mentioning that the number of non-cooperative countries is shrinking, and by the end of 2005 only five countries remained on the list.

Transactions in 1997 – which naturally coordinates anti-money-laundering efforts.[17]

Finally, if negotiations fail, the international community (or even individual countries) can as a last resort exclude non-complying countries from financial transfers. In other words, the international AML system either cures or quarantines non-complying countries. The analogy is obvious with how contamination is treated, not least because money laundering similarly contaminates through international transfers.

Deterrence and Prosecution

International deterrence and prosecution is built on similar principles to domestic deterrence and prosecution. Hence, most of the discussion in the previous chapter can be used directly. However, there is an important difference: enforcement agencies now have to compile data both from domestic and foreign banks, and potentially from foreign law enforcement agencies. Such data acquisition is not easy, and that makes international AML efforts more difficult than domestic ones.

Data acquisition is made difficult by fragmented institutions and divergent privacy and data protection rules. First, countries have very different privacy and data protection rules for reasons unrelated to money-laundering enforcement. For instance, European countries have much stricter rules on how data on their citizens can be collected, stored and used than the United States. It can create tensions, as post 9/11 US officials are more interested in using European data to fight terrorism.[18] Furthermore, much of the data generated by AML procedures, such as CTR or SAR reporting, is on law-abiding citizens. Sharing this information with foreign law enforcement officials is obviously sensitive.[19]

---

[17] Though action against foreign bribery was – unsurprisingly – rather slow. As it was discussed earlier, those who are harmed by corruption are usually the least represented in decision making.

[18] Something similar happens in air traffic, where American officials ask for (and store) more data than would be acceptable in Europe – even on European passengers. Yet the situation is somewhat different from money laundering enforcement, as these European travelers fly to the US. Hence, one could argue that they subject themselves to US laws as well. However, providing data on European citizens who do not leave their countries is a somewhat more sensitive case.

[19] Finally, in some countries the police investigations serve political goals such as prosecuting political opponents. Obviously, democratic countries should not lend

Second, different institutions gather in different countries and information flows are slowed down by this fragmentation. To abuse this, money launderers might transfer dirty money from country A to country B, and then to country C before transferring it back to country A to a different bank. Even if the money is obviously dirty at the beginning of this journey, it might take years to follow the money on its way. Country A's law enforcement agencies need to receive information from financial institutions and law enforcement agencies in two countries. Without that information they might not be able to prosecute the launderer (or recognize the illicit origins of the money) even if the money is in their jurisdiction.[20]

Furthermore, very different discretionary reporting can result from institutional fragmentation. Even the subject of reporting can differ: in the United States suspicious activities are reported, whereas in most other jurisdictions suspicious transactions are reported. [21] The Swiss AML system is very special in that it focuses on the customer, not on the transaction or the activity.[22] As a result, the Swiss system generates far fewer reports (only 417 in 2001) than the US system. In 2001 there were 0.06 reports per thousand citizens in Switzerland, whereas the same figure was 0.73 for the US – even though one would expect a higher figure for Switzerland given the relative size of its financial sector.[23] These differences make the databases hard to compare. Law enforcement officials trained to understand a country's reports might find it difficult to

---

support to such practices. Yet they might do so by providing access to their AML databases.

[20] An additional problem is that in a domestic AML setting arbitration between conflicting agencies (such as the FBI and CIA, for instance) can be done by higher level officials of the executive branch. In international settings similar arbitration needs to go through diplomatic channels, which can slow down resolution considerably.

[21] On one hand, the US system is more comprehensive, as attempted or discussed transactions can also be reported. On the other hand, reporting only actual transactions makes reporting more focused. Maybe suspicious transaction reporting is less prone to exhibit excessive reporting patterns, though most SARs are also linked to actual transactions. In any case, the relative merits of suspicious activity vs. transaction reporting are yet to be explored.

[22] See further Pieth and Aiolfi (2003) on this subject. Note that these differences might even warrant a different economic modeling framework to specifically study the Swiss system.

[23] Data from Reuter and Truman (2004, p. 116).

understand another's reporting. Thus, reporting differences alone can hinder international cooperation.

There are also further differences in what is exactly expected to be reported. In the Netherlands, financial institutions report all 'flagged' or unusual transactions to the Dutch Financial Intelligence Unit (FIU), which further reports the suspicious ones to law enforcement agencies. Dutch reporting is somewhat different from the US system, where financial institutions are supposed to report only the suspicious activities (and not the flagged, unusual ones).[24] As a consequence, there are even more reports – of course only proportionally – in the Netherlands than in the United States. There were 1.56 reports per thousand citizens in the Netherlands, whereas the same figure was 0.80 for the US in 2002.[25] In other words, the Dutch system provides roughly twice as many reports as the US.

In spite of the differences, the general lesson drawn in the previous chapter on discretionary reporting seems to hold in other countries as well. Most importantly, an optimal amount of discretionary reporting is desired: too many or too few reports can hinder law enforcement efforts. Consequently, signs of excessive reporting are not limited to the United States. In the United Kingdom, a KPMG (2003) government sponsored study found that a sudden increase in reporting did not have positive effects on enforcement. Based on accumulated evidence since the KPMG (2003) study, it would be worthwhile to study the UK system for empirical evidence on excessive reporting.

Preserving Integrity

Preserving the integrity of the international financial system serves the same purpose as in the domestic setting. Financial institutions should stay on the legal side of financial transfers and should not willingly facilitate money laundering. Unfortunately, preserving the integrity of financial service providers can be more difficult in an international setting.

The main reason is that supervisory efforts have significant positive externalities. If a country's supervisors force an international bank to

---

[24] Yet, the two systems are not that much different as FinCEN (the US financial intelligence unit) also forwards those reports that it considers really suspicious to law enforcement agencies. Hence, in both countries FIUs screen reports further. The difference is that the Dutch system does not require screening from banks.

[25] Data from Reuter and Truman (2004, p. 116).

preserve its integrity, then other countries where the bank also operates will benefit from these costly supervisory actions. Thus, other supervisors can 'free ride' on the enforcing supervisors' efforts. The situation is similar to the laundering externality discussed earlier. Once again, international cooperation is needed to ensure cooperation.

The case of the Bank of Credit and Commerce International (BCCI) exemplifies how the integrity of an international bank can be compromised.[26] BCCI was founded in 1972 in Pakistan and developed an international presence fairly quickly. Soon, it was willingly involved in transferring illicit funds for both money launderers and terrorists with the full knowledge of the management. It was a thoroughly corrupt institution specifically designed to evade and hinder regulatory scrutiny. Though it had been operating in major countries and had been investigated by the supervisors of these countries, the illicit activities remained hidden for quite a while. BCCI collapsed in 1991 and its collapse cause substantial disruption in international finance and payments. As much as $13 billion was left unpaid after the downfall of the bank.[27]

Equal Marginal Deterrence

Equating marginal deterrence across different transfer channels was important in the domestic case in order to avoid channeling money laundering into certain less regulated channels. Money launderers are ideally not deterred from laundering *only through banks*, but from laundering in general.

A similar concern does exist in international settings. Money launderers should not be deterred from laundering in a single country, but rather deterred from money laundering in general.

Money launderers have a choice not only across different transfer providers, but also across different countries. Certain segments of money laundering are linked to a given country. For instance, drug dealers in a country need to launder most of the resulting low denomination funds there. However, significant segments of laundering monies are free to go wherever it is the easiest to launder monies. For example, drug dealers

---

[26] For further details please refer to *The BCCI Affair* (1992) and Beaty and Gwynne (1993).

[27] The downfall also highlights how the fight against money laundering is connected to financial stability. This link is highly interesting from a central banking perspective, and worth further research.

might smuggle their cash revenues from one country to another and launder them there. Hence, the global AML regime needs to deter laundering globally. International organizations, such as the FATF and the Egmont Group, aim at establishing such uniform global deterrence.

Furthermore, if compliance cannot be established in any other ways, non-complying countries should be excluded from the international financial world so as not to contaminate others. As has already been discussed, the FATF reviews countries and their compliance. Based on this review they publish the Non-cooperative Countries and Territories list. Importantly, this blacklisting is not limited to 'name and shame'. The FATF might advise policy reform and countermeasures such as warnings to FATF non-financial businesses dealing with these countries. Countermeasures were applied to Burma/Myanmar and Nauru, and countries like Russia and the Philippines were threatened with them.

In sum, international AML should aim at keeping money laundering equally difficult in all countries. Where this equal marginal deterrence proves to be impossible, limiting the financial contacts might stop money-laundering contamination.

REVERSING GLOBALIZATION?

The fight against money laundering can sometimes involve severing the financial ties between countries or institutions, so as to stop contamination and preserve the integrity of the global financial system. An unintended negative consequence of such decisions could be a reversal of globalization. Countries or institutions might be excluded from the global financial world due to money-laundering concerns.

This can happen through two main channels. First, banks might exit from certain markets voluntarily. Second, countries might be excluded from the international financial markets because of AML non-compliance. In the following these will be discussed in detail.

Banks might find doing business in certain countries unprofitable because of the costs of monitoring and reporting, and not least because of the costs of expected sanctions. Certain areas are more likely to be infected with money laundering or terrorism financing. For instance, in the Gaza strip even the most honest banks might unwittingly participate in serving suicide bombers, would-be terrorists or transfers monies to their families. Not surprisingly, Western banks are leaving the region as reported in the *Economist* (2005a). The costs of litigation and the associated compliance costs can exceed the operating profits in these areas.

Furthermore, not only might Western banks pull out of the Middle East, but Middle Eastern banks might have to withdraw from the West. The *New York Times* (2005a) reported that the Arab Bank decided to gradually close its New York branch. Groups of suicide bombing victims sued the bank for transferring funds for suicide bombers' families. In addition, FinCEN fined the bank later with $24 million (FinCEN, 2005g). What is worrying here is not that the Arab Bank violated AML rules (in which case, of course, all sanctions are justified), but the possibility that US AML laws are not compatible with honest banking in some parts of the Arab world.

Finally, formal sanctions (such as the FATF blacklist) can also sever financial ties between countries. These sanctions have yet to be used; hence they cannot be precisely evaluated. However, it is important to note from an economic perspective that their usage involves a trade-off: gains in international money-laundering enforcement efficiency must out-weigh the costs of receding financial integration.

CONCLUDING REMARKS

This chapter reviewed some of the most important additional challenges international money-laundering enforcement faces compared to those faced by domestic AML regimes. The main lesson from this chapter is that international fund transfers are unfortunately well-suited to concealing the origins of funds. Three important factors play a role in that. First, international enforcement creates a powerful externality, the laundering externality, which leads to a Prisoner's dilemma-like situation for enforcement agencies. Hence, incentives are not per se well-aligned between different law enforcement agencies. Second, legal differences (and the above externalities) can lead to different predicate crime definitions. This eases money laundering as some types of it will escape prosecution in certain countries. Third, cross-border transfers are opaque even without the above problems. Hence, money launderers are naturally inclined to transfer funds through several jurisdictions.

The most interesting result is that international anti-money-laundering regulation can reverse financial globalization. This can happen directly, as regulators might want to sever ties with particularly lax regulated countries. The reason is that if negotiations (and peer pressure) cannot achieve compliance, then sovereign countries cannot be forced to implement AML measures. The only measure left is to deny their access to complying countries' financial markets. More importantly, however, financial globalization can reverse as an indirect consequence of overly tough AML regulations. Fearing prosecution banks might systematically withdraw from certain markets and thereby reverse financial globalization.

Concluding, on the surface weak international AML enforcement seems to be the relevant danger to the international community. The laundering externality pushes the system towards a suboptimal level of enforcement. Yet excessively strong local AML regulations might result in unforeseen consequences, most importantly reversing global financial integration. Hence, even in international money laundering both extremes, too weak or excessively strong enforcement, should be avoided. In this regard, the main lessons for both domestic and international AML systems are strikingly similar: optimal policies are needed, and excesses – even overly strong enforcement – backfire.

References

American Banker (2005a), *Too many SARs? Not according to the FBI*, by Michael Heller, May 31, 1.

American Banker (2005b), *Senators: Agency Overreacted*, by Damian Paletta, July 14, 6.

Aninat, E., D. Hardy and B.R. Johnston (2002), 'Combating Money-Laundering and the Financing of Terrorism', *Finance and Development*, 39 (3), September, 44-47.

Beaty, J. and S.C. Gwynne (1993), *The Outlaw Bank: A Wild Ride into the Secret Heart of BCCI*, Random House.

Becker, G. (1968), 'Crime and Punishment: An Economic Approach', *Journal of Political Economy*, 76 (March/April), 169-217.

Blunden, B. (2001), *The Money Launderers: How They Do It, and How to Catch Them at It*, Chalford, England: Management Books.

Bolton, P. and M. Dewatripont (2005), *Contract Theory*, MIT Press.

Camdessus, M (1998), *Speech to the Financial Action Task Force*, Paris.

Economic Perspectives (2001), 'The Fight against Money Laundering', US Department of State, *Electronic Journal*, 6 (2), May.

Economist (2005a), Financing Terrorism – Controversial Customers, January 18, 64.

Economist (2005b), *Pointless Efforts Against Terror Finance*, October 22, p. 15 and pp. 73-75.

El-Qorchi, M. (2002), *Hawala, Finance and Development*, December, 39 (4).

FATF Report (2005), *Financial Action Task Force – Money Laundering and Terrorist Financing Typologies 2004-2005*, June 10, http://www.fatf-gafi.org/dataoecd/16/8/35003256.pdf

FBI (2001), 'Money Laundering', FBI *Law Enforcement Bulletin*, by William R. Schroeder, May, 70 (5), 1-9.

FinCEN (2004a), *$25 Million Civil Money Penalty Against Riggs Bank N.A.*, May 13. http://www.fincen.gov/riggs6.pdf

FinCEN (2004b), *In the Matter of AmSouth Bank*, October 12 http://www.fincen.gov/amsouthassessmentcivilmoney.pdf

FinCEN (2005a), *Joint Statement on Providing Banking Service to Money Services Businesses*, March 30, http://www.fincen.gov/bsamsbrevisedstatement.pdf

FinCEN (2005b), *The SAR Activity Review, Trends, Tips and Issues*, #8, April http://www.fincen.gov/sarreviewissue8.pdf

FinCEN (2005c), *Statement of William J. Fox, Director, before the United States Senate Committee on Banking, Housing and Urban Affairs*, April 26, http://www.fincen.gov/foxtestimony042605.pdf

FinCEN (2005d), *Joint News Release Announcing the Guidance and Advisory Issued on Banking Services for Money Services Businesses Operating in the United States*, April 26, http://www.fincen.gov/nr04262005.pdf

FinCEN (2005e), *SAR Activity Review*, 4, May, http://www.fincen.gov/sarreviewmay2005.pdf

FinCEN (2005f), *FinCEN's 314(a) Fact Sheet*, June 08, http://www.fincen.gov/314afactsheet.pdf

FinCEN (2005g), *FinCEN and OCC (Office of the Comptroller of Currency) Joint Release*, August 17, http://www.fincen.gov/pressrelease08172005.pdf

Freeman, S. (1996), 'The Payment System, Liquidity and Rediscounting', *American Economic Review*, 86, 1126-1138.

GAO (2004), *US General Accounting Office: Anti-Money Laundering: Issues Concerning Depository Institution Regulatory Oversight*, GAO-04-833T, June 3, http://www.gao.gov/new.items/d04833t.pdf

Garicano, L. and R.A. Posner (2006), 'Intelligence Failures: An Organizational Economics Perspective', *Journal of Economic Perspectives*, forthcoming.

Gordon, N.J. (2005), 'The Rise of Independent Directors, 1950-2000: Towards a New Corporate Governance Paradigm', Columbia Law School, mimeo.

Grossman, S.J. (1981), 'The Role of Warranties and Private Disclosure about Product', *Quality Journal of Law and Economics*, 24, 461-483.

Grossman, S.J. and O.D. Hart (1980), 'Disclosure Laws and Takeover Bids', *Journal of Finance*, 35, 323-334.

Holmström, B. and P. Milgrom (1991), 'Multitask Principal-Agent Analyses: Incentive Contracts, Asset Ownership, and Job Design', *Journal of Law, Economics, and Organization*, Spec. Issue, 7, 24-52.

IMF – International Monetary Fund (2003), *Offshore Financial Centers – The Assessment Program – A Progress Report and the Future of the Program*, Washington, DC: International Monetary Fund.

Kofman, F. and J. Lawarrée (1993), 'Collusion in Hierarchical Agency', *Econometrica*, 61, 629-656.

La Porta R., F. Lopez-de-Silanes and A. Schleifer (2006), 'What Works in Securities Laws?', *Journal of Finance*, forthcoming.

KPMG (2003), *Money Laundering: Review of the Regime for Handling Suspicious Activity Reports*, London: National Criminal Intelligence Service.

Lal, B. (2003), *Money Laundering: An Insight into the Dark World of Financial Frauds*, Delhi, India: Siddharth Publications.

Lilley, P. (2000), *Dirty Dealing: The Untold Truth About Global Money Laundering*, London: Kogan Page.

Looney, R. (2003), 'Hawala: The Terrorist's Informal Financial Mechanism', *Middle East Policy*, 10 (1), Spring, 164-167.

Money Laundering Special Report (2003), 'Bureau of Justice Statistics', compiled by M. Motivans, July 2003, NCJ 199574.

Masciandaro, D. (1999), 'Money Laundering: The Economics of Regulation', *European Journal of Law and Economics*, 7 (3), 225-240.

Masciandaro, D. (ed.) (2004), *Global Financial Crime, Terrorism, Money Laundering and Offshore Centres*, Ashgate, Burlington, VT, USA: ISPI.

Masciandaro, D. and U. Filotto (2001), 'Money Laundering Regulation and Bank Compliance Costs: What do your Customers Know? Economics and the Italian Experience', *Journal of Money Laundering Control*, 5 (2), 133-145.

Masciandaro, D. and A. Portolano (2002), 'Inside the Black (list) Box: Money Laundering, Lax Financial Regulation, Non-cooperative Countries. A Law and Economics Approach', Paolo Baffi Center, Bocconi University and Bank of Italy.

Milgrom, P. (1981), 'Good News and Bad News: Representation Theorems and Applications', *Bell Journal of Economics*, 12, 380-391.

Napoleoni, L. (2005), Terror Incorporated: Tracing the Dollars behind the Terror Networks, New York: Seven Stories Press.

New York Times (2005), *Company News: Arab Bank of Jordan to Close Branch in New York*, February 9.

OCC (2005), *Memorandum, Subject: Bank Secrecy Act, From: Wayne Rushton, Tim Long, and Doug Roeder*, Committee on Bank Supervision, April 25.

Pieth, M. and G. Aiolfi (2003), *Anti-Money Laundering: Leveling the Playing Field*, Basel Institute of Governance, Basel, Switzerland.

Posner, R.A. (2004), *The 9/11 Report: A Dissent, The New York Times*, August 29, S7, 1.

Prendergast, C. (1993), 'A Theory of "Yes Men"', *American Economic Review*, 83 (4), September, 757-770.

Prendergast, C. and L. Stole (1996), 'Impetuous Youngsters and Jaded Old-Timers: Acquiring a Reputation for Learning', *Journal of Political Economy*, 104 (6), 1105-1134.

Reuter, P. and E.M. Truman (2004), *Chasing Dirty Money – The Fight Against Money Laundering*, Washington, DC: Institute for International Economics.

Savla, S. (2001), *Money Laundering and Financial Intermediaries*, The Hague and Boston: Kluwer Law International.

Schneider, F. (2002), 'The Size and Development of the Shadow Economies of 22 Transition and 21 OECD Countries', IZA Discussion Paper (514).

Shavell, S. (2004), *Foundations of Economic Analysis of Law*, Harvard University Press.

Stein, J. (2002), 'Information Production and Capital Allocation: Decentralized versus Hierarchical Firms', *Journal of Finance*, LVII (5), October, 1891-1922.

Tanzi, V. (2000), 'Money Laundering and the International Financial System', in *Policies, Institutions and The Dark Side of Economics*, Cheltenham, UK and Northampton, MA, USA: Edward Elgar, Chapter II.

Takáts, E. (2006), 'A Theory of "Crying Wolf": The Economics of Money Laundering Enforcement', mimeo.

Time (2001), A Banking System Built for Terrorism, October 05.

Tirole, J. (1986), 'Hierarchies and Bureaucracies: On the Role of Collusion in Organizations', *Journal of Law, Economics and Organization*, (2), 181-214.

The 9/11 Commission Report (2004) by the National Commission on Terrorist Attacks, US Government Printing Office, Washington DC.

The BCCI Affair (1992), A Report to the Committee on Foreign Relations, United States Senate by Senator John Kerry and Senator Hank Brown, December, 1992, 102d Congress 2d Session Senate Print, 102-140. http://www.fas.org/irp/congress/1992_rpt/bcci/

United Nations Office on Drugs and Crime (2005), *Money Laundering* http://www.unodc.org/unodc/en/money_laundering.html

US Attorneys' Manual (2005), http://www.usdoj.gov/usao/eousa/foia_reading_room/usam/

Wall Street Journal (2004a), *Bob Dole Goes Banking – and Trips the Alarm*, Sept. 3, C1.

Wall Street Journal (2004b), *Expanding in an Age of Terror*, Western Union Faces Scrutiny, October 20, A1.

Wall Street Journal (2005), *US Banks Overreport Data for the Patriot Act*, July 07, C1.

Verrecchia, R.E. (1983), 'Discretionary Disclosure', *Journal of Accounting and Economics*, 5, 365-380.

Verrecchia, R. E. (2001), 'Essays on Disclosure', *Journal of Accounting and Economics*, 32, 97-180.

Index

ABN AMRO Bank, Netherlands 123,
124–5, 134, 136
Aiolfi, G. 236
al Qaeda 136
Alessie, R. 152
AML (anti-money laundering) *see* law
enforcement
AmSouth Bank 210
Anderson, J. 76, 86
Annunzio-Wylie Money Laundering
Act 1992 (US) 202, 209
Arab Bank for Investment and Foreign
Trade (ARBIFT), UAR 125, 210,
240
Arlacchi, P. 157
arms trade 146
ATM machines 196
Australia
money laundering definition(s) 106,
109–10, 113, 116
as money laundering destination
161–2
Austria
BAWG Bank 123, 125–6
as money laundering destination
107, 112, 115, 118, 119–22,
124

back-to-back loans 137
bank audits 206–8
bank cheques/drafts 136
bank closure 222
Bank of Credit and Commerce
International (BCCI) 203, 238
bank integrity/ethics 36, 203, 220–22,
237–8
Bank of New York 221
bank regulation 31–5, 35–52
compensation incentives *see*
regulatory sanctions *below*

cost of 37, 38–9, 40–42, 43, 44, 48,
50, 58
effectiveness of 31–2, 34–5, 39, 40,
41, 43–4, 50–52
government-driven 35, 36–7,
39–52; of criminal banks
53–60
incentive constraint in 52
industry-driven 35–6
model of 39–52; of criminal banks
53–60; of honest banks 39–52
regulatory sanctions 38–9, 42–52,
209–10
risk analysis 36, 42, 43–4, 46, 47–8
Banking Security Act 1970 (US) 201,
202, 210
banking system/banks
ATM machines 196
cash deposits 195
client contact information 203
collective accounts 136
confidentiality issues 34
correspondent banking 134–6,
231–2
as criminal 30–31, 36, 203, 220–21;
economic model of 53–60
customer due diligence (CDD) 203,
204–5, 208, 211, 218, 219
e-cash 147
economic models of 39–60
fund transfers *see* correspondent
banking *above*
hawala transfers 195, 199, 230
as honest 30–31, 33, 35–52;
economic model of 39–52
informal value transfer systems
(IVTS) 195, 198–9, 232
information assets 36, 37, 38, 40,
51, 61, 203; *see also* reporting
role

law enforcement role 30, 31–2, 33, 210
money laundering and 27, 28, 29–60, 134, 195, 196, 198, 201–2
on-line 146
payable through accounts 136–7
payment system 29
reporting role 203, 205–6; discretionary 208–18; rule-based 206–8
reputation 34–5
services offered by 29
underground 142–3
vulnerability of 27
wire transfers 138, 195, 198, 232
see also financial sector; individual banks
Barone, R. 174
Barro, R. J. 171, 172
BAWG Bank (Bank für Arbeit und Wirtschaft) 123, 125–6
Becker, G. 1, 2, 5, 56, 204, 207
Bergstrand, J. H. 76
Bermuda 79, 80
black economy *see* shadow economy
black finance *see* money laundering
Blomberg, S. B. 179–80
bond market 159
border related costs 86
see also trading partners
borders/frontiers 88–9
see also cross-border
Bosma, S. 171
Boyrie, M. E. 140, 167
bribery *see* corruption/bribery
Broadway National Bank, New York 210, 221
Burma/Myanmar 239
business finance 141, 145, 146, 196
Busuioc, Madalina 111, 114–15, 130, 131

camouflaging effect 6, 30, 131–2
capital flight 167
capital market investments 143
Capone, Al 103, 145
cash deposits 195

cash smuggling 195, 232
cash-intensive businesses 145
casinos *see* gambling
catering industry 144
Cayman Islands 78, 79, 80, 88, 105
China 78, 80
clean money 6–8
investment of 3, 6, 14–15, 17–18, 20–22
see also dirty money; money laundering
Colombia 175
Medellin Group 156
colonial background 84, 89
Commerzbank, Germany 136
compensation incentives *see* regulatory sanctions
competition *see* unfair competition
competition, for dirty money *see* Seychelles strategy
competitive advantage 76, 157
see also trade theory; unfair competition
Conference on Global Drugs Law, 1997 106
construction industry 158, 159
see also real estate acquisition
contamination effects 123–4, 157, 160, 220
see also impact studies
correspondent banking 134–6, 231–2
corruption/bribery 82, 96, 149, 230–31, 234–5
Council of Europe Convention on Laundering, Search, Seizure and Confiscation of the Proceeds of Crime, 1990 and 2005 106, 129–30
credit card payments 196
Credit Lyonnais 136
crime increase 173–8
criminal banks 30–31, 36, 53, 203, 220–21
model for regulation of 53–60
offshore (OFCs) 54; *see also* offshore financial centres
social losses caused by 53–5
see also banking system/banks

criminal money *see* dirty money
criminal organizations/criminals 4,
    5–6, 197
  decision making 3, 6–16
  hoarding of money by 151–4, 175
  legal profession and 123–4
  mafia 157, 158, 178
  money laundering by *see* money
    laundering
  risk analysis 3, 4, 5–6, 16–24
  spending patterns 150–55, 162, 166
  supply side economics and 28, 29,
    30–31
cross-border flows 74, 78–90, 118,
    225–32
  attractiveness indicator 79, 81, 82,
    83–4
  colonial background and 84, 89
  cultural differences and 86, 87
  distance deterrence indicator 79, 81,
    82–3, 84, 86, 87
  fund transfers 231–2
  language differences and 84, 86, 87
  laundering externality concept
    226–8, 229, 231
  offshore financial centres (OFC) 54,
    79, 80, 88, 95, 132, 147–8, 228
  paper trails 226, 232
  prisoner's dilemma application
    226–8
  see also trading partners
cross-border law enforcement 129–30,
    232–41
  aims 225, 235–7
  bilateral 233
  data protection issues 230, 235
  deterrence/prosecution role 235–7
  harmonization of 232–5
  information flows 235–7
  marginal deterrence concept 238–9
  multilateral 233–5
  unilateral 233
cross-border prosecutions 129–30
currency hedging 137
currency and other monetary
    instruments reports (CMIR) 106,
    219
currency smuggling 132

currency transaction reports (CTR)
    203, 205, 206–8, 209, 219, 235
currency transactions 138–9, 145
customer due diligence (CDD) 203,
    204–5, 208, 211, 218, 219

data protection issues 230, 235
Deardoff, Alan V. 76–7
demand side economics 1–26
  decision making in 3, 6–16
  demand curve 16
  model of 2, 3, 4–5; macroeconomic
    16–24; microeconomic 6–16
  opportunity costs 3
  optimal value concept 3, 5–6, 7–12
  price/quantity relationship 15
  as a process 3, 4–6
  transaction costs 1, 2, 4, 25–6, 28
  zero-value concept 7
  see also economic analysis
derivatives 143
diamond market 144–5
dirty money 2–3, 5, 6–7, 14
  cross-border flows *see* cross-border
    flows
  destination countries 74, 78–9, 80,
    81, 82–90, 170–71, 229–31
  international competition for
    (Seychelles strategy) 90–96,
    226–8, 234
  money dirtying process 25–6, 175,
    179
  originating countries 74, 78, 81,
    169, 170–71
  spending patterns of criminals
    150–61, 162, 166
  welfare gains from 91–6
  as zero value 7
  see also money laundering
distance
  as a deterrent in cross-border flows
    79, 81, 82–3, 84, 86, 87
  in trade theory 87, 88
Dixit-Stiglitz trade theory model 77,
    89
domestic law enforcement
  deterrence/prosecution role 202–22
  protection role 220–23

in US 193, 200–224; legislation
   200, 201–2, 209, 218
drug trafficking 129, 132, 134, 143,
   149, 194, 197, 238–9
   in Latin America 229, 230
   profits from 151, 153–4, 169, 175,
      194
   terrorism increase and 178
   transport facilities for 159–60
   in US 200, 201, 229–30
due diligence *see* customer due
   diligence
Dutch Banking Association 147
Dutch National Bank (DNB) 128, 139,
   141, 175
   see also Netherlands

e-cash 146–7
economic analysis 1–4
   demand side 4–26
   international implications 74–96
   supply side 2, 27–73
economic growth 170–72
economic impact, of money
   laundering 150–78
Egmont Group of Financial
   Intelligence Units 81, 234, 239
e-gold 147
Egypt 234
Eichholtz, P. 159
employment/unemployment levels
   161–5
Endstra, Willem 157–8
environmental factor, in money
   laundering 37, 40–41, 42, 48
European Central Bank (ECB) 158
European Communities (EC)
   Convention on Laundering,
   Search, Seizure and Confiscation
   of the Proceeds of Crime 110,
   114
European Union (EU)
   money laundering definition(s) 106,
      107, 108, 112, 115–16, 118,
      119–21, 124; attempted
      harmonization of 103, 115,
      128–30
   as money laundering destination 78,

   79, 80, 88, 90, 91
   Schengen countries 88
   tax fraud/evasion 167–8, 230
   see also individual countries
European Union (EU) Directives on
   Money Laundering 115, 116–17,
   128–9
exchange rates 170
exports *see* trading partners

fake invoicing 139–40
fake sales/purchases 139
Federal Bureau of Investigation (FBI)
   220
Ferwerda, J. 84, 85, 106, 112–14, 171,
   172
Fijnaut, C. J. C. F. 159
Financial Action Task Force (FATF)
   on Money Laundering 105, 106,
      126, 132, 144, 233–4, 239
   aims/purpose 234
   definitions used by 118, 194,
      195–6, 197
   Forty Recommendations 109, 112,
      117, 119–21, 128, 234
   Non-cooperative Countries and
      Territories List 234, 239, 240
financial integrity 45, 160–61, 203,
   220–22
financial intelligence units (FIUs) 31
   Administrative Unit model 65–6,
      67–73
   control of 66, 67–73
   creation/design 60–66; models of
      61–6
   definition 65
   Egmont Group of 81, 234, 239
   function/purpose 64–5
   Hybrid model 66, 67–73
   information assets 64, 65
   international list of 67–73
   Judicial Unit model 65, 67–73
   Law Enforcement model 65, 67–73
   in Netherlands 237
financial sector
   bond market 159
   as cooperative 31–2
   customer due diligence (CDD) 203,

204–5, 208, 211, 218, 219
foreign exchange market 230
money laundering and 27, 28, 30,
32; impact of 149, 160–61,
201–2
offshore centres (OFCs) 54, 79, 80,
88, 95, 132, 147–8, 228
opacity in 28, 29
reporting role 203, 205–6;
discretionary 208–18;
rule-based 206–8
securities market 196
vulnerability of 27
working relationships in 29
see also banking system/banks;
monetary sector
financial service regulation 31
financial stability 238
FinCEN *see* US Treasury Financial
Crime Enforcement Network
foreign currencies 138–9
black market in 143
foreign direct investment (FDI) 76, 89
foreign exchange markets 230
France, Credit Lyonnais 136
fraud 149, 151, 197
in EU 167, 168
losses from 167
risk of 160–61
tax fraud/evasion 149, 167–9, 194,
197, 229–30

gambling 133–4, 195
Garciano, L. 219–20
Gaza Strip 239–40
Germany
Commerzbank 136
money laundering definition(s) 107,
112, 115, 116, 118, 119–21,
124
globalization, reversal of 239–41
gold market 144
e-gold 147
gravity model, of international trade
theory 75–86, 88, 89–90
criticism of 76
development of 76–7
money laundering estimation using

78–86
remoteness factor in 76, 78
Tinbergen's formula 75–6, 88
transport costs in 76–7
Greece 116

hawala bank transfers 195, 199, 230
Head, K. 77, 78
Heckscher-Ohlin trade theory model
76, 77, 89
Helpman, E. 76
Holleeder, Willem 158
hot money *see* dirty money

illicit money transfer *see* money
laundering
immigrants
hawala bank transfers 195, 199, 230
illegal 106
as money launderers 195
impact studies 3, 6, 37, 53–5, 80,
149–80
contamination effects 123–4, 157,
160, 220
direct 149
indirect 149
macroeconomic 161–78
microeconomic 150–55
sector 155–61
terrorism increase 144, 178–80
imports *see* trading partners
income levels 161–5
income tax payments 167–8
see also tax fraud/evasion
India 230
Indonesia 230–31
Bank Indonesia 127
Indover Bank, Netherlands 123,
127–8, 183–4
industrial sectors, money laundering
impact on 161–6
informal value transfer systems
(IVTS) 195, 198–9, 232
information assets/distribution 28–9
as asymmetrical 28, 30, 33, 34, 39,
40, 51
in banking system/banks 36, 37, 38,
40, 51, 61, 203

in cross-border law enforcement
235–7
in financial intelligence units (FIUs)
64, 65
see also data protection issues;
reporting role
Information Laffer curve 213, 214,
215, 216
information overload 219–20, 223–4
insurance market 139, 196
interest rates 170
interest-free loans 137
international economics 74–96
tax competition 74, 90–96
trade theory 74, 75–90
international law enforcement *see*
cross-border law enforcement
International Monetary Fund (IMF)
169, 228, 234
estimates of money laundering
activity 78–9, 80
money laundering definition(s) 106,
109, 113
international organizations 106,
108–11, 112–13, 114
see also individual organizations
internet financial transactions 146–8
Interpol 106, 109, 113
investment(s) 156–61
in capital market 143
foreign direct (FDI) 76, 89
irregular 151–4, 155
legitimate 143, 151, 152, 153–4,
155
in luxury goods 150, 151, 152,
153–4
in real estate 144, 157–60
Iran 123, 124–5
Italy
bond market 159
as money laundering destination 78,
80, 159
ITERATE data base 179–80

Japan 229

Kageman, Dirk 132
de Kam, F. 169

Karayannis, M. 155
Kleemans, E. R. 139, 178

language issues 84, 86, 87, 89
Lankhorst, F. 160
Latin America 229, 230
laundering externality concept 226–8,
229, 231
see also cross-border finance
law enforcement 58–9, 61, 105
banking system/banks role in 30,
31, 32, 210
cost of 167
cross-border 129–30, 225, 232–41
domestic 200–224
financial intelligence units (FIUs)
and 60–66
marginal deterrence concept 223
predicate offences 114–15, 117–18,
129, 167, 194, 196–8;
cross-border 229–31;
definition 229
probability of incrimination concept
56–7
punishment 5, 8, 13, 55, 116, 117,
129–30
sanctions 3, 8, 56–7, 74, 140
legal profession, contamination of
123–4, 160
Libya 123, 124–5
Liechtenstein 79, 80
Liquid Opportunity 126
loans 137
lotteries 195
see also gambling
luxury goods, purchase of 145, 150,
151, 152, 153–4, 166

the mafia 157, 158, 178
see also criminal organizations
Marcos, Ferdinand Edralin 127,
230–32
marginal deterrence concept
cross-border 238–9
domestic 223
Masciandaro, D. 95, 173, 174, 175,
177, 178, 179
McCallum, J. 88

Medellin Group, Colombia 156
Meloen, J. 150, 151, 152
Middle East 239–40
monetary sector 149, 169–70
   see also financial sector
monetary value *see* optimal value
   concept
money
   definition 11
   demand for 169
money exchange offices 138
money laundering
   action against *see* law enforcement;
      regulation
   amounts involved 78, 80, 105, 123,
      151–4, 168, 199, 215;
      estimation techniques 74,
      78–86, 199
   banking system/banks and *see*
      banking system/banks
   between trading partners 86–90,
      166–7, 233
   camouflaging effect 6, 30, 131–2
   case studies in 103, 123–8
   clean money 3, 6–8, 14–15, 17–18,
      20–22
   as complex 1
   cost of 13, 14, 15, 17, 25–6, 32, 60,
      86, 174–5
   cross-border *see* cross-border flows
   definition(s) 2, 4–6, 32–3, 103–22,
      194, 197, 229; EU
      harmonization of 128–30
   demand for 17, 19, 32
   detection of 2, 3, 5, 13, 33; *see also*
      law enforcement
   effects of *see* impact studies *below*
   environmental factor 37, 40–41, 42,
      48
   fees charged for 200
   financial sector and *see* financial
      sector
   immigrants involved in 195, 199,
      230; illegal immigrants 106
   impact studies 3, 6, 37, 53–5, 90,
      149–80, 201–2
   international *see* cross-border flows
   international economics and 74–96

local 84
polluting effect 3, 6, 23–4, 27, 37,
   60
punishment for 5, 8, 13, 55, 116,
   117, 129–30; *see also* law
   enforcement
purpose *see* definition(s) *above*
self-laundering 115, 126
social impact 53–5, 149, 194, 199
transforming effect 6
see also dirty money; shadow
   economy
money laundering consensus 230–31
money laundering destinations 74,
   78–9, 80, 81, 82–90, 170–71,
   229–31
   amounts involved 78, 80, 81
   corrupt dictatorships 230–31
   income per capita in 88
   list of 80
   offshore financial centres (OFCs)
      54, 79, 80, 88, 95, 132, 147–8,
      228
   see also dirty money
money laundering methods/process 3,
   4–6, 32–3, 44, 89–90, 103–48,
   194–200
   case studies 123–8
   integration phase 104, 105, 143–8
   layering phase 104, 105, 134–43
   placement phase 104–5, 131–4
   underground economy and 103,
      118, 122, 123
   see also demand side economics;
      supply side economics
money transfer offices 138–9
MoneyGram 138
multinational corporations 141–2,
   167–8

Nauru 239
Nelen, H. 158–9, 160
Netherlands 127, 128, 131, 132, 137,
   138–9, 141–2
   ABN AMRO Bank 123, 124–5,
      134, 136
   Dutch National Bank (DNB) 128,
      139, 141

Financial Intelligence Unit (FIU)
237
gambling in 133–4
Indover Bank 123, 127–8, 183–4
money laundering definition(s) 107,
110, 112, 118, 119–21
as money laundering destination 79,
80, 84, 85, 90, 91, 116, 165–6
real estate purchase 157–60
spending patterns of criminals
150–55, 157–60
tax fraud 167–9
trust offices in 141
underground banking 143
Newton's theory of gravity 75, 76
Nigeria 230–31, 234

OECD Convention on Combating
Bribery 234–5
offshore financial centres (OFCs)
anti-money laundering regimes 228
money laundering by 54, 79, 80, 88,
95, 132, 147–8, 228
on-line banking 146
optimal value concept 3, 5–6, 7–12
originating countries, of dirty money
74, 78–81, 169, 170–71

Pakistan 238
paper trails 226, 232
passports, false 131–2
Patriot Act 2001 (US) 201, 202, 218,
231
Philippines 127, 230–31, 239
phone cards, pre-paid 147
Pieth, M. 236
Pinochet, Augusto 221
political impact, of money laundering
149
polluting effect, of money laundering
3, 6, 23–4, 27, 37, 60
Posner, R. A. 219–20
predicate offences 114–15, 117–18,
129, 167, 194
cross-border 229–31
definition(s) 229
types of 194, 196–8
see also law enforcement

price increases 156, 158, 166–7
principal-agent theory, in bank
regulation 34, 35
proprietary systems 147–8
Public Investment in Private Equity
(PIPE) schemes (US) 126
public sector, impact of money
laundering 149, 167–9
punishment, of money launderers 5, 8,
13, 55, 116, 117, 129–30
see also law enforcement; risk
analysis

Quirk, P. J. 157, 169, 171–2

Rawlings, G. 90–91, 93, 94, 174
RBTT (Royal Bank of Trinidad and
Tobago) 154
real estate acquisition 144, 195
construction projects 158, 159
in Netherlands 157–60
Refco (US securities trader) 125–6
regulation
of banking system/banks 31–52,
209–10; economic models of:
criminal banks 53–60; honest
banks 39–52
cost of 32, 55
effectiveness of 31–2, 34–5, 39, 40,
41, 43–4, 47, 50–52
financial intelligence units (FIUs)
and 31, 60–73
government driven 35, 36–7,
39–52; of criminal banks
53–60
incentive constraint in 52
incentives for 34–5, 38–9, 42–52
indifference to 45–6
industry driven 35–6
principal-agent theory of 34, 35
of supply side economics 31–3
regulatory sanctions 38–9, 45–52,
209–10
rent-bearing costs 86, 87
see also trading partners
reporting role, of financial institutions
203, 205–22, 223–4
currency and other monetary

instruments reports (CMIR)
206, 219
currency transaction reports (CTR)
203, 205, 206–8, 209, 219, 235
discretionary 208–18, 236–7
economic problems of 210–11
excessive reporting 219–20, 223–4,
237
fines/incentives, effects of 206–8,
212–16, 218–19, 223–4
information on request 218, 219
maximum deterrence theory and
207–8
numbers of reports 211–12, 216–17,
219–20, 223–4
policy issues 211–12
rule-based 206–8, 211, 219
suspicious activity reports (SAR)
205, 206, 209, 210, 211, 216,
219, 235, 237
uncertainty in 210–11
Reuter, P. 175, 202, 236, 237
Riggs Bank, Washington 210, 221
risk analysis
of bank regulation 36, 42, 43–4, 46,
47–8
of money laundering 3, 4, 5–6,
16–24, 86–7
Russia 140, 234, 239
as money laundering destination 78,
80
US and 167

Sacoccia, Stephen 200
sanction incentives 38–9
see also bank regulation
sanctions
against money laundering 3, 8,
56–7, 74, 140
AML (anti-money laundering)
agreements 74, 140
Saudi Bank 136
Schneider, F. 178
securities market 196
Seychelles 234
Seychelles strategy 90–96, 226–8, 234
see also dirty money
shadow economy 103, 105–6, 118,
122, 123
money laundering and 118, 122,
123
shell companies 136, 140–41, 196
Siegel, M. 133
Simpson, O. J. 201
Sinn, H. W. 91, 93, 94
smuggling *see* currency smuggling
smurfing/structuring 131, 136, 209
social impact, of money laundering
53–5, 149, 194, 199
Special Purpose Entities/Vehicles
(SPEs/SPVs) 140–42
spending patterns, of criminals
150–61, 162, 166
amounts involved 151–4
investments 151–4, 155–6, 157–61
luxury goods 145, 150, 151, 152,
153–4
in Netherlands 150–55, 157–60
Sudan 136
Suharto, Thojib N. J. 127–8, 230–31
Sullivan, Martin 142
supply side economics 2, 27–73
banking system/banks 27, 28,
29–60; *see also* financial
sector *below*
criminal organizations and 28, 29,
30–31
financial intelligence units (FIUs)
and 31, 60–73
financial sector 27, 28, 29, 30; *see
also* banking system/banks
above
intermediaries in 27–31, 37;
criminal 30; honest 30
as a process 28, 32–3
regulation of *see* regulation
see also economic analysis
Suriname 116, 133, 134, 135, 137,
138, 208
suspicious activity reports (SAR) 203,
205, 206, 209, 210, 211, 219,
235, 236
numbers of 216
SWIFT payment system 135
Switzerland 140
anti-money laundering regime 236

money laundering definition(s) 107, 111, 112, 116–17, 118, 119–21, 124

Takáts, E. 193, 208
Taliban 178
Tanzi, V. 169, 170
tax competition 74, 90–96
tax fraud/evasion 194, 196, 197
  in Latin America 229, 230
  in Netherlands 149, 167–9
  in US 229–30
taxation
  income tax 167–8
  value added tax 168
terrorism finance 64–5
  al Qaeda and 136
  financial flows 25–6
  money laundering and 4, 24–6, 105, 129, 135, 136, 196–8, 199, 201
terrorism increase
  drug trafficking and 178
  funded by clean money 179
  funded by money laundering 149, 178–80
  internal conflict and 179–80
Tinbergen formula 75–6, 88
  see also gravity model
trade theory
  bilateral 77; *see also* trading partners
  distance indicator in 87, 88
  Dixit-Stiglitz model 77, 89
  foreign direct investment (FDI) 76, 89
  gravity model 75–86, 88, 89–90
  Heckscher-Ohlin model 76, 77, 89
  money laundering and 74, 75–90
  predictive models 76
  Tinbergen formula 75–6, 88; *see also* gravity model *above*
trading partners 75–6, 82, 84, 140
  borders between 88–9
  colonial background 84, 89
  costs incurred by 86–7
  distortion between 166–7
  language issues 84, 86, 87, 89
  money laundering flows between

86–90, 233
trade-related costs 86, 87
transaction costs 1, 2, 4, 13, 14, 15, 17, 25–6, 28, 32, 60, 86, 174–5
transforming effect, of money laundering 6
trans-national *see* cross-border
transport sector, drug trafficking and 159–60
travellers cheques 132
Truman, E. M. 175, 202, 236, 237
trust offices (Netherlands) 141

underground banking 142–3
underground economy *see* shadow economy
unfair competition 156
Unger, B. 79, 80, 81, 82–3, 90–91, 93, 94, 119–21, 131, 133, 149, 166
United Kingdom
  anti-money laundering regime 237
  money laundering definition(s) 115–16
United Nations, money laundering definition(s) 106, 109, 112, 114
United Nations Convention against Illicit Traffic in Narcotic Drugs and Psychotropic Substances (1988) 129
United States 131, 140, 145
  ABN AMRO Bank, fining of for money laundering 124–5
  anti-money laundering regime 193, 200–224, 230, 233, 234, 236, 237, 240
  drug trafficking 169, 175, 229–30
  Iran and 123, 124–5
  Libya and 123, 124–5
  money laundering definition(s) 106, 108, 111, 112, 117, 118, 119–21, 124, 229
  as money laundering destination 78, 80, 90, 91, 106, 193, 215, 230
  multinationals based in 142
  Public Investment in Private Equity (PIPE) schemes 126
  Russia and 167
  tax evasion 229–30

US Government Accounting Office (GAO) 197
US Internal Revenue Service (IRS) 140, 147–8, 167–8, 206
US Treasury Financial Crime Enforcement Network (FinCEN) 206, 209, 212, 215–16, 217, 220, 222, 237, 240

value
  optimal 3, 5–6, 7–12
  zero 7
value added tax 168
van Wincoop, Eric 86
Vatican City 79, 80

Walker, J. 78–9, 80, 81–2, 83–4, 85, 87, 88, 89, 110, 114, 119–21, 161–2, 165
Weissink, Alexander 127
welfare gains, from dirty money 91–6
Western Union 138, 198, 232
wire money transfers 138, 195, 198, 232
World Bank 234
  money laundering definition(s) 109, 113

Yaniv, G. 167–8

Zaire 230–31
Zdanowicz, J. 140
zero value concept 7